AD Non Fiction
306.7663 C659e

Cogswell, Kelly. Eating fire : my life as a
Lesbian Avenger   9001088240

EATING FIRE

EATING FIRE

MY LIFE AS A
LESBIAN
AVENGER

KELLY COGSWELL

University of Minnesota Press
Minneapolis • London

Portions of "A Laboratory of Identity" previously appeared as Kelly Cogswell, "Herstory Live: The Lesbian Avengers School You on Their Ass-Kicking Roots," http://www.autostraddle.com, October 12, 2012.

Copyright 2014 by Kelly Cogswell

All rights reserved. No part of this publication may be reproduced, stored in a retrieval system, or transmitted, in any form or by any means, electronic, mechanical, photocopying, recording, or otherwise, without the prior written permission of the publisher.

Published by the University of Minnesota Press
111 Third Avenue South, Suite 290
Minneapolis, MN 55401-2520
http://www.upress.umn.edu

Library of Congress Cataloging-in-Publication Data
Cogswell, Kelly.
Eating fire : my life as a lesbian avenger / Kelly Cogswell.
Includes bibliographical references.
ISBN 978-0-8166-9115-9 (hc : alk. paper)
ISBN 978-0-8166-9116-6 (pb : alk. paper)
1. Cogswell, Kelly. 2. Lesbians—United States—Biography. 3. Lesbians—Political activity—United States. 4. Gay rights. I. Title.
HQ75.4.C64A3 2014
306.76'63092—dc23 [B]
                                    2013038697

Printed in the United States of America on acid-free paper

The University of Minnesota is an equal-opportunity educator and employer.

20 19 18 17 16 15 14   10 9 8 7 6 5 4 3 2 1

9001088240

To Ana

CONTENTS

I. ACTIVIST HONEYMOON

Unscrew the locks from the doors!
Unscrew the doors themselves from their jambs!

—WALT WHITMAN

1.

In 1992, when the Lesbian Avengers started, I was living in a loft on Avenue B with my ex-girlfriend Amy, and her roommate, Rennes, who would pick up closeted fags and have noisy, slurpy sex. I shouldn't complain. He'd agreed to let me live there for cheap, the broke poet with some weird disease that had me crying out with feverish dreams, disrupting his postcoital sleep. Drag queens had been there first, and it took days for me and Amy to clean the eye shadow ground into the bathroom grout. Above us was our tequila-soaked landlady whose overflowing Jacuzzi sometimes came through our ceiling. Below us were a pit bull, a large iguana, and two tattooed musician dykes. And on the ground floor, the Tu Casa recording studio and rehearsal space that gave all our lives the same irregular 4/4 beat.

Every Saturday night, the pioneering Korean deli owners across the street would shout, "Call the police, call the police!" And every Saturday night, one of us would call 911 and wait for the blue and white to turn up, siren blaring, cops laconic as a crackhead ran down the street with the till. Every block had two or three gaps where buildings had burnt to the ground. In between, in grimy graffitied buildings lived poor Latino families sprinkled with an assortment of artists and queers. Once, Rennes organized a brunch and I ended up making pancakes for some elderly British neighbor in a broad-brimmed hat and purple cloak that he introduced as Quentin Crisp.

A couple blocks north, in the rapidly gentrifying East Village, was Tompkins Square Park with its dealers and drummers. In the summer, it hosted the likes of Wigstock, Lady Bunny, and every wannabe beatnik in the world. At all times, it held the homeless, along with a full complement of squirrels, other rodents, and dogs. My friend Kathryn lived up at the northeastern edge in a basement apartment. I'd visit at night, scurrying past the rats when she didn't have a late shift waitressing or a gig with her band. I saw her once at CBGB's, thin and energetic on her traps, but she played guitar, too, and wrote her own stuff. She'd give me a couple puffs off her weed, and we'd talk about all our failures with girls, then sometimes mess around with her instruments. For a while we called ourselves The Sextets, randomly picking poems from a volume of Anne Sexton with me wailing the lyrics and thunking away on the bass, and Kathryn playing guitar. We never tried to get any shows, and only had one witness that whole time, but it made us happy. We weren't afraid yet of squandering our lives and dying poor, alone, in the crappiest hospitals reserved for the uninsured.

I think we met at an action for ILGO, the Irish Lesbian and Gay Organization, though she's about as Irish as I am, meaning hardly at all. She went because of an Irish ex. I went because of Marie Honan, an Irish girl I met when I was temping at Philip Morris. She had leopard-print glasses and a handbag big as a kitchen sink. Marie lived in Brooklyn then, with Anne Maguire, her girlfriend, and for a couple of years I followed them around like a barely housebroken pup. They were the first lesbian couple I ever knew, cool, smart, pretty, and composed, even under a fire of beer cans and garbage that we'd caught along with Mayor Dinkins when we walked for the first and only time as out Irish queers in the St. Patrick's Day Parade. I adored them both, tried to be them, really, the way I'd tried to be my oldest sister trailing around in her T-shirts that dropped to my knees. I bummed cigarettes, borrowed clothes and accents, learned to warm a teapot and drink tea, listened to their stories of girls on the rampage in Dublin and heroes in Belfast, slept often in their spare room, slept with Marie a few times until Anne found out. I only understood the betrayal when I saw it on her face. I don't know why she didn't hold it against me. I guess she saw how young I was in many ways and decided to treat me kindly. And I'm a sucker for kindness, even if it ends.

But it hadn't yet, not then. One night, when I was hanging out with them at their new place on Fifth Street, they announced they were going to dinner at some Cuban playwright's house because she wanted to start a lesbian action group. I tried to invite myself along, but they weren't having any of it: "We don't really know her. That would be rude." But what's meant to be is meant to be, and I still ended up in the Lesbian Avengers. And had my dinner with that playwright, Ana Simo.

2.

If I mention Kathryn first, it's because I'm trying to remember what those days were like, what I was like, actually, when the East Village really did seem like a small town, and my dyke friends lived just around the corner, dragging their politics and art into the street. I remember neighborhood fixtures, like a homeless black man down near Fourth who ranted about honkeys and The Man and would spit at anything that moved. There was a cracked white woman, too, on St. Mark's Place, who would set up a card table with tattered antiporn pamphlets and a faded blow-up of that *Playboy* illustration that had a woman going through a meat grinder. There were also the ambulatory skeletons of people dying from AIDS, and I ventured into a couple of ACT UP meetings at Cooper Union, but there were so many people, so many men. I also tried a Women's Action Coalition meeting, but WAC was stuffed with those good-smelling SoHo types who had never applied for Medicaid. Closer to me was that young black woman who went around the park with Band-Aid–colored leggings smeared in the crotch with an enormous bloody stain.

Mostly I traced the neighborhood one concrete block at a time with my notebook and pen, looking for a moment or two of grace. Like that time in the middle of the night I saw this man playing Bach on his guitar in front of the Most Holy Redeemer Church, all around crumpled brown bags and pools of piss. He played with such concentrated joy even the drunks halted in their reeling dance back home. That grace is gone now, gone for me, anyway. Like Keith Haring's funny fucking figures, the anguished cries of David Wojnarowicz, and the tower in the community garden at Sixth and B that rose up bit by bit until it reached two or three stories, all scrap lumber, broken dolls, and old shoes strung on. It got too high. Aspired too much without permits. And probably was a menace.

Amy moved to Boston a long time ago. Ana and I went to France for a while. When we came back in 2010, Kathryn was one of the few old timers left who I'd kept up with, though she splits time with San Francisco. Not long ago, we ate big greasy burgers at Paul's, which still has the giant plastic hamburger outside. Afterwards, we went back to her place near the park, and listened to a little music—though not the Indigo Girls or Sinéad O'Connor—and talked a lot, about art and politics, the big scar on her chest, and the tiny ones on my belly. When I walked home, to Ana's, to ours, this time, through the silent streets, I tried to erase the chic restaurants, all the fancy apartment buildings, and cute little shops and feel what lay beyond.

Probably it happened like this. Amy came home from her job at the advertising agency doing Photoshop and Illustrator, changed into shorts, and we walked together to the Community Center over on West Twelfth, passing from artistic grunge and Latino flash to the bourgeois respectability of the West Village, though the center hadn't achieved that yet. It was crumbling and dirty, but very alive. Since coming to New York a couple years before, I'd only been there twice. Once, for a meeting of the Irish Lesbian and Gay Organization (ILGO) where I felt totally out of place despite my name. Again, for a thing put on by queer Puerto Ricans where I got all choked up at their fight for independence from the United States. They showed an image of Pedro Albizu Campos' body broken by jail and torture, and pictures of Lolita Lebrón, who had fired a few rounds into the House of Representatives and then rotted in a U.S. pen for twenty-five years before she was amnestied out.

The meetings were listed in front of the desk. I blanched

a little at the name. *Avengers* was great, but *lesbian* seemed a label of no return. Not that others hadn't stuck it on me. There was that summer after my sophomore year when I was working in Yellowstone with a skinny insecure "friend," and some afternoons the other girls would stand outside our dorm room howling, "Lezzies, lezzies, lezzies" like a pack of wolves. In Cincinnati once, a carload of guys with scrawny white necks threw beer bottles at me, yelling, "Fucking dyke." I knew I mostly liked girls, but I'd hedged my bets when I'd written to my mother to come out and named myself *bi*. She fired off a disgusted response, writing *prostitute* was more like it if my changing addresses were anything to go by. She didn't want to hear from me "until you're the girl God wants you to be."

Yet there I was in the Gay and Lesbian Center going to a meeting of the *Lesbian* Avengers. It was on some upper floor, and the air got hotter every couple of steps as we crept up the decrepit wooden staircase covered with posters. The funky bathrooms that intentionally mixed the signals for girls and boys were also covered with flyers, photos, postcards, and graffiti, queer history on the hoof. We picked our folding metal chairs, and I tried to look around without meeting anybody's eyes. I was there mostly because I was still trailing Anne and Marie and didn't want to miss anything. Chubby, brainy Amy probably would have gone anyway. She'd already been involved in feminist and queer stuff. She helped start a lesbian group in the Performance Studies Program at NYU where we met, and her bookcases were full of women writers from the academic Judith Butler to the dyke mystery guru Barbara Wilson and sci-fier Octavia Butler. Me, I'd dip into her shelves, then pass on, a fish searching for a different hook.

Gradually, the room filled up with women. Some were around my age, twenty-six. Others still in college. Some old enough to have grown kids. But all a little nervous and eager. Nobody foamed at the mouth or anything, though. Nobody brandished a sword or cape or breast. The first meeting of the

Lesbian Avengers was actually kind of bureaucratic, the way somebody officially called the meeting to order and the six organizers introduced themselves. I already knew the funny freckled Marie Honan and Anne Maguire with her riotous red hair. The writer, Sarah Schulman, and professor, Maxine Wolfe, had worked with ILGO, so I'd met them, too. Sarah was more blunt than the yearning narrator of *After Dolores*. Long-haired Max was efficient and expansive, the born teacher. There was also an angular androgynous dyke, Anne-christine d'Adesky, who turned out to be a journalist, and a short one with dark hair and bright-red lipstick who spoke so softly you could barely hear her. That was the playwright, Ana Simo.

After them, it was our turn. None of the names stuck at first, but I remember the multitude of accents: Hispanic, British, Irish, East Coast, West Coast, flat Midwestern, my faint Kentucky twang, and even a few homegrown New Yawk drawls. Then Sarah or somebody talked just enough to lay out what the Lesbian Avengers was supposed to be, "a direct-action group focused on issues vital to lesbian survival and visibility." And I nodded my head like I understood, though that phrase "direct action" didn't mean much to me. The closest I'd come to organizing anything was the time back in Louisville when I tried to get the kids in my youth choir to protest the sudden firing of the minister of music. Deb was a kind, energetic woman; I babysat her kid. When I came to her defense, the pastor denounced me in private as a confused little girl, then in public as an agitator, and I'd faded in shame.

"Visibility" didn't really mean anything either, except in the most basic sense. I'd never thought about how the world changed. Or about the world at all, for that matter. Martin Luther King gave a speech, and that was that. Public schools were desegregated. White teachers were horrible to black kids, and young white girls got their asses grabbed in the hallways by young black guys getting their own back. I'd been to NOW's March on Washington in '89 to photograph the marchers for an installation I was doing with some artist friends in Cincinnati, but they had to identify the VIPs in the shots. "Oh my god, you got Gloria Steinem." "Really?" But this idea of going to the source, aiming to change what people thought, how they saw each other, saw us, was something new to me.

That first Avenger meeting, sweating in that metal chair, I was really just there to be among girls, and to find out if I belonged. I wanted to. Anybody would. I can almost feel the gape-mouthed awe of watching the organizers talk about something called the Rainbow Curriculum, and why they'd decided our first action should be in support of it. I didn't say much, though plenty of others did. All the dykes there seemed so incredibly smart, creative, beautiful, adventurous, ready to take their place in the world. And there I was with them.

Pretty soon, we broke up into five or six groups and got to work. There was research to do, flyers to design, interviews to place, money to raise, and strategies and ideas to hash out— preferably involving balloons. Successful actions don't organize themselves.

The other day I was in the Lesbian Herstory Archives out in Brooklyn and saw the sign-up sheet for that first meeting. Something like fifty women attended, and forty-six were brave enough to put their John Hancocks down, along with phone numbers and addresses. Remarkably, most were still in the room two years later when we'd already mobilized twenty thousand lesbians for a '93 Dyke March in D.C., and sparked sixty other Avenger groups. I'm tempted to read out the names, one by one, and summon them back to me as they were in those days. Ready for anything, fearless, open, generous, and kind. Before the bitter end.

More dykes came every week as the word spread, cramming their bodies into the hot, dusty room, jockeying for spots near the window as flies buzzed around the place and our sweaty legs stuck to the seats. There hadn't been any action yet, but you could feel it coming, even in the committee reports. The Research girls came with two pages analyzing possible targets until they finally recommended a grade school in Middle Village, Queens, the heart of District 24. They talked a lot, but there wasn't much discussion afterward. We said, Excellent. Great. Who the hell really cared? Let's just get moving.

We rapidly approved draft flyers, including an alternative list of ABCs to hand out to parents and kids that featured lots of names I'd never heard of, like Urvashi Vaid, who was running something called the National Gay and Lesbian Task Force, which I'd never heard of either. Though, why would I, coming from Kentucky, writing poems, crisscrossing the streets of New York? I watched cop shows on TV, and baseball. The Mets lost. They always did. Nobody was inviting me to black-tie fund-raisers. Still don't.

The Rainbow Curriculum that the Board of Ed had developed used games and songs, from an Irish ballad to the Mexican hat dance, to teach little kids there were lots of different kinds of people in the world, and they should all be respected. We whipped ourselves up with scorn for the homophobic assholes, denouncing the whole project as "gay" because out of its 443 pages a whopping six mentioned queers, including the book *Heather Has Two Mommies*. Which was only on an additional reading list, and for that matter was about as insidious as a glass of milk. We also sneered a little at the dykes who would turn up as regularly as Cassandra to point an irate finger and accuse us of setting back the movement a hundred years by going anywhere near children. "My god, they already think we're pedophiles," they'd wail. We tried to keep it civil but didn't give an inch. Their discomfort, their desire to play it safe, avoid confronting taboos, seemed to confirm the rightness of what we were doing. Maxine Wolfe, the college professor, was the kind, but firm, diplomat. "Maybe this action isn't for you. Why don't you check back in afterwards?"

A few walked out and never returned, but most stuck around to see what we did next. They were a little like an audience at an air show, half marveling at our high-flying antics, half hoping we would crash and burn.

It would be dark when we left the center. Most Avengers would head to the nearby Art Bar or somewhere else to get cold beer. Amy and I would head home to the grunge of the East Village and the inferno of the apartment so she could get to work early and I could get to bed. It was like walking through water. The air was still full of heat, and the faint scent of the Hudson lurked underneath the exhaust and pollinating trees. Gradually, I began to sense other forces in the city besides the cracked sidewalks I walked every day, and the figures moving through the streets. Over everything, through it, and all around were the invisible filaments of politics, of bureaucracy, of a decaying decadent culture that looked under and into its beds and was afraid, and made us queers the scapegoats, drafting laws, defunding art, banning books that merely acknowledged our existence. As if they could force us into moral and physical exile.

But we refused to go.

We shaped our renegade lesbian identity action by action, flyer by flyer. A fund-raising poster featured little giggling girls in front of a blackboard. Like a public service announcement, it demanded, "Do you know where your daughters are?" (At the Lesbian Avengers' back-to-school party!) Carrie Moyer, this bleached blonde artist, did a flyer with a drawing of a superhero dyke flying over the city. She held a balloon reading, "I ♥ lesbians." And the caption screamed, "THE LESBIAN AVENGERS ARE COMING TO MAKE THE WORLD SAFE FOR BABY DYKES EVERYWHERE." It wasn't meant to reassure. Not with kids on the same page as LESBIAN. Not with the dyke in cape and tights jetting down from the sky.

We laughed our heads off, there in the center, but were a little more muted when it was time to go out to Queens and wheat-paste Carrie's flyer on lampposts and fences. Especially me. I might strip naked and shave myself for art, or wander the streets of the East Village at all hours, but I wasn't ready to claim either the word or the image. Still, I went, giggling nervously and sweating in the New York dusk. One of us stood lookout, while another swabbed the nearest flat surface with wallpaper paste and the third slapped a poster on before we all scampered away. The newbies among us laughed the loudest, almost hysterical with happiness and fear. The Lesbians are coming. The Lesbians are coming.

3.

On September 9, 1992, the first day of school in New York City, I scrounged a token and took the subway out to Middle Village, Queens, with Amy. Most of the school district was racially mixed, with shops as likely to have Mexican tortillas as Turkish preserves, or cartons of kimchi. Middle Village, though, was a mostly white working-class neighborhood that couldn't boast much except a cemetery housing Lucky Luciano and Don Carlo Gambino, and the Long Island Expressway.

We were the most interesting thing to happen there in ages. And while we would have made a splash if we'd come in black leather and raising our fists like the Black Panthers or ACT UP, the Lesbian Avenger Concept Committee decided what we really needed was Sousa. Sousa, and lavender balloons reading, "Ask about lesbian lives." It was ridiculous, absurd, delightful, though I wouldn't have admitted it then.

Jenny Romaine, an artist Amy knew from Performance Studies, pulled together a brass band, kitting them out in the knee socks and plaid skirts of Catholic school uniforms. She herself carried a big bass drum. Some Avengers wore T-shirts that read, "I was a lesbian child." I turned one down, saying I couldn't afford it, but refused even when Ana Simo, that mild-mannered Cuban playwright, offered me a discount. I still cringed at the word *lesbian*.

When we were all there, the sixty of us marched down Metropolitan Avenue to the elementary school, P.S. 87, singing at the top of our lungs, "Oh when the dykes, oh when the dykes, oh when the dykes come marching in." We revised a few other

Dixieland standards and proclaimed, "We are family. I've got all my sisters with me." One banner read, "Teach About Lesbian Lives" and another "The Lesbian Avengers." Somebody clutched an enormous bunch of the balloons, which had created a ruckus at the printer's, who kept misspelling l-e-s-b-i-a-n. We were met with disbelief, anger, fear, a few approving nods, but mostly the typical New Yorker's disinterest. Like them, I pretended I was totally cool with it. Hell, I did this kind of thing four or five times a week. No big deal. Like it was no big deal that when we got to the elementary school, the cops came with their thick blue arms and shiny shoes and tried to get us to leave.

At the civil disobedience training session, Maxine Wolfe explained it was perfectly legal to have a picket and hand out flyers. It was a public sidewalk, for crying out loud. And she'd been doing demos since the sixties, first for workers' rights, then women, then people with AIDS. But who knows what cops will do? Nothing, as it turned out. Maybe it was our unshakeable knowledge of our rights, or how we continued singing, handing out balloons, giving interviews and flyers, while our negotiators negotiated with them. Or maybe they just took one look at this group of relatively innocuous females in knee socks and plaid skirts and thought, "What the heck. It's New York. Let's go get donuts."

More than one kid got their first lesson in the real world when an Avenger handed them a balloon and their red-faced mother grabbed it away. No way is my little Sean or Antonio or Karen gonna be like *that*. As for the Xerox of our alternative alphabet—A for Acceptance, Action, and W. H. Auden; B for James Baldwin, Rita Mae Brown, and boycotting bigotry—some got tucked into pockets, others pointedly ripped into shreds. Though not in front of me. I stayed with the other picketers tracing that tiny oval on the sidewalk and avoiding confrontation. Maybe I held a sign for a while, feeling goofy and embarrassed, as I always did, at so much emotion being displayed.

The weather was nice, anyway, one of those perfect fall days with dark blue skies and white fluffy clouds that did not send forth lightning bolts or hail or anything at all to kill the lesbians. Nope, nobody died, there in front of the school yard. Neither were kids converted, or perverted, or particularly traumatized except when their angry moms grabbed their shiny balloons and let them float away. We just signaled to the world we existed. We'd been kids ourselves in school. The only thing different about us as adult lesbians was a few additional years. And self-awareness. Which was just beginning on my part.

Funny, I write that like it's nothing. *Just signaling to the world we existed*. When it was like setting off a bomb. What else could it be? Lesbians plus elementary schoolchildren.

We left en masse when the last student entered the school. In those days, bigots would sometimes haunt queer demos, grab a few stragglers, and beat the crap out of them. So, together, Avengers set off for their day jobs, or classes, or coffee shops. The media dykes went to send more press releases. And I remember at the next meeting, Maxine or Ana or somebody arrived triumphantly waving copies of *Newsday* and other rags that had covered the demo. We'd done it. We'd launched the Lesbian Avengers, and the city had taken note.

Not everybody was happy about it. Homophobe-in-chief, Mary A. Cummins, worked twice as hard to kill the Rainbow Curriculum. She was a white-haired grandmother and president of the school board in District 24 where we'd taken our balloons, and she worked that white hair for all it was worth. "Look how nice I am, how innocent. How mean the homos are to me." Her specialty was forging unholy alliances, and she pulled one off with Cardinal John O'Connor, and the evangelical Pat Robertson. But the real coup was dragging in New York's African American and Latino churches in a kind of rainbow of hate.

Of course, Cummins and her lily-white board had no ulterior motives, like seeing the whole multicultural thing dumped. It was just a fluke a few years later in '94 when District 24 elected Louisa M. Chan, its first minority school board member, and Ms. Cummins immediately attacked her behind closed doors as a know-nothing chink. Cummins denied the allegations, though in another session packed with press she went on to call Chan "an evil, wicked woman," declaring, "I'll say what I like, as long as I'm an American!"

Chan responded, "I'm an American, too."

That's what we were saying also, just by taking to the streets. But Republicans didn't accept it. Played one minority against each other, defining just who a real American was. Sometimes immigrants were. Sometimes not. In his speech to the '92 Republican National Convention, Pat Buchanan used the "brave people of Koreatown" to slam the (black) welfare-ridden mobs of the LA riots, setting everybody against the bra-burning feminists, tree-huggers, and of course, homosexuals. It was a Culture War, a holy war, he declared, for the soul of America. Extremist Christians would do anything to save it. Including bombing abortion clinics and dipping into their filthy minds to create videotapes "proving" lesbians and gay men did nothing but have orgies with animals and babies and assorted inanimate objects, snacking on fecal matter between rapes.

In California, antigay activists perfected divide-and-conquer when they defined lesbians and gay men as "a rich class demanding 'special rights' at the expense of *true* minorities"— which didn't seem like a lie because the visible leaders of the movement were almost exclusively white and privileged (and male). In New York City, plenty eagerly swallowed the hook. The mostly black District 29 decided it was better to dump the curriculum, let their kids pay the price, than extend a mere six pages of respect to queers. Thousands of black and Hispanic parents marched on the Board of Ed and flooded every hearing. No way they had anything in common with rich white pervs. No way they were gonna let that Chancellor of Schools Joe Fernandez turn their kids into sodomites. He even wanted to hand out rubbers in high schools. What was the world coming to?

The Avengers who attended the hearings would come back shaken at seeing the whole gamut of human faces so contorted with hate. When we spoke in favor of the curriculum, they screamed at us, stomped, threw chairs, and pumped fists in dyke and faggot faces, even if some of us were black or Latina like them.

I signed up to go but chickened out. I didn't want to be there when it finally erupted, the mass antigay lynch mob. Everybody knew about the murders of black kids at Howard Beach and Bensonhurst, but queers were getting killed, too. And not just by AIDS. The year 1992 had started with a student in Alabama shooting members of Auburn's lesbian and gay organization from his dormitory window. In March, a gang of kids—the youngest eight years old—shot a bartender at a Norfolk, Virginia, gay bar just because they wanted to "mess with some gays." In April, an off-duty cop and his pal attacked a couple of dykes in Methuen, Massachusetts. In May, in the Detroit suburbs, a lesbian couple was shot and killed in their front yard by a neighbor. And these were just the cases that got attention. In New York, queers were regularly murdered and dumped in the Hudson. Transgendered people and drag queens, many of them black and Hispanic, disappeared without a trace. We'd all been harassed. Some of us beaten.

If you'd have gotten out a U.S. map and colored in a bright red dot for every attack, huge crimson smears would have covered places like Oregon, where the Christian Right was in the throes of an antigay campaign. They wanted it set down in the black and white of their constitution that we were child-molesting monsters, not worthy of homes or jobs or even life. Their foot soldiers destroyed the offices of LGBT organizations, beat up queers. In Salem, Oregon, skinheads spent months harassing Brian Mock, a white, gay disabled guy. First they just called him names, then they threw things at the rooming house where he lived. They finally beat him so badly he could barely move and his face was unrecognizable. When his friend, African American lesbian Hattie Mae Cohens, tried to step in and protect him, she became a victim, too. On September 27, 1992, at 3:18 a.m., the four wannabe Nazis tossed a Molotov cocktail at their rooming house, burning them both alive.

"Nigger dyke," the skinheads jeered, as they watched the building burn, uniting us minorities as objects of hate, whether we wanted it or not.

4.

Not long after the murders in Oregon, the New York City Anti-Violence Project (AVP) asked the Avengers to join them in a protest march on October 30, the night before the big Halloween parade. I saw it for the first time in '89. I was on my way to get a falafel after a class at NYU when I got caught up in a shocking mob of drag queens all dressed up as the pope and his cardinals with enormous red hats and robes. There was also a bloody Marie Antoinette and her courtiers with giant wigs and sequins. Huge puppets. Practically fresh off the bus, I'd only seen drag queens at the one gay dive in Lexington where I went to college. They were like my furious sister Vikki, who also had big hair, extravagant blue eye shadow, and sometimes drew her knife-like fingernails down whatever was nearest, my arm, neck, back.

It was dark and there were barriers everywhere, sending me off into a maze of narrow streets that were stuffed with white suburbanites loaded with plastic cups and beer bottles and flasks trying to get a glimpse of the freaks. They wore Batman or Catwoman masks or powdered white faces made up as sadistic Jokers. Others came as themselves, with the acid-washed blue jeans and matching jackets of the bridge and tunnel crowd. I was the hickster ingénue, authentically shabby in my army jacket and holey shoes that the Irish girls made me throw away a year later. "How can you wear these stinking things?"

Music blasted from the floats and the bars, along with laughter, shouts. Glass shattered in the distance. People smashed up against me, sometimes excusing themselves, mostly not. I couldn't breathe, never made it to Mamoun's Falafel, just got the hell out of the crush, and descended into the nearest functioning subway station. The train had already been pelted with eggs and whatever else the mobs of teenagers found. There was that plastic string stuff everywhere, and graffiti scrawled on seats and subway maps. All the working people looked warily at the platforms when the train stopped and doors opened. They were still full of kids unleashing chaos, covering the city with garbage, broken bottles, broken egg shells, the tempera of drying yolk, and blood.

I learned that was a typical Halloween, with the blood often belonging to queers.

That was why AVP was holding the antiviolence march, and also warning every queer they could find to skip the Halloween night parade. The year before, there had been even more anti-gay attacks than usual. The Avengers said "yes" to the march, and a big fat "no" to staying home when things heated up. It would make a mockery of any effort to Take Back the Night, as the protest march was called. Otherwise you'd have to rename it Take Back One Night, or Take Back the Nights That Aren't Too Troublesome and Don't Require Very Much Effort.

Remembering the Oregon murders, we decided to build a shrine to Hattie Mae Cohens and Brian Mock at Father Demo Square in the Village and plant ourselves there from the chaos of Halloween Eve through Election Day. Jennifer Monson, a wiry dyke with strawberry blonde hair and a sideways way of talking, suggested we transform the image of their deaths by learning to eat fire. She turned out to be a dancer and choreographer, with a bunch of friends in alternative circuses. A couple of days before the march, Amy and I and some others found ourselves out in Brooklyn with jars of lighter fluid, rags, and a bunch of metal hangers in a room filled with juggling pins, and swords, and stilts. I hadn't meant to learn. I was mostly tagging along with Amy, who was really into it, and seeing who else would turn up.

There were a dozen or so of us, all about my age or younger. All white, too. When I'd asked Marlene Colburn, this older African American dyke if she was going to learn because she was as tough as anybody and had a lot of flair, she just laughed and said, "Are you kidding?" Another black woman said it was nuts, too, that *her* people had better sense than that, though she was even younger than me. And paid her tuition dancing in a bar.

When we got there, Jennifer Monson introduced us to her friend Jennifer Miller, the director of Circus Amok, the one-ring, gender-bending spectacle of political agitators, jugglers, and tightrope walkers. She showed us all how to wrap a little bit of rag around the end of a hanger (not too big or the flame will be enormous), then dip it in lighter fluid or kerosene (lighter fluid tasted less gross). You tilt your head back so the approaching flame doesn't burn off your nose or hair and insert it into your mouth as you exhale slightly. Close your lips, it's extinguished. Make a mistake and inhale—your lungs explode and you die.

It was harder in Jennifer Miller's case because she was a bearded lady and her face was flammable. But I still balked when it came down to it, even with my short hair and smooth cheeks. If you want to talk about unnatural acts, bringing fire toward your face clearly qualifies. Sticking it in your mouth is downright nuts. But I didn't want to look like a wimp in front of the others, so I grabbed a torch, lit it, tilted my head back, and opened my mouth, exhaling in a great gust.

I could eat fire. It was nothing at all.

We practiced until we could do it with aplomb, in unison. We even learned to light the torches from each other's flaming tongues. We started to pick up each other's names: Sara, Michelle, Alison were all roommates at a loft on Avenue D. Then there was Cindra, Rachel, Lysander, the Jennifers. It was a bonding experience. We became friends. Some of us, lovers.

It was chilly and dark at Father Demo Square. The streetlights barely shone. You could hear the march coming from blocks away with whistles and chants, the call and response of "Whose streets?" "Our streets!" as we reclaimed the Village, making it safe. Suddenly, the marchers were around us, a nervous, angry crowd with signs, "No on Nine" (the antigay Oregon measure), "Bigots Go Home," and "Justice for Marsha," a murdered black drag queen and transactivist the cops were ignoring.

Lysander climbed up on a plastic milk crate in front of our homemade shrine, and we formed lines off to her right and left. She was a deeply religious person who wore an Elmer Fudd cap. Other Avengers handed out candles, and the small crowd lit them as Lysander began to read from her notes. It was as much a homily as an activist's speech. Her voice shook a little, but the people fell silent as she talked, first about the nearby dyke bashing where a gang of kids attacked two lesbians just for embracing, then about Oregon, where Hattie Mae Cohens and Brian Mock had been burned alive.

"We Lesbian Avengers have built this shrine. It stands for our fear. It stands for our grief. It stands for our rage. And it enshrines our intention to live fully and completely as who we are, wherever we are. We take the fire of action into our hearts. And we take it into our bodies. And we stand, here and now, to make it known that we are here, and here we will stay. Our fear does not consume us. Their fire will not consume us. We take that fire, and we make it our own."

And Lysander touched the torch to her tongue where the flame stayed lit long enough to light a second torch. And the Avengers to her right and left lit their own. And so, the fire passed down the line from tongue to torch to tongue. On my side, from Rachel to me, then Sara, then Alison, her roommate. And we raised our flames triumphantly into the air, leaned back, and swallowed them down. The crowd cheered, a little uncertainly, at watching a circus trick transformed into a sacrament.

I took a couple of shifts at the shrine encampment. The Village was one of the most gay-friendly places in the city, and also the most dangerous, because the homophobes knew where to find us. And there we were, handing out leaflets with the words *gay* and *lesbian* smack-dab on the front, explaining how violence and murders followed hateful antigay campaigns like sharks follow the scent of blood.

I remember being cold and sitting on scrounged cardboard to keep the damp from rising up from the concrete. An outreach worker to the homeless brought warm blankets that we returned when it was all over. We peed in the coffee shop at the corner. The revelers of Halloween came and went like the fading light. We stood vigil and bled into the gray city. Sometimes, other queers joined us for a while, lighting candles to their friends who were dead from violence or AIDS. The sidewalk was a constellation. People bought us slices of pizza and paper cups of coffee. Somebody brought the news that the Vatican had finally lifted the Inquisition's edict against Galileo. The world *did* revolve around the sun. More than one romance was born when Avengers huddled together. It became hard to leave after your shift. Part of you wanted to stay there forever, claiming, at the very least, that corner of the city, inserting yourself as a speck in the public eye.

We packed up on Election Day and took stock of things at the next meeting. The liberals' darling, Bill Clinton, dethroned George Herbert Walker Bush, but queers still got creamed. In Oregon, where Hattie Mae and Brian were murdered, tons of local antigay laws got passed, though the statewide initiative failed. A lot of cities like Tampa dumped pro-gay ordinances. Probably the biggest victory for the Christian Right was in Colorado, where they passed a statewide amendment making it legal to kick us out of our jobs, our apartments, even the hospital.

We hissed in frustration. Queers couldn't keep up. More antigay campaigns started every day, and each was followed by violence. If we were going to get anywhere, we had to rouse a national press that was mostly ignoring the story. Somebody had to knock on their door, beat on it if they had to, and announce the casualties of the "Culture War." What good was it being in New York if the Avengers didn't answer the call?

On November 19, a couple of weeks after the encampment, we met outside the Plaza Hotel in midtown Manhattan. It was rush hour, and Fifth Avenue was a river of angry light. Our marshals quickly blocked the traffic, and before the cops could do anything, we'd taken the street. A bunch of us had torches made out of small sticks gleaned from the trees at Tompkins Square Park in the East Village and wrapped with rags. When we lit them, the cops moved in, warning us we weren't allowed to have open flames.

Hell, we weren't allowed to do a lot of things, but that wasn't going to stop us. There, on Fifth Avenue, the skyscrapers rising up on either side, we burning dykes took off down the street with the cops in hot pursuit. At first, when they caught us, they'd just put out the torch, drop it on the ground, then move on. It took them a while to notice somebody else would pick it up, relight it, and take off again playing cat and flaming mouse. I was just about the last one with my torch held high, the crowd cheering as I refused to relinquish it to the cops. How could I, in the city's twilight, surrounded by dyke voices calling out for justice, for freedom? For once I was brave. I didn't let go and move on. I held tight to what I had.

Even after the cops wrestled away the last torch, we continued marching to Rockefeller Center, home to NBC with plenty of other media outlets nearby. There, other Avengers had reassembled the shrine to Hattie Mae Cohens and Brian Mock. And Marlene Colburn, with Mandela's high cheekbones and same angry resolve, raised her bullhorn and condemned the antigay amendments in Colorado and Oregon, calling out the names of dead queers and demanding attention be paid as the antigay measures, written on flash paper, went up in flames.

That was the first time we stepped out as lesbians onto Fifth Avenue, the symbolic heart of the city, and the first time in decades lesbians owned the street. Something shifted in me. With the Avengers guarding my back, I was briefly, fearlessly myself. I was transformed. And these early actions, with their rituals changing hate and fear into a kind of resolve, bound us together in ways I didn't understand until a long time after the group itself combusted.

5.

A few days later, just before Thanksgiving, the Avengers held a Speakout Against Violence over at the Center. I'd never seen so many dykes in one place, especially African Americans and Latinas. It was like subway cars from the Bronx and Brooklyn all got tipped out in the West Village. Everybody had stories to tell. Mostly worse than mine. I was already gone from the house when I told my mother I was bi so there was a limit the damage her rejection could do. I'd been harassed and insulted on the street but never ended up in the hospital like some of these dykes, put there by random strangers. Or worse, by their families who attacked them inside their own homes. They had mothers and fathers and brothers and sisters who didn't just snicker or sneer or pray. They beat the holy crap out of their own flesh and blood. Or raped them, kicked them out into the streets when they were just kids so they had to beg or turn tricks. We were the experts in family values.

The mike went from hand to hand to hand. The voices were raw. Some hesitant. Some self-pitying and whiny. Others piti-less and enraged. All as suicided by society as Van Gogh ever was. I can still hear their voices. Maybe because we're still being attacked, no matter how many times we climb on the deck of that metaphorical destroyer and wave a giant banner, "Vic-tory." No matter how many legal bones we're tossed.

That year we had no illusions about what America thought. What we had were friends like us, and in the best queer tradi-tion we celebrated Thanksgiving with a gathering of the homo-clan in the Avenue B loft. Somebody brought a Tofurky sort of thing. Somebody else did potatoes. Stuffing. Then there was cranberry sauce. Assorted casseroles, curries, salads. The whole deal except the bird, which even now I avoid in my return to meat-eating. We joked about green beans slimed with cream of mushroom soup and opened bottle after bottle of Beaujolais Nouveau. And put on loud music. And laughed and ate and drank all day. The only traditions we skipped were the red-faced fights, bitter squabbling, broken crockery, and tears.

We even gave thanks. That we'd found our true families, queer ones. And that we weren't in Colorado where more and more lesbians and gay men were getting the shit kicked out of them, even before Amendment 2 took effect.

Colorado queers fought back tooth and nail, filing lawsuits, and organizing an economic boycott, which mostly meant getting people to avoid Coors beer and cancel ski trips. That wasn't a problem for me since I didn't like Coors, anyway, and skiing wasn't at all on my agenda. In early December, the Avengers decided to be more proactive when we heard the Denver mayor was coming to New York on December 7 and 8 to promote tourism. There wasn't much time to plan, so the meeting just settled on a boring picket outside the Regency Hotel where the guy was having a power breakfast. I didn't see the point of standing there with a poster and shivering in the cold, so I didn't sign up to go. Apparently the handful who turned up agreed. One Avenger just asked the obvious, "Why don't we go in?" A few moments later, eight dykes burst into the hotel conference room tossing leaflets to the journalists and chanting, "We're here, we're queer. We're NOT going skiing!"

The mayor's mouth hung open in shock. There was an uproar. It was scary, fun, and it worked.

I should say up front that Wellington Webb wasn't a bad guy. He was Denver's first African American mayor and was actually pretty gay-friendly himself, appalled at the amendment. But he'd come to plug Colorado tourism in the midst of a gay boycott and that made him a target. Small groups of Avengers followed him for the next two days, busting in on meetings and making their point, then getting out before security arrived. After the first day, a dyke from the mayor's own office leaked the Avengers a copy of his schedule, and his pursuers would get to his appointments before him and goad bored reporters into grilling Webb about Amendment 2. He added more and more police protection, but intimidation didn't work. Neither did stealth. Once he sent his limo around to the entrance while he took a cop car and tried to sneak into the back, but the Avengers figured it out and zapped him anyway. We laughed our asses off when Avenger and journalist Ann Northrop came to the meeting and told us about it in her sardonic, East Coast drawl.

After he was a guest on a radio show and Avengers bombarded him with calls, he retired in defeat, canceling not just the rest of the New York trip, but the six-city extravaganza he had planned. And on December 21, the *New York Times* finally published an editorial. After declaring their sympathy for the liberal Mayor Webb, and bemoaning how economic boycotts hurt everybody, they admitted it was necessary in this case. Not just to change the law in Colorado, but to discourage other states from passing similar measures: "The boycott is a legitimate weapon in a democratic society and, historically, one of the most effective."

We passed the newspaper clipping around at the meeting, amazed at the power of a handful of big-mouthed dykes. The action wasn't as dramatic as fire-eating, but it was effective. And unexpected. We broke as many taboos. Imagine intruding into that fancy hotel and screaming when the only sounds you hear are the clink of cutlery, the polite murmur of power.

A couple of weeks after targeting the Teachers Union for their lukewarm support of the Rainbow Curriculum, Avengers hit *Self* magazine on January 25, 1993. We'd sent a letter asking them nicely to respect the Colorado boycott and skip their ski weekend in Aspen. When they didn't respond, we paid a house call, chanting awkwardly over the muted clatter of fingers on keyboards, the ka-ching of advertising dollars pouring in. That was enough for Alexandra Penney, the editor, to storm out of her office, absolutely freaking: "Why are you doing this to us?"

The *New York Times* thought it was hilarious. So did *Newsday*. And the *Daily News*. Hell, everybody did. Because Penney wasn't just any old editor, but the author of *How to Make Love to a Man*. And she'd been zapped by the Lesbian Avengers. Afterward, *Self* pulled their trip, proclaiming it had nothing to do with us. Nope, nothing at all.

Hearing about the actions was almost enough to redeem the season of sanctimonious good cheer and endless focus on the family, no matter how dysfunctional. For Christmas, I'd been to Pennsylvania with Amy, tucking away my grandmother's two holiday cards. She'd peppered descriptions of dental work with complaints about my attitude. "Maybe you want to forget us, but we can't forget you. We love you." It set my teeth on edge, that little forgotten grain of truth. Yes, I'd once been loved. Propped between my sisters on the couch for holiday photos. Sprawled on my dad's big belly and listening to the beating of his sentimental heart.

But what do you want from a mixed marriage, the poor Southern Baptist woman putting all her hopes on the genial Catholic bourgeois man? Enough ink's been spilled on the usual heterosexual misery. By the time I was twelve, my bright, sensitive mother was lost to bitterness and hate. My oblivious father drifted further away. Everybody suffered. Though it was good for a few horrible stories. The time my mom flipped out and threatened to run her car into a brick wall—and then denied it. That time in high school, after the divorce, when my dad dropped me from his insurance and refused to pay up when I had to have a bone tumor chopped off. The doctor said it was benign, after all. But a few months later when he found a lump on his dog (nothing at all, said the vet), he still paid to have it removed. And proudly told me so at his Derby Party, tears welling up in his eyes.

Which is why I fled to the Parkers' even if it meant shivering in a cold colonial attic and being quoted at by Amy's two skinny little sisters and tiny beanpole brother who knew all of Monty Python and had, as a result, a particular fascination for the sex lives of mollusks. Short, round Amy looked like the mailman's kid next to them, though she could quote Monty Python, too. Her mother interrupted her Christmas cookie baking mania just long enough to make a lemon meringue pie because she knew it was my favorite. Which made me tear up because it was more than my own family did.

During the Christmas Eve party, I drank gin and tonics in the kitchen with Amy's father and I made him blush with extravagant curses this Scottish girl Melanie had taught me at the Halloween encampment. I guess I wanted to bust a hole in all that season's familial pressure, expectations, and disappear into the ether. But her dad didn't freak out, just teased me back with jokes about some disgusting lentil burgers I'd made once when I was still Amy's significant other a couple of years before.

It sounds kind of sappy. It was. But it was nice to let my guard down a little. Eat cookies. Get drunk. Rely, again, on the kindness of strangers.

6.

In February, somebody, possibly me, suggested a stink-bombing campaign. Not everybody was thrilled. Fire-eating may have been a circus trick, but it was really impressive, transformative even. But what kind of gravitas do stink bombs have? I didn't care. When it came to self-image, I didn't need to spring from the head of the virgin huntress, Athena, like plenty of old-time feminists. Give me Medusa or Loki any day, the Merry Pranksters, the glorious Dadaists, or the irreverent Van Dykes with sex workshops and T-shirts sporting a gun-toting Patty Hearst.

In no time, the working group came up with the perfect slogan, "Homophobia stinks," identified plenty of smelly targets, and we were off. I paired up with Melanie Fallon, the curly-headed Barnard student with a slight Scottish accent and the gawky elegance of a colt. She was the one I'd met at the Halloween encampment who had shared her foul-mouthed mother's creative curses. Her father was a scientist. Her younger sister very American. Our target was St. Patrick's Cathedral, the epicenter of antigay activism in New York. ACT UP had made their own stink there a year or two before, invading a mass at the drippy neo-Gothic building to protest how the Catholic Church spread HIV with their campaigns against condoms and queers.

When Melanie and I got uptown on February 12, 1993, there were tourists everywhere, and plenty of security guards. I was sweating and nervous, sure I had a sign indicating "trouble-making dyke" on my back. We whispered in the corner, giggled, and tried to think it through. The committee had mostly considered the metaphorical aspects, not the practical ones.

The space was too enormous for a little stench to penetrate. We needed a crew of twenty and a crate of stink. We decided to go ahead anyway. I dropped a couple of glass vials on the floor, but when I stepped on them with my tennis shoes, they wouldn't break. Melanie finally crushed them with her big Doc Martens boots. But in the big cathedral, the vials barely had the impact of a fart. We slapped a sticker on the back of a pew and left.

Another Avenger cell had more impact in their attack on the rancid Jack Hale. He was a lawyer for the archdiocese of New York, and they loaned him out to whatever bigot needed him next. Like the antigay granny Mary Cummins. Or the Ancient Order of Hibernians, which was responsible for banning ILGO from the upcoming St. Paddy's Day Parade. The plan was to break a huge amount of stink bombs in the elevator of his office building and put a sticker on the inside doors. People would get in, notice the stench, and see the sticker when the doors closed. It went better than anybody dreamed because when Mr. Hale went on TV that night to slam Irish queers, he was stupid enough to complain at length about the stink bombing, holding up the sticker the whole time, just as if he were paid to. So thanks to Mr. Hale, all of New York got to see the Lesbian Avenger logo and read our message, "Homophobia stinks!"

We barely had time to celebrate before we were on to the next actions, focusing on St. Valentine's Day. It was tempting to massacre a few assholes, but what we did on the 13th was take the train out to a neighborhood in Queens armed with lyrics for a serenade. It was snowy, dark, and cold. There weren't many streetlights among the row houses, just the yellow squares from windows, so after ringing the doorbell of the white-haired, homophobe Mary Cummins, we could barely see our lines to sing, "Cupid, get out your bow, la, la, la, Shoobey-doo-waa."

It was enough. A hook-nosed Irishman charged out, bellowing, "Why the hell don't you go home? You're disturbing the peace." His voice shook with anger and fear, though the only real affront was the key we tried to sing in. Still, I can imagine what he and Mary thought in their dirty minds. "First those lezzies turn up at the grade school, and now at our own door. Singing!" Which was somehow more offensive and terrifying than anything I could have dreamed up, like egging their house or setting bags of burning shit on their doorstep that they'd have to stamp out.

On St. Valentine's Day itself, more mittened Avengers made their way to the New York Public Library in midtown where enormous stone lions stand guard over rare books and researchers housed inside. The Avengers were more interested in the snowy Bryant Park in back, where there is a statue of Gertrude Stein.

I can't remember when I first heard of her. In art history, I think, when they flashed that portrait Picasso did where she was more boulder than woman. The professor didn't say much about her, just repeated the legend that when someone told Picasso that Stein did not look like her portrait, he replied, "She will." And she did. Later on, when I found out she was a dyke, and a writer, and I was, too, I carried around a postcard of her and Alice B. Toklas. I didn't read anything by Stein until that year between college and New York when I was living in Cincinnati, writing poems, and doing rogue performances. Like having a handful of women stand up to crunch apples in the midst of an audience expecting poems.

It was around then that I gobbled down so much of *The Making of Americans* I almost made myself sick. That rhythm got in my head, repeating Americans endlessly repeating themselves, and I couldn't sleep for weeks. What audacity, grappling with what an entire country was, what humans are, at the same time she was upending the novel, turning words into hallucinogens. It couldn't have been easy keeping at it. Her own brother scoffed, nobody published her work for years, and when they did, most critics sneered. Not just because her writing was experimental, but because she was a big dyke and didn't hide it.

The Avenger goal outside the library was to reunite that statue of Gertrude with one of her lover, Alice, and, as Maxine Wolfe put it in her opening words, to celebrate the connections between dyke love, dyke art, dyke activism. It looked pretty good, that Alice statue. The committee had been working on it for ages, besides rehearsing a Thespian Avengers version of Stein's poem "Lifting Belly." The bill also boasted experimenting dykes like our own Sarah Schulman, and a ton of others like Yvonne Rainer and Eileen Myles, whom I'd met during those few months I kept company with the dancer Jennifer Monson.

I think we got together over Mason jars of kerosene and bits of old sheets during the fire-eating lesson. We played on the swings at Tompkins Square Park and traipsed out to see the ducks in Jamaica Bay. It wasn't just how they floated and flew, but the invisible paths they traced in migration. A kind of globe-trotting dance. Jennifer lived in Williamsburg, which was still full of abandoned buildings, and we'd go to explore, sliding under ribbons of yellow warning tape. Light streamed through broken roofs. Holes gaped in the floor. She'd grab me by the hand and pull me forward past the dirty needles and condoms until we could barely see. If we had to, we could almost navigate by the burnt-sugar stink of the Domino factory a few blocks away.

Her apartment was a loft bed in the dance studio she and her roommate DD Dorvillier built in the old matzoh factory on Bedford Avenue. If I was still there when rehearsals started in the morning, I'd join in warm-ups when all the dancers started squirming across the floor or throwing themselves around on it. Sometimes I'd stay to watch them collide as hard as they could in the air, waltz upside down on their hands, try on the furry legs of fauns instead of tutus and tights, and disrupting, if you will, the time-space-gender continuum I'd always accepted as dance. Once, I went with her and her posse of dancers to the foot of the bridge. It was night. We began climbing. I only made it a little way, but they kept inching their way up, from one handhold to the next. Jennifer went furthest. She always did, hanging on like she hadn't forgotten her evolutionary roots and had that much more connection to the starry, threatening sky.

It was around then we took a workshop with her friend Eileen Myles, this amazing dyke poet who wasn't exactly what you'd call an activist but in '92 had campaigned as a write-in candidate for president, claiming America in her own way, like Wojnarowicz had and the Avengers were beginning to. The class was in a loft somewhere farther east in the East Village. I remember one girl who had tattoos and piercings, or should have, and played in a band. And Eileen would hand out Xeroxes of John Ashbery or whoever she was into that day, and we'd read our own poems. She didn't mind it when I handed over sonnets—yeah, sonnets—all typed out, the rhymes doing their best to nail together my own uncontrollable life. She was one of the first dyke poets to write about her own, and dare leave her life so messy and raw only the poetry itself redeemed it. Later on, I read with her a few times, including at Mona's on Avenue B way up near Fourteenth Street. I always liked hearing Eileen read. She didn't get too singsong or pretend to be incanting anything. She just set her jaw and got going, letting all the sounds of working-class Boston spill out.

That afternoon, the crowd was stuffed with Avengers. And the words were working for me, too, every poem lodging in the audience like pleasant little hooks that bound us briefly together. It was the same feeling I got running around with fire, when every other voice amplifies yours. Every body delivers the message you exist.

I don't know what Jennifer thought of me. I was kind of a mess, writing about being broke and sick, pressing this burning body against hers that could do back flips. We never were good at communicating. She was a dancer. I was a writer. And writers aren't the best with words when they don't have a blank page in front of them, and time to revise. More than once, Jennifer bit me in the throws of some emotion that may have been passion, maybe not. Sometimes I suspected she was a maenad considering the best way to rip me limb from limb to get the poetry out. I gave consent to be devoured. We all did. She persuaded a couple dozen Avengers to be in a dance at P.S. 122. When it was time, we ran from the audience to the stage, threw ourselves on the floor, pounded and screamed, then left after the tantrum. She also tucked away that image of a small group of burning figures surrounded by the rising buildings of Fifth Avenue. It echoes through her work even now.

Filmmaker Su Friedrich saw the Avengers in front of the elementary school wearing "I was a lesbian child" T-shirts and was seized by the idea for *Hide and Seek,* part documentary, part fiction. Sue Schaffner and Carrie Moyer—who designed so many of our flyers—took Avengers for their Dyke Action Machine posters, posing us as *American Gothic,* as spoofs of Benetton ads. Sarah Schulman inserted us in her book *My American History.* And haunted by the burning deaths of Hattie Mae Cohens and Brian Mock, Ana Simo wrote *The Table of Liquid Measures.* Maybe it was a continual summer, after all, this incredible fecundity. Rage and joy ripening on the vine. No matter what the season. And Gertrude Stein was the mother of us.

When her snowy statue was united with Alice, and the last poem read, somebody cranked up a boom box, and the Avengers danced their own experimental versions of foxtrots and tangos, first upright, then horizontal, rolling around like puppies, like pigeons in the snowy grass.

A couple days later, Lower Manhattan shook with an enormous explosion and sirens went off all over the city. There'd been a bombing downtown at the World Trade Center. Six dead, a thousand injured. More than one preacher blamed queers for it as if all we had to do was exist with our lesbian bodies, and lesbian voices, and lesbian jeans, and lesbian coats for the inhabitants of Jericho to shake with terror, and the walls of Jericho fall.

7.

Not that gestures don't have their power. What is that gazillion-dollar endeavor of advertising (or politics, or activism, or art) but an almost religious manipulation of images?

Just before Lent started, I got some 2x4s and built an enormous caduceus in the living room to explore my own concerns about lesbian bodies. Barbed wire snaked up the form instead of a reptile, and the double arms of the cross hinted at abstract wings. I hung relics here and there, used lacquered tampons and test tubes filled with toe jam, fingernails, chunks of hair, or my own mysterious blood that doctors grabbed sometimes hoping to cure my mysterious fevers, later, my tangled guts. The treadmill came mail order, maybe from Amy's credit card points, and every day during Lent I walked in front of the caduceus for as long as I could stand it, sometimes two or three hours, sometimes more, but never until I dropped. I called the performance *Surviving Salvation,* got blisters, and bruises on my heels, new aches, fevers, and nightmares, and a case of boredom so profound I could've died of it.

On Sundays, visitors were encouraged, but not essential. I wore a hospital gown with my ass hanging out and made guests put on those surgical latex gloves with talcum inside to make them feel complicit with the stern and snickering gods of the medical establishment. I only invited Avengers, tossing a few postcards in the center of the room at the end of meetings when people made announcements. Some came and wrote comments in the comment book. One woman asked me if I prayed. Another picked a fight about alternative medicine and said I could be perfectly healthy if I only wanted. "Try this for fever. That for joints. You should meditate."

Some freaked out at the enormous cross-like thing. Others were disturbed that I chatted while I walked in front of it, as if I were a hostess. Su Friedrich videoed for a little while, though there wasn't much to shoot. I was pretty much just walking in place, without emotion or anything. It was cold so I didn't even sweat. I didn't realize she was a real filmmaker until later. Nobody in the Avengers waved their creds. She was just this long-haired woman who kept the books and had a cranky New York sense of humor, a blunt naïveté. Jennifer came and draped Guatemalan amulets on the barbed wire.

Fire-eating friends turned up one day bringing beer, and smoking cigarettes in the dusty hallway because it was banned in our apartment. I joined them for a while, leaving the treadmill running, and considered counting the movement in absentia. But I couldn't make myself do it and went back in, climbed on, and walked. I didn't mind when they called me a wuss. It was something to write down in my notebook.

Sarah Schulman came, too, and in her abrupt way asked if I'd shaved my head to make myself look sicker. "I'm not sorry for you."

"Good," I said. "That's not the point." Though if she'd wanted to pat me on the head and buy a round, I would've drunk it, no problem. The shaving was mostly to signal the end of one thing, the beginning of another. Or at least induce a moment of contemplation. In Nepal, that's what you do when a relative dies. I'd done a whole unscheduled shaving performance at NYU when I figured out that most of grad school was about taking whatever was natural and true and stuffing it into inaccessible language and appropriate, official forms. Pretty much like my mother tried to stuff me into the shape of a proper girl. It was infuriating. What was the point of thinking things and trying to know things if you were only going to communicate them to people just like you? Maybe they didn't notice the gap, those other students of the academic caste whose parents were professors. Not clerk-typists like my mom, and whatever it was my father did. He was not an engineer, no matter what my mom taught me to tell the other kids in elementary school.

I reserved the rounded, windowed classroom at the intersection of two hallways, put up a few notices, and when the moment came, plugged in the razor, stripped naked, and buzzed myself from toe to legs, crotch, underarms, arms, head while the audience gaped from outside. They gasped loudest at the eyebrows. "Is she really going to...? Omigod, she did." Afterwards I applied pantyhose, skirt, deodorant, blouse, lipstick, and eyeliner, with a quick spritz of breath freshener. That, I called *Art-Official Ritual*.

The chair of the department flipped out and called me into her office with her co-chair to see if I needed counseling. "You understand this is an academic program?"

I should have known better. I'd already had a run-in with the official art authorities when I'd visited with my contemporary art class from Transylvania University in Lexington. During a tour of MOMA, or the Guggenheim, maybe, I went bananas when I saw a Dadaist work stuck behind a barrier with a Do Not Touch sign on it, even though it was a card catalogue type thing, whose whole point was to be touched, browsed through, and smudged. And I sneered aloud, "They've killed it. They've killed it. What a horrible place. They don't understand art at all." And went on in that vein until the whole tour came to halt, so I could get chewed out. A friend comforted me by saying one day we'd come back with water pistols full of acid and liberate the spirit of the thing by dissolving it entirely. Later, though, I heard he'd become an art conservator.

The night after that performance in grad school, I got kicked out of the apartment I shared in Corona, Queens, with Jorge, the brother-in-law of an ex-girlfriend's ex, and Rosa, an elderly Colombian lady that I used to help with errands. Jorge told me, "Rosa called the landlady and told her you're a child of the devil. You have to be out of here tomorrow morning. She only let you move in because I told her we were engaged. I'm really sorry." So at dawn I was squatting outside Tisch School of the Arts, waiting to stash my bags at the *Women & Performance* journal where I'd been working for a whole two weeks.

I'd mostly walk on the treadmill when everybody was gone, glancing occasionally at the video camera to see if it was still watching. I only ran it for an hour. After that it was just me. A discussion with the universe, gestures on one side, silence on the other. I filled the emptiness with bookkeeping: taking notes of distances walked, calories burned, songs played, time putting my mediocre suffering on display, while elsewhere people were dying of AIDS, and my roommates pretended I was doing something as normal as watching TV. When Rennes' latest boyfriend, Paul, would come over, he'd call out, "How's it going, Sport?" as he passed through to Rennes' room in the back where they'd put Sinatra on really loud, and fuck, squish, glop their way to the moon, the stars, old Jupiter, and Mars. I sent them subliminal messages, "Isn't that what public toilets are for?" "How about a nice back room in a bar?"

The only day I skipped was drizzly disgusting St. Patrick's. The street corners were still marked with patches of calcified snow that looked more like coal deposits than something you'd want to put in a cone. Uptown, a sparse crowd shivered on Fifth Avenue, while queers gathered in front of the Plaza Hotel with their own Irish band of bagpipers and drums and kilts getting ready to protest ILGO's exclusion from the parade. It was getting to be a tradition, for me anyway. I'd been there since '91, the first year they applied to march. When the Hibernians turned down their request, a participating group invited ILGO to join them. I'd just met Marie and Anne and joined the fun, along with David Dinkins, New York's first African American mayor. To show his solidarity, he walked with us instead of out in front, and for his trouble got hours of insults, catcalls, and abuse, plus a couple of beer cans tossed at his head by a vicious crowd.

The year afterward, ILGO's application was refused again, but the city gave us a permit to hold a countermarch going up Fifth before the official parade. The crowd had at us again, screaming insults and threats. "You should all die of AIDS" was popular. So was, "You have your own parade" and "This is our parade, not yours." As if *queer* cancelled out *Irish* and Lucy Lynch hadn't had brothers in Long Kesh, and Anne Maguire had never worked on the campaign of the legendary Bernadette Devlin McAliskey. Nope, not Irish enough. Disqualified. Visa canceled. Even though the parade was begun in the first place to fight bigotry against the Irish.

When we got to the end of the parade route, the cops trapped us in a pen with those wooden blue sawhorses and wouldn't let us out until we'd seen every last Irish bar, county association, and monstrous step-dancing troupe where little girls wore false everything from hair extensions to eyelashes. The worst were the lines of cops and firemen who passed in their dress uniforms all shouting threats and insults, flipping us the bird. A reminder that queers couldn't count on the people who were supposed to protect us, who we were supposed to turn to after getting attacked on the streets.

That was '92. In '93, when the Avengers were at full tilt, the city was refusing to let ILGO even do a countermarch. "We can't guarantee your safety," was the excuse, though Dinkin's sinking poll numbers probably had something to do with it, along with pressure from the archdiocese in an election year. After all, queers lived unprotected every day in New York. In the time I hung out with ILGO, this big guy Tarlach MacNiallais got beaten to within an inch of his life. Little fairyish Brendan Fay lost his job teaching religion at a Catholic high school for girls after he marched with ILGO the first time. Later on in '93, he'd get stabbed while he was walking home in Brooklyn, the blood from a punctured lung spilling out all over the sidewalk.

The cops said it wasn't a bias crime, though the first reports had Brendan's attacker shouting antigay slurs. Anonymous callers regularly left violent messages on the answering machine for Anne Maguire and Paul O'Dwyer, who co-founded ILGO. After threatening to kill them, they'd say, "I know where you live."

But when it came time to ban us from the parade, suddenly the city was worried about our safety. And for our own sake threatened to arrest any of us who even stepped foot onto the street.

When the band switched to a jig, we got ready for action. Demonstrators without green cards skedaddled to the far sidewalk, so they couldn't get grabbed by mistake and put on the next plane out. And the rest played the Hokey Pokey with the cops. You put your right foot in, you put right foot out, you put your right foot in, and the cops slap cuffs on your ass and drag you away to the St. Paddy's Day wagon.

Two hundred twenty-eight got booked, hands twisty-tied behind their backs. Mine were cutting off circulation, so climbing on the bus, I shouted, "My cuffs are too tight," and the pissed-off cop behind me gave a hard shove and I fell face forward onto Maxine Wolfe's shoes. And that was that. The parade took place just the way they wanted, as if nothing had happened and queers didn't exist. Just baton twirlers and marching bands and cops and firemen. All the Irish with their county banners, all the crowds of gaping tourists and fraternity boys getting drunk and celebrating the one day everybody in New York was Irish. Except for queers. Queers weren't Irish. Queers had their own parade.

The other conspicuous absence was Mayor Dinkins. He didn't go to the parade at all that year. He had a convenient case of diverticulitis.

At the cop station, they were nicer than I expected, giving me a copy of my mug shots when I boldly asked. Later, I stuck them up on the caduceus. After fingerprinting, they gave us brown paper towels and put us in cells off to ourselves, segregated by gender. We swapped names, talked, tried to get the ink off our hands. Some of the girls had been arrested a bunch of times, mostly with ACT UP. They were practically connoisseurs and seemed almost disappointed the arrests had been so peaceful, and that the toilet with no seat in the corner didn't even really stink.

I thought a lot about lunch. And peeing. Alone.

I finally broke down and used the toilet, making everybody turn away but still shield me from view. We got out after a couple of hours.

ILGO threw a big bash that night, but I didn't go. I didn't do a stint on the treadmill either. Ana Simo had been arrested, too, and when we were leaving the precinct I asked her if she thought I had to walk. When she said, no, I proclaimed her the Pope of New York. She shook her head in embarrassment, but it was too late. I was absolved.

8.

Easter came, and the performance ended. Something felt resolved, though I didn't know what. I couldn't figure out what to do with the caduceus and just left it standing in the living room, entangling the members of the Dyke March committee in barbed wire and rotting tampons. We'd already been meeting for ages, since somebody came to the center raging that the March on Washington people had scheduled almost nothing for dykes except a couple of artsy events, and power breakfasts where lesbians dressed for success would drink mimosas and honor each other.

We decided to hold our own march, a Dyke March, and when my hand shot up to be co-coordinator, it surprised me as much as anybody. Like that time they'd asked for someone to facilitate an Avenger meeting and I volunteered because I'd once read Robert's Rules of Order after getting elected Governor of Kentucky Girls State, that mock government thing, in high school. After the first session, Maxine Wolfe said I was the best facilitator she'd ever seen, getting consensus, moving things along. After several more, efficiency became tyranny, and they got out the hook.

The Dyke March prep went better, mostly because the Avengers were running like the well-oiled machine you hear so much about and almost never see. It helped that at the end of meetings we'd go around the room and say what our task for the week was. You'd be ashamed not to say anything, or let it slide. Ana Simo and Carrie Moyer were in charge of promo and media, dubbing themselves the Ministry of Propaganda.

Maxine did the marshal training and logistics. Lidia, a visual artist, did the amazing banners. A committee organized fund-raising parties that pulled in hundreds of dykes to drink beer and watch go-go dancing activists and videos of our first actions. And when we sent out notices across the country to every dyke bar, bookstore, and newsletter we ever heard of, Marlene Colburn, who spoke so strongly in front of Rockefeller Center, fielded the calls. It was like magic, how vans got rented, hotel reservations made. Blonde fire-eater Alison had a crew working on sewing machines in the street outside the loft on Avenue D, I think, and they made Avenger capes and painted shields. Somebody taught line dancing.

That's right, line dancing. What kind of dykes was I mixed up with, line dancing?

That androgynous, slow-talking journalist Anne d'Adesky organized the writing of the manifesto that was going to convert the lesbian masses to the Avenger cause. She invited everybody to her place on Seventh Street, laid in a supply of Rolling Rock, and a handful of us gathered around a Formica table like one my grandmother had. I couldn't tell if it was a kitschy sneer or a celebration of the America I came from. I didn't ask. Anne had a way of slouching back in her chair after making a point that made her seem irrefutable. At any rate, there was me and KT, who was an artist and musician, and Kat, a girl she hung out with, and Anne's roommate, Brenda, a dyke with long blonde hair and a cherubic face who used to play the snare at demos. Maybe Jennifer Monson was there, too, though neither of us is quite sure today. And we popped open green bottles and tossed out lines dipping into our collective semi-consciousness, which was full of Emma Goldman, who wanted a revolution you could dance to, and Rosa Luxemburg, who wanted freedom to dissent, and Valerie Solanas, who wanted to cut up men, and the Futurist Marinetti, who wanted to demolish libraries and museums (and feminism). My brain had goofier stuff, too, like TV jingles for dog biscuits (activism builds strong bones) and bible verses I'd memorized since I was three. (We are the Apocalypse and Rapture.)

It became part political manifesto, part lesbian love poem, audacious, whimsical, sincere. Like the Avengers. And when we brought it back to the group, they loved it. Or seemed to. Especially when Carrie Moyer put it on a broadsheet in blood red with the manifesto on one side and a Lesbian Avengers 101 on the other, offering a brief history and basic organizing tips. I still have a few squirreled away, their crimson fading but not the words.

A group of Avengers went down a little early to D.C. for a demo about lesbians and AIDS. The rest of us followed in a convoy, everybody excited and nervous, especially me. I was afraid that things would go wrong and it would be mostly my fault. I hadn't written my speech. I scratched notes in a notebook, chewed my cuticles trying to prod a feverish, empty brain. When Sarah Schulman told me I had to say something in front of the White House, she didn't give me much help: "You're a poet. It's going to be great." Maybe she envisioned some MLK moment, with the crowd spread out on the lawn, a mike, and TV cameras as I eloquently described the Lesbian Dream. But I drew a total blank.

Back then, I didn't dream of a future, lesbian or not. I'd started college sure I was going to be a medical missionary. Within months, I started having strange pains in my feet and hands, and a rheumatologist in plaid golf pants offered his warning, "Pick a profession where you don't use your hands or feet." He'd mistakenly decided I had rheumatoid arthritis or lupus. Which almost seemed cool, because lupus is what killed Flannery O'Connor. I think that was also the year a girl first lifted my hand to her mouth and kissed it in the half-dark of the Greyhound bus somewhere between Texas and Lexington. And the year I'd tagged along to a women's studies course and had that shock of recognition you only get once or twice a lifetime when they showed me the list of presidents and I suddenly understood what it meant—that there were no women on it. Almost none in the Senate, a few in the House. None again among the pastors and preachers and brothers I knew. Which was why they'd dumped Deb as minister of music, the only woman ever to hold a responsible position, and why they'd humiliated me when I protested. Yeah, they kept me in my place, and my mother in hers, which didn't absolve her of complicity, for watching me curl my fingers around a coffee cup and screaming in horror, "YOU'RE HOLDING YOUR CUP LIKE A *MAN*!"

It inspired a kind of Huck Finn moment when I decided it was better to risk hell than shrivel in the midst of a toxic Southern Baptist morality. I cut my ties. Soon left Kentucky. Unmoored, I moved from one city, one thing to the next. Waiting for hours in free clinics. Writing poems that were all intuition and rhythm and feelings deeply, but quickly, plumbed. Making these mute gestures in front of 2x4s. Still grappling with being a lesbian, no matter how it seemed. Half the reason I'd volunteered to facilitate meetings was that I'd have to use the word. The first thing we said every meeting, after asking if there were any cops in the room, was the tag line: "The Lesbian Avengers is a direct-action group focused on issues vital to lesbian survival and visibility." It was a mouthful, but it meant I had to say the word, *lesbian, lesbian, lesbian*. And it came down to me, trying to articulate the Lesbian Dream? Good luck with that. Somebody turned up the radio. The vans got trapped in D.C. traffic. It was going to be a disaster. Not just my speech. The whole fucking thing. I was sure of it.

When we got to D.C., I was a nervous wreck, and the Avengers didn't help much, most scattering like cats when they were supposed to be blanketing the city with the Lesbian Avenger broadsheet and our club cards for the Dyke March. Finally, the handful of people who always did the shitwork, like Alison and KT, saw what was happening and pitched in. After a while, people began to turn away the flyers, but with big smiles, "We already have one. Yes, we're coming." I was still nervous. People always say that and never do.

We went early to Dupont Circle. We didn't have a permit, and the ACT UP women and Avenger marshals went over tactics one more time. The goal: to keep everyone safe, block streets when they had to, negotiate with the cops who would no doubt be nervous. Especially near the White House. Just a couple days before, the feds had stormed the Branch Davidians' compound in Waco, Texas, and ended up with seventy-six corpses on their hands, including twenty kids, and David Koresh. A lot of people were angry with the government. Not us particularly, but who knew what the cops would assume?

I did the math while we waited. We only knew for sure we'd have a couple hundred marchers between the Lesbian Avengers and dykes from the ACT UP Women's Network that Maxine had invited to join the Dyke March party. We were also entangled with a West Coast group that had emerged after we'd already announced the march and done a lot of work on our own. When they said they had a similar idea, I agreed we should work together instead of throwing competing marches. It was a fiasco from the start. They skipped half the conference calls with us and the ACT UP women, and when we were forced to make decisions without them, they bitched it was all an East Coast plot. Still, I was glad when they finally turned up with their portable sound system, the only real responsibility they had.

At first the marchers came one by one, then in droves. By 7 P.M., on April 24, 1993, Dupont Circle was filled to bursting, spilling over like a dyke Times Square on New Year's Eve. Young ones, old ones. Suburban dykes in their khakis, city dykes in their boots, softball dykes with the little rat tails in the back of their short-cut hair, shaved Sinéad heads like mine, the big hair of die-hard femmes in dresses, butches dressed to the nines. People who knew about the march before they got to D.C. brought their own banners and signs. The rest dragged each other. I was supposed to be in charge, but how can you manage a hurricane? A tsunami of twenty thousand dykes? You don't. You just try to get out in front. The Avengers gathered the fire-eaters and drummers together and with the banner pushed our way to the head of the crowd. When that huge entity started moving, what a roar.

The only glitch, if you can call it that, was when we got in front of the White House, the Left Coast girls and the sound system were nowhere to be found. Later, I heard, they were pissed at all the attention the Avengers were getting and decided not to share. At any rate, I bellowed the few words I had to say into a bullhorn. Probably no one understood, though it didn't much matter because all those dykes knew where we were (in front of the White House), and how many we were (enough to fill the streets of the entire city), and that together we were Dyke America taking over the capital.

After I got done shouting, a dozen of us Avengers stood on the plastic crates we'd toted from New York. The crowd around us grew quiet. It was getting dark by then. You could hear voices shouting in the background, others yelling, "I can't see. What are they doing?" We dipped our torches into lighter fluid, lit them, and raised the flames in the air. Then, silhouetted against the familiar glowing white form, we brought them slowly toward our faces, which were lit up, too. Exhaling, as the heat approached our lips, fire entered our mouths and disappeared. The crowds hollered and screamed. And we did it again, while Marlene Colburn tried to get a chant going, "The fire will not consume us. We take it and make it our own."

That moment, of dykes eating fire in front of the White House, endured as the image of the Avengers. Photographers sent out their photos. The Ministry of Propaganda shot off their press releases. Journalists from major venues beat down our doors for interviews, marveling at the turnout, at the drama and life compared to the same old, same old of the official March on Washington for Lesbian, Gay, and Bisexual

Rights and Liberation with all the groups lined up and orderly. All the speeches predictably moving.

The message of the Dyke March was in our bodies. All twenty thousand of them there together in front of the White House, lit up with flame. We were disorderly, raucous, happy to be behind our own lesbian banner for a change. I can almost hear a couple of dyke readers murmuring as they turn the pages, "What's the big deal? I don't need anybody's validation." But if you don't think it makes a difference, it's because you don't know. Maybe you're dulled a little by seeing one or two lesbian faces on TV, in your local politics. One among thousands. Well, imagine what it's like to suddenly be the majority. Not even the one in ten on the street or whatever it is. But the 100 percent. I suppose that would be my Lesbian Dream if I could describe it now. To be big enough to count. To take up space in the great brain of the country, for even ten minutes a day. To be free.

At the official march the next day, I walked in a daze, a little off to the side, feeling too shy for the Avenger capes and shields and line dancing, though I have to say we looked good. Everybody along the route cheered us. The sun was out. Girls took off their shirts and slathered on sunscreen. And the Avengers danced and danced. All the way to the mall's vast expanse of green.

We climbed back in our vans with the sense that anything was possible. Twenty thousand dykes in the street today, a million tomorrow.

9.

And why not? Why not be hopeful for a change? I'd sit in that dusty room and positively beam as Marlene read the latest excited letter from some teenage dyke in the heartland who was thrilled to know there was someone somewhere as disgruntled as she was. New chapters sprang up everywhere from San Francisco to Minneapolis and New Orleans. Some were already planning more Dyke Marches to coincide with local Gay Pride marches in June. The motto for New York's was Lesbians Lust for Power. I was one of the organizers again, and two artist members, Martha Burgess and Kathleen McKenzie, volunteered to build an enormous bed to push down the street. Somebody else was stitching together a giant vulva costume. And Amy—Amy Parker!—who usually looked like a bespectacled Velma from Scooby-Doo, agreed to wear it. The march was going to be absolutely amazing, even better than D.C. We'd knock their socks off. Flood the streets. I can't describe the exuberance, the sense that the whole thing was more than an incipient lesbian movement; it was a kind of Dyke Awakening. With lesbians everywhere rubbing the sleep from their eyes, and shouting with joy.

It was buoyed, for once, by a mainstream media tired of all the fire and brimstone and hate. In June, as cities across the United States began to celebrate gay pride, *Newsweek* would even run a cover story on lesbians, highlighting the Avengers and our success in D.C. Three million copies containing our fire-eating lesbian faces turned up on newsstands, in people's mailboxes, pushing back against the Christian Right with our provocative cry, "Ten percent is not enough, recruit, recruit, recruit!"

Lesbians were suddenly, and briefly, chic.

There was something intoxicating about seeing our faces there, blurry as they were, even if I knew other dykes were going through hell. Like skinny, sick Dee DeBerry who came back from D.C. to find her home in ashes. Her neighbors in the Tampa trailer park had threatened to burn the place down if she didn't shut her mouth about AIDS and gay rights, and when they did it, Dee was left with nothing much but the clothes on her back, a dwindling T-cell count, a hostile insurance investigator, and the Avengers hot line number. When we decided to help, I felt like we really did have capes hanging from our shoulders.

Tampa was already on our radar screen. It was almost as bad as Colorado or Oregon, with violence rising after the city's own antigay campaign. In a shooting case, the trial judge had just accepted a "gay panic" defense, arguing a straight guy was justified in blowing away the fag who happened to flirt with him. That's what you get for unwanted advances. Imagine if dykes used the same rationale, killing every annoying guy who hit on us. We'd have filled whole graveyards, depopulated cities.

We set up a committee and started making plans with Tampa dykes to fly down in June. I wanted to go. I wanted to do everything back then, but my budget didn't stretch much beyond lentils and rice and rent. I remember talking about it to Phyllis on the way down to Baltimore for a commitment ceremony of two Avengers. I was gussied up for the occasion in clothes that actually had color. I'd borrowed fuchsia cutoffs and put on this tiara kind of thing with cloth roses, smeared my lips with pink.

Phyllis Lutsky was a curly-headed, cab-driving New Yorker who seemed very placid and calm until she got behind the wheel of a car. "We're holding fund-raisers," she encouraged me, swerving into traffic. "Look into it. Anybody can go that wants." I made indifferent sounds. I wasn't sure I'd work up the nerve. I mooched with the best of them, hinted around, "borrowed," but almost never asked outright.

It was a moot point after Baltimore.

We parked on the street of a typical suburb. The house was a one-story thing, with a yard front and back, driveway on the side, if I remember right. You imagined paperboys riding their bikes at dawn, and men driving off to work at 8:30 A.M. in suits and ties. Not in high finance, but something that you didn't have to dirty your hands with, like accounting or insurance, though maybe they were plumbers made good. Who knew? I hadn't seen that kind of neighborhood in a long time.

The wedding crowd was a peculiar mix of New York Avengers and Baltimore folks, including aging straight relatives who had been persuaded to come. Lisa and Cyn, the happy couple, had gotten cute matching tattoos in addition to swappable rings. After the ceremony, we ate cake and finger sandwiches and goofed around. I tried to avoid that Avenger who had come to my performance and harassed me the whole time about alternative medicines, and my failures in positive thinking, all while I was stuck there on the treadmill. In Baltimore, she and her friends started tossing around this tennis ball, all worked up like kids on a sugar high. Laughing when it smacked people.

After they hit me the second time, I took it and stuffed it down my shorts. Which was a big mistake. There in front of the other Avengers, in front of the aging relatives and Baltimore straights, they pushed me to the ground, drug my pants down, and stuck their hands in fumbling around until they grabbed the ball. It seemed to go on forever. Me on the ground with my pants half down while these fumbling, laughing girls restrained me, howling with that combustible energy and anger that the Avengers uncovered. That could explode at any moment. Against themselves. Other activists. Against me. Whom nobody helped. While old ladies watched.

When I finally got to my feet and pulled my shorts up, I saw the looks on their faces. Or imagined them. "Those brutes," the old ladies were thinking. "Those dykes." And because I always do, I kept on laughing, pretended like it was nothing. Getting thrown down to the ground, my pants yanked down in public. Yeah, I was so tough. Drank more punch. Ate more cake. Swallowed it whole. It sat in my stomach for a week. On the way back to the city, I was adamant about Tampa. I wasn't going. I was sick of the Avengers. "Why? What happened?" Phyllis asked.

"You didn't see?"

When I got home, I wiped off the lipstick, threw away the flowers I'd worn in my hair, called the other chair of the New York City Dyke March committee to tell her she was on her own, and quit the Avengers for the first time. I didn't send a letter or anything, just didn't go. I got a hammer and ripped down the caduceus, cutting myself a little on the razor wire, boxed up the tampons and amulets, and started tracing the streets again. Walked until I was sick. Until the season started changing and heat radiated up off the sidewalks stinking again of beer and piss and rotting garbage, and melting tar clung to my shoes like shit. Sometimes I'd pause at the river, drop on a bench, and stare at the Domino Sugar factory on the Brooklyn side. Sometimes I'd stop by Kathryn's. It was cooler in her basement than in our third floor.

A postal worker shot up a post office. Somebody else shot up a McDonald's. And I'd eye the cars that parked along Tompkins Square Park and wonder what it would be like to take a baseball bat and smash their windows, what it would be like to take a blade and slice spirals into my legs, instead of getting a tattoo like everybody else. Yeah, I'd take a blade and make neat cuts and the blood would curl down my legs.

All that because my pants got yanked down at a wedding party.

I blame it on the eyes. The eyes and thin, pinched lips of those older pin-curled ladies who stared at my vulnerable body while the hands of "those brutes, those dykes" groped around in my pink shorts. They were echoes of my mother who tried to shame me with monthly letters riddled with bible verses and feverish adoration of her delightful Christian friends whose lovely Christian daughters landed terrific, good-paying jobs and then delightful god-fearing husbands. "I pray for you every day," she wrote. But she was mute about my sister Kim nursing a struggling marriage. Vikki with a divorce and her own address changes moving from Kentucky to Florida to Texas where she wasn't quite the girl God wanted her to be. And even though my mother had told me a million times what a mistake it had been for her to get married, "and have you girls," she kept enclosing wedding announcements, births, and deaths neatly torn from the *Louisville Courier-Journal*.

I'd forgotten about them. They are brittle yellow scraps that fall from old letters as I retrace my steps. Little messages of yearning and fury on her part, inspiring in me—what else can you call it?—but a sudden, total grief.

When I was too tired to walk, too tired almost to climb the stairs, I'd visit tar beach with our two new roommates. Rennes was moving to London with his boyfriends and Sinatra CDs. Boy Kelly, a skinny young ACT UP fag, was taking his old room facing the Korean deli. Cindra, a fire-eating Lesbian Avenger, claimed the office room in front. We swapped clothes, cutoff jeans, sleeveless flannel shirts, necklaces and bracelets made out of leather strips and bits of thread. None of us had regular jobs, and we'd sometimes spend whole days on the roof, roasting in our underwear while Amy was at her air-conditioned office at the ad agency. At night she'd prop an icepack on her head with two or three fans going and edit the Avenger handbook, *A Handy Guide to Homemade Revolution*. Sarah Schulman had whipped out the bulk of the text, handing Amy a brown paper bag stuffed with handwritten notes.

"I'm quitting, too, after this," Amy said. "Seriously. I want to have a life." She'd learned banjo and was cooking up a blue-grass band.

Still, on Tuesdays, she and Cindra would go off to the Center for the Avenger meeting, and I'd turn on the television and scribble in my notebook, watching the Mets bobble balls or cars explode, until I heard them come up the stairs. Boy Kelly was hardly ever around, busy with the needle exchange or his ten million pals from Brown that would stop him in the street if he ventured out of doors. A couple of times his friend John came over to the house with a bushel of pills, and if he could hold it down, sipped a cocktail as he attached himself to the IV that was supposed to keep him from going blind before he died of AIDS. I liked John a lot. He was a flaming queen, with the quick wit, high-pitched voice, and all the mannerisms people make fun of. He'd learned to sneer right back.

"Embrace your inner faggot," he tried to teach Boy Kelly, twirling his glass. "Never be ashamed."

I ran into Ana Simo around the Fourth of July. She seemed smaller than usual, sweating there in the street, in her white sleeveless blouse. She told me Tampa had gone well. They'd put together a pretty good march on City Hall and forced the mayor to at least make a statement denouncing hate crimes. Tampa dykes had really opened their arms to the Avengers, shaved heads and all. Then she asked why I hadn't gone. Either to Tampa or the Dyke March. "Weren't you co-chair?" And I told her what happened at the wedding party in Baltimore. She got upset, wished I'd said something. But I just shrugged. We stood awkwardly, shifting around.

Ana made me uncomfortable. I'd felt something that time she worked the door for a party at P.S. 122, and I gave her a hug and felt the curve of her waist under a silky dress. Nothing happened, though, not then. We didn't click either, that time or two during the prep for the Dyke March in D.C., when I went over to her apartment on First Street to check in with the Ministry of Propaganda. She always asked such terrifying questions, had I done this or that, though she always said, "Never mind. I'll do it." Or "I think Carrie's already working on that." And we'd begin to talk about other things, like what it was like to be seven years old with your personality already in full bloom. And purely yourself because you weren't on anybody's radar as a female yet, not even your own.

We wondered if we could ever get back to that. I still do.

I flirted once, or tried to, during one of these sessions. We were standing in her kitchen looking for food, but there wasn't much unless you liked bananas or raw tofu dripping from a bag. But when I made my carefully deniable approach, she immediately brought up her most recent ex. "Those olives were hers. Want some?" I turned some interesting shade and ran all the way over to Kathryn's apartment where I got stoned and complained bitterly, as always, about my incompetence with girls.

When we got done dithering, Ana and I made a date to see *Orlando* that Sunday at the Angelika. We met in the lobby, which was so cold I started shivering. I couldn't remember the last time I'd seen a movie. There was always the TV to watch. Or the river. Our small talk was riveting. "God, it's hot." "A scorcher." We bought our tickets and deferred nervously to each other when it came to choosing seats. "Wherever you want." "I don't care," she fibbed. "Me neither," I lied.

Quentin Crisp was Queen Elizabeth. I whispered to Ana he'd been in my house just the year before eating pancakes with a cloak draped over his chair. Then I mustered up what courage I had, inched my hand over, and took hers. She didn't scream or invoke her ex-girlfriend, so that was good. And we left them there, the two hands, like a Berlin Wall, marking the point we were joined and separated, getting sweaty, holding us together. I hoped she would do something. Because I didn't know what to do next, except sit there, my hand going numb, until the credits ended.

It was still broiling when we left, walking west to the Hudson piers where it smelled of salt and fish and rotting wood. From a distance, Lady Liberty watched over the cruising men like a kind of saint, and blessed them as they looked for lovers or, having found them, locked mouths or hands or got hand jobs beneath a brutal sun. There was something comforting about it. All that faggy sexual energy, none of it directed toward us. We walked toward the end of the pier, admired the water, and began to kiss. Kissed some more. Sat weak-kneed down on the soft splintering planks as the gulls screamed. After a while of that, we got up again to hail a taxi and stumbled to Ana's soft, air-conditioned bed where we stayed for about a week until she had to go to a meeting for Dyke TV, and I went back to Avenue B.

II. ENEMIES WITHIN

*Workers of all countries unite in peacetime,
but in war—slit one another's throats!*

—Rosa Luxemburg

10.

I courted her with pints of chocolate Häagen-Dazs and lines from Calderón de la Barca, "¿Qué es la vida? / Un frenesí. ¿Qué es la vida? Una ilusión/ Una sombra, una ficción..." What is life? A frenzy. What is life? An illusion, a shadow, a lie. I took her to Kathryn's where we gave a command performance as The Sextets.

Once, I recited the litany of all the places I'd stayed after the shaving performance when the Colombians kicked me out of the Rego Park apartment. There was the house in Long Island packed with South Asians that I came to by way of a Filipina woman from Performance Studies. Then there was the house-sitting gig in Flatbush where a bunch of young black men surrounded me on the train once, asking "Happy about Benson-hurst, you racist skinhead?" Until one guy finally said, "It's just her 'do, man, like that singer," and they moved off, reluctantly. Then the sublet in Park Slope. Then a retreat to Cincinnati. Then back for a studio on SoHo's Grand Street. And a room in Astoria with a Basque–Puerto Rican dyke who taught me how to make pasta. Then a share in Harlem, with a heterosexual Bengali poet who dated an ex-boxer, drank nothing but scotch, and made me dinner in exchange for the Marlboros I got as a perk for temping at Philip Morris where I fortuitously met Marie. Then an illegal hostel in a West Village brownstone run by a Dubliner dyke, before Ireland itself, where for a month I was the first out dyke everybody's parents met. Then an all-Hispanic building in Williamsburg infested with rats so big they only left paw prints on the glue traps. Finally Avenue B.

I still thought it was an adventure, all those worlds I passed through, my around-the-world trip in 690 days. Though maybe when I told her those stories I was hedging my bets again, offering a warning that I was a rolling stone, wouldn't last. Ana's friends, too, were skeptical. Maybe because I was quite a bit younger than her. And had no roots. Ana herself told me, "I keep waiting for a shoe to drop. First one, then the other." But the relationship took, like an unexpected graft.

Ana even stayed sometimes in the loft, pushing Audre Lorde and H.D. and Artaud off my mattress to sweat in solidarity, though her bedroom eight blocks away was cold with air conditioning and complete with a real bed, real walls, a door, and a son in the room across the hall who departed from the story as quickly as possible. There was an ailanthus in the backyard. You could hear it rustling in the wind like a jungle creature. When it rained, the heavy green leaves pressed up against the window. I discovered bright red lipstick in Ana's medicine cabinet.

We talked sprawled out on her living room floor because there was no couch until I demanded it years later, and if you didn't want tetanus you'd avoid the chairs around the table that were made of skins and twigs and rusty nails. There wasn't much besides that but a piano in a niche, tons of plants, a few paintings. The empty space was handy for rehearsals, she said. And meetings. Delivery guys asked if it was a dance studio. And we would sometimes turn on the music and fling ourselves around the room. I did a mean rendition of Isadora Duncan trapped by her own scarf.

We told each other all our stories. I'd still go off on my mom, who was occasionally joyful but mostly ranted and raved, all strung out on Jesus and tranqs and gallons of Maxwell House Instant brewed in the dangerous cup. Then it was my multiply married sisters, and my father who was barely there, working out of town when we were kids, and after the divorce was such a schmuck about that tumor thing.

But I also told her about that summer after college that

Heather and I went up to her mother's farm in northern Kentucky and had to kill hornets in the attic and replace panes of glass. There was a garden with basil, lemon basil, purple basil, lemon balm, oregano, peppers, squash, and corn. In the heat, the fragrance of the herbs rose up to the house where we slept with old sheer curtains pulled up over us to keep off the ticks and mosquitoes. In the mornings, fog covered the mountains. I churned out poems. Once, when I went upstairs to write, there was a five-foot snake draped over the baseboard. I read a poem to it about Moses and snakes and God's rod. It listened, then slithered away.

And Ana, at first, told charming, innocuous tales about her hometown of Cienfuegos, Cuba, and the nuns at school who made the little girls wear wool socks even in the tropical heat, and how she'd gum up her sewing exercises with her sweaty little fingers and bring them home for her grandma to fix. She said she never was very good at crafty things like that, but I figured the problem was simpler. If she didn't learn, she'd never have to do it. Still, she admired the nuns. They were from Philadelphia, sweating, red-faced, and independent. If something difficult needed doing, like lifting a heavy record player or a film projector, they rolled up their sleeves and did it themselves. They didn't bullshit. Weren't ashamed of being smart. They taught the girls English along with the Hokey Pokey. Put your right foot in, pull your right foot out. Though when the electricity went out, they declared such a thing would never happen in Philadelphia. A colonialism-lite that fed an ambivalence in Ana that would bug her later. On the other hand, they were right, she said, Pennsylvania wasn't known for its blackouts.

By the time we met, her grandmother lived in Queens with Ana's mother, with one brother not far away and another safely in France. I learned that her grandmother and mother had both been grade school teachers and never took to cooking or cleaning. Which was why Ana ate raw tofu and bananas standing in her kitchen, or whipped out the credit card for restaurants that actually had wine lists. It excited me, three generations out of the kitchen.

Ana took me to her tiny cabin in the Catskills where we ripped each other's clothes off and rolled around on the floor until my skin started stinging from what we discovered were horrible little ants, and proceedings were discontinued for extermination. After night fell and the yellow moon came out, we went for a walk up the dirt road that climbed a rib of Scotch Mountain. And she told me about moving to Havana with her grandmother, only the two of them, right before the end of the revolution in '58. Afterwards, a young soldier just down from the Sierra Maestra taught all the neighborhood kids how to make Molotov cocktails. Later on, the high school took students on marches, sometimes at night when they could barely see a thing. Girls were suddenly allowed to do everything. Not like in Cienfuegos when she'd fought with her parents who wanted to keep her under lock and key.

She whispered in the shadows, "You'd walk with an arm outstretched to touch the person in front of you. Like this. And the one behind would do the same. No talking." She pushed me in front of her the length of an arm, and we walked in silence, stumbling over stones in the dark. When I giggled, she shushed me fake sternly and whispered soldiering tips, "If you pause for a rest, never take your boots off because your feet swell and you can't get them back on."

"Let's go back. I'm tired."

"Just a little further."

Ana was smaller than the others and worked hard to prove herself. When she could, she took a crash course in journalism, got a gig at a newspaper. After work, she'd meet up with a bunch of teenagers who had started a publishing project, *Ediciones El Puente*. José Mario was the pied piper attracting all the talent. He'd roped her in as co-director. She did some editing but also managed the grunt work, making sure deadlines were met and typesetters got clean proofs. They published chapbooks and held readings and performances that were dangerously popular.

She showed me a photo once of four of the crew standing in front of the print shop in Old Havana. José Mario was smiling at something off to the side, slick in his pressed white shirt, with his dark hair falling daringly past his ears. He was the oldest at nineteen or twenty. Ana Justina was a plump black poet with a sweater draped around her shoulders and her arms stuffed with papers and books. Gerardo, an Afro-Cuban guy, was posing with each thumb hanging through a belt loop, satisfied with the world, and his own literary revolution. His shoes showed a high shine even in this faded sepia print. Ana was the most restrained, staring stiffly into the camera, all femmed up in pointy heels and a sweater set. I didn't recognize that young girl at first. Something essential about her face had changed. Even now, when I see the picture, I wonder who she is, then remember, "Ana. It's Ana." And I want to reach out and touch the side of her face.

When she told me what happened, we were sitting in bed, leaning back against the smooth, dark wood of the headboard. Yellow light arrived in bars through the window blinds. Our bodies seemed dark against the cream of the twisted sheets. This was the gist of it—that some goons from state security grabbed her from her apartment and took her to jail. At first they stuck her in the general population, which was mostly poor white women busted for illegal abortions or squatting in abandoned houses. Then they moved her to a smaller cell packed with murderers, thieves, a nut case. Most of them were black, all seemingly dykes. It was supposed to be an object lesson. "Keep associating with counterrevolutionary degenerates, that's where you'll end up for good." It stank of urine, sweat, damp stone, and bloody rags. The women stared at her from their overcrowded bunks. The only space left in the cell was a foot or two by the bars, where she was supposed to put her mattress.

When night fell, Ana burst into tears, but a middle-aged black woman told her not to worry. "The girls are just silly. They won't hurt you. You'll be out soon." Not like her. She was doing twenty-five-to-life for killing a man, though her girlfriend still visited her.

Two or three times, guards fetched her in the middle of the night and marched her to a brightly lit office where she was interrogated by a military officer who laid his big pistol on the desk while he fingered through her teenaged diaries and demanded to know who was queer. "Tell me about Gerardo, Nancy, José Mario. That Rimbaud you write so much about." Ana herself had a boyfriend and had never really considered the others. Suddenly, a lot made sense, the cryptic comments, and giggles. She kept mum, or defended them.

Then it was back to the cells, and more mind games. A guard would wake her up and force her to march through the serpentine halls of the old Spanish fort. He kept behind her and ordered her not to turn around. Sometimes he'd pause for no reason, then resume. She waited to be put against the wall and shot.

I couldn't listen properly. I remember looking at the curve of her arm, the flesh of her rounded belly, and muscular shoulders. I held her hand. It seemed like a story we'd have read in a women's studies class back in Kentucky, the classic Third World woman's nightmare that poet Carolyn Forché described. Ana's voice seemed more and more distant. She told me the big purges happened a year later. She'd been arrested early because of her mother. Things had been okay as long as Ana was alone in Havana with her grandmother. But when her mother came from Cienfuegos, the battles resumed about what girls could and couldn't do, especially with young men. Gerardo used to walk her home sometimes, and two dyke neighbors spread the rumor she was pregnant with his black baby. She was also too close to the flamboyant José Mario. And in fury, anger, and shame, Ana's mother went everywhere complaining about her unruly underage daughter, her degenerate friends.

State security, already eying *El Puente,* had been thrilled to help.

They dumped Ana in a mental hospital after what seemed like weeks of getting grilled. When she told the shrink she was a political prisoner, they diagnosed her as paranoid and gave her electroshocks until she couldn't shape the letters of her name. By the time they let her out, months later, she'd decided to flee from her parents' house and sleep with a girl as soon as possible. If she was going to be accused of things, they might as well be true.

I've thought a lot about this since 9/11, and the War on Terror. How we never learn. Homophobes conceive a lesbian activist. A son kills his father at a Theban crossroads.

Ana only told me because she had to. That was her life, and we were getting serious. She asked me not to spread it around, but even then I was a blabbermouth. I told Amy as soon as I got home. I think I actually made notes, too, trying to create some distance, kill it with the filter of history. It was cool and horrible at once, like a train wreck. I was twenty-seven, an ignorant American who couldn't have found Cuba on a map. I wished above all I could have swooped in and saved her, that teenage girl. But all I could do was wipe away a few stray tears.

I feel weird spilling it now but have to. Because after a while, it took root, the way shared stories do when you live with them long enough. They affect your DNA like radiation. They give birth to you.

I met her mother shortly after she told me. Ana swung by the Avenue B loft with her and her grandmother in her little red Hyundai. I remember standing there with my shaved head. Behind me the shabby building with a mural of palm trees on the front and music blaring from the open door. When she got out of the car and saw me, Faustina's square jaw tightened like a vise. She managed a hello, but boy how it cost her.

We drove to Veniero's on Eleventh Street and sat outside where there was room for her grandmother's wheelchair. Ana and María Luisa, her grandmother, ordered Tartuffo, that two-flavored ball of ice cream. I got a slice of almond cake. Faustina ordered a baba rum. She and I exchanged a few remarks while Ana and her grandmother joked and laughed. Ana squeezed her half to death but didn't touch Faustina, who still seemed frozen at the shame of a dyke daughter. Still enraged that Ana had escaped, but she hadn't. After all those years she had fought her own husband whenever she wanted to leave the house by herself, when she wanted to work.

She only bit her tongue, I figured, because Ana had gotten them out of a hungry Cuba soon after the "Special Period." I pretended I didn't know anything. Spoke politely in Spanish, made those meaningless sounds that appear to be conversation. I'd had practice after all. That's what families are for.

11.

Now and then we'd go back to the Catskills where we'd bake in the sun and read Whitman, or drive to a town forty-five minutes away to see a movie, preferably with car chases and exploding things. Ana helped me get my driver's permit, and back in the city I crashed into a sedan near Canal Street, and an angry Asian guy in a blue suit charged out and screamed for a while but didn't call the cops or demand insurance. We'd been heading to the Dyke TV office in Chinatown where Ana ran the news department and tried to keep the empty take-out cartons from overrunning the desks.

She'd helped start that too, roping in videomaker Mary Patierno and stage director Linda Chapman, so the Avengers wouldn't have to depend on mainstream media. It had grown into a real weekly show, with art and culture, and other segments featuring important dyke skills like how to change a bicycle tire. Pretty soon Dyke TV played all over the country on public access stations. I'd leave her at the office and walk back home past the fruit and vegetable markets. In the evening, the streets stank of fish when the ice got dumped in the gutter and the big metal trays were hosed down. Musty spicy smells came from the open doors of Chinese apothecaries.

Trailing after Ana, it was inevitable that I'd return to that room upstairs at the center with the folding metal chairs, and heat, and occasional buzzing fly. I entered tentatively, found a seat off to the side, afraid I'd have to explain where I'd been. But so many people had been on vacation, nobody noticed one more missing dyke. I stared around the room and was greeted by smiles, only relaxing when the meeting started and she wasn't there, the one who yanked down my pants in Baltimore. "The Lesbian Avengers is a direct action group focused on issues vital to lesbian survival and visibility." It sounded different after a year, now that I knew what the words meant.

For several Tuesdays, I didn't do anything but sit in that dusty room and watch. There wasn't much going on, a picnic here, a picket there against Clinton's idiotic Don't Ask, Don't Tell compromise about military queers. Almost every week new chapters were announced: Atlanta, New Orleans, Minneapolis, San Francisco, and Tampa. Colorado dykes were the first Avengers to be arrested, chaining themselves to the fence of the governor's mansion during a protest against antigay Amendment 2. They got busted again gate-crashing a party of Focus on the Family, a big backer of the antigay legislation. We thought it was cool, but there in Colorado activists were getting slammed. The boycott was working, and the queers losing money were as quick to hate them as straights.

Ana threw a party when Su Friedrich and videomaker Janet Baus had finished editing the Avenger video, *Lesbian Avengers Eat Fire Too.* She persuaded her mother to make enormous pots of black beans and rice, and everybody brought beer. I didn't eat anything, even though Ana swore the beans were meatless, or almost. I'd been a vegetarian for almost a decade. Ethical reasons, if you have to know. Screw health. I hung out in the kitchen and bummed cigarettes from the Avengers blowing smoke up the airshaft and annoying the neighbors. When they turned on the TV and slipped in the fat VHS cassette, I said a quick good-bye to Ana and went back to Avenue B. I couldn't bear to see my own face on the screen, wondering what it would betray as I talked about those twenty thousand in front of the White House. About growing up dyke in Kentucky. I'd done an interview with Su and Janet after the D.C. March. It had been shot there at Ana's in front of a brick fireplace with a quilt hanging on it. I was still nearly bald from my performance. Still so high on what we were accomplishing. And feeling whole for the first time ever.

One Tuesday in August, Sarah Schulman swung by a meeting. She almost never came anymore, spending a lot of time out of town on book tours where she still pitched the Avengers. She grabbed a spot at the top of the agenda and talked for a few minutes about the communities that were absolutely swamped with antigay legislation. Many had no idea how to fight back. She'd concluded that the Avengers should share skills. Offer our organizing services to whoever wanted them. Maybe do a kind of Freedom Ride to call attention to the latest wave of hate coming our way. She left immediately afterwards, and we rolled our eyes a little bit at her abruptness but decided it was a good idea. The Christian Right sent forth their minions. Why not us?

One of the first requests for help came from Lewiston, Maine, where a local gay rights ordinance was under attack. When the moderator asked for volunteers, two of my fire-eating friends, Sara Pursley and Michelle Kelley, put up their hands, along with a newbie, Chanelle Mathews. By September 1, they were already in Lewiston, ready to work with local queers, and Equal Protection Lewiston, the struggling organization that was running the show. The Freedom Ride would end there after a tour through New England doing actions in cities where there were Avenger chapters, like Boston and Albany. We started to fax around press releases. We got tons of enthusiastic responses.

We also got a letter from an African American lesbian in Albany practically forbidding us to use the name "Freedom Ride" unless we focused on questions of race. It was more than a letter. It was an injunction, a campaign. The author circulated her demands as widely as possible before we even had a chance to respond. Her heavy-handed tactics led our most experienced activists to wonder if it was as much about territoriality and homophobia as it was about race. She was a big deal in Albany, famous, actually, and we hadn't paid her our respects. But the youngest took it at face value. If she said something was racist, it had to be. It was Barbara Smith, for fuck's sake. The grand dame of black feminism, co-founder of Kitchen Table: Women of Color Press and the Combahee River Collective. She was an icon, almost as much of a saint as Audre Lorde. We couldn't admit the possibility that a lifetime of fury at racism could possibly miss its target, that we ourselves didn't always aim true.

We agreed on changes to the press release, still keeping the name, but acknowledging our debt to the earlier Freedom Ride. Younger Avengers organized a teach-in. Smith was informed. Nevertheless, when she published the article "Blacks and Gays: Healing the Great Divide," Smith renewed her attacks on the Lesbian Avengers, essentially characterizing us as a white, insensitive, racist group. The proof was that we refused to relinquish the name after a lesbian of color had ordered us to.

Like half the group, I was still ready to concede. When bits of the article were read aloud, I'd felt a wave of shame rise up from my knees and go straight to my eyes. I looked around the room and everybody *was* white, including Marlene and Valarie, Gail, Maura, Andrea—all bleached by contagion. And Ana and Lidia and all the other Latinas also became not just white but Anglo. And Maxine became young and Christian, and a blank slate. And all the other little quirks of language, or age, or origin that I had perceived until that moment were erased by the indelible power of that word, *white.*

But then Sarah Schulman and Maxine Woolf said it was a ridiculous idea, thinking anybody could plant a flag in that word *Freedom.* Ana with her accent agreed. Marlene Colburn, too, shook her head, adjusted the baseball cap over her own black face, and said sadly, "That's Barbara." We kept the name. Our elders had spoken, two Jewish dykes, a Latina, and an African American woman, who were not ashamed to admire MLK, who admired Gandhi. Some were actually acquainted with Smith. But you could see it on some of the faces, especially us younger ones of all colors, that we in fact accepted the charge, the Avengers *was* a white group and by definition racist. We didn't look at each other the same way after that.

In October, the Avengers rented a van or two and draped them with banners calling for Lesbian Freedom, and a group set out for Boston. It was okay at first. They got lots of friendly honks on the way up, and a warm welcome before they got down to the serious business of eating fire and pamphleteering outside the public library. But when the Avengers arrived at the Boston OutWrite conference to screen our video, *Lesbian Avengers Eat Fire Too,* we found Barbara Smith had set the place ablaze, distributing her damning article to all the professional queers and arbiters of the LGBT community, who attacked us under her banner, accused us of "appropriating" the name, of getting black dykes in trouble with their communities, as if "white" dykes were responsible for inspiring black homophobia.

When Gail asked, with her dark face betraying her Panamanian–West Indies roots, "What about me? I'm an Avenger. Don't I count?" The answer was pretty much a resounding, nope. Afterwards, she, who had been so proud to be an Avenger, became horribly anguished at having to defend the "white" group she belonged to.

At the next meeting, Anne d'Adesky, who was herself a French-Haitian-American dyke, tried to give it a good spin: "It's just as well to air things out, confront the 'divide-and-conquer' techniques of the Christian Right."

Except we didn't really confront anything: not the real problem of racism in the queer community, not the homophobia in the assumptions dykes would dirty up the name "Freedom Ride," not the hubris of activists. Or even how denouncing us as "white" actually erased Avengers of color along with the differences between, for instance, a Catholic Irish immigrant, a Jewish New Yorker, and a white Southern Baptist dyke from Kentucky. Instead, we became terrified accountants looking only at skin. How many African Americans are in the room today? How many Asians?

Which was too bad, because we could have used a real discussion about race and power, but also class and education. Sure, Sarah Schulman could breeze in and get the group to do anything, but there were also certain African American and Latina and Asian voices that had authority, too. But when the merely beige Ana started to speak in her marked Cuban accent, the eyes of newer Avengers seemed to glaze over almost immediately. Nobody listened either to this glowingly white Russian girl who was still struggling in English. Or even noticed that Denise, a young black dyke, rarely opened her mouth. Maybe because she didn't seem to have a degree from one of the Seven Sisters or was kind of fat.

I wonder now what would have happened if we had responded differently. Allowed Smith to assume the Freedom Ride was hers. That the Avengers were all white and had never mourned Hattie Mae Cohens, or acted on behalf of the Rainbow Curriculum. What would have happened if instead we had asked if African Americans were such misers, freedom in such scarce supply, that they couldn't spare a little for us, too? In those divide-and-conquer days, would she have responded to a plea for generosity? Or was it inevitable to wait twenty years for an African American president to see Seneca Falls, Selma, and Stonewall as three faces of one struggle for freedom and human rights?

12.

I missed Sara and Michelle, two of my fire eating friends, and took the Greyhound up to Maine, meaning to help out a couple of weeks. But I arrived with a scratchy throat and bloody underwear because I always got my period when I climbed onto a plane or a bus. I only lasted long enough to draft a flyer or proofread something before they sent me home, pale and feverish. Still, I got a good look at the place, and Lewiston was nothing to shout about. Decrepit, urban, gray. A rotting town abandoned by the textile industry and the bluebird of hope. The apartment wasn't much better, damp and filled with bits of paper, notebooks, empty pizza boxes, neon green buttons, and a handful of depressed dykes who wanted to change the world and ended up stuffing envelopes full of crap that they didn't even get to put on some asshole's doorstep and set on fire.

The newbie was Chanelle Mathews, a young black woman who was the epitome of elegant urban cool. She came to the Avengers fresh out of the Army, and at her first meeting when they were calling for Lewiston volunteers she just stuck up her hand and was on her way. Why the hell not? The smiling Mary Lou came from Austin, I think. Sara and Michelle had been part of the New York Avengers from the beginning, fire-eaters like me, and roommates at the loft on Avenue D where we held our legendary fund-raising parties. Michelle was a pastry chef, trained up in Paris. She had glasses and thick, curly black hair, and horse sense galore. Sara taught English as a second language and barely made enough to pay the rent and keep herself in smokes. She was a ringer for the young Leonardo DiCaprio, though far too laconic to climb on the prow of anything and shout.

Sara and I had kept company for a while after my thing with Jennifer. We didn't do much. Hung out. Messed around. Once, after a hurricane passed over the city, we struggled along the East River promenade in the gusting wind. Waves jumped over the rusting, crumbling handrails and in some places claimed the highway. We leaned into each other as ballast, kissed each other's salty lips. Another time, we dressed up for a party, her in a blue wig, me in a blonde one and gold-sequined dress that sweet Alison leant me, which I balanced out with a pair of big Doc Martens. I should have played it cool and sophisticated, but instead went around like a three-year-old demanding, "Guess who I am. Do you know who I am?"

Nobody really knows with dykes. Especially ones like Sara who masked herself in an army jacket, and blue jeans, and a wreath of cigarette smoke. But then you'd find out she went to Dartmouth and had done stuff in Africa that she'd tell you about like it was nothing. If you didn't know better, you'd dismiss her, dismiss us all because we preferred shabby to chic, and often camouflaged ourselves as butch on the street.

Equal Protection Lewiston's straight consultants couldn't see her at all, even if they were heading up the fight to preserve the town's pro-gay statute. They had actually thrown a fit when Britain's BBC News wanted to interview the Lesbian Avenger Freedom Riders as part of their coverage. When the Freedom Riders got to Lewiston, EPL shoved them into a room with the windows papered over so that they weren't visible from the street. And when the Avengers got sick of stuffing envelopes full of ugly promises that we queers wouldn't try to adopt kids, EPL people said they could go hand out pamphlets as long as they didn't look too dykey. After all, everybody hates queers, especially the poor, which Lewiston was full of. The best way to win civil rights was to hide just who was going to get them.

When I was there, Sara introduced me to one of the EPL

consultants. She was about what you'd expect, appropriately coiffed and made-up and perfumed. She smiled even more than I did and said how happy she was to have the Avengers on board. Then she told the story of how Sara had raised all this money for them, leaving out the part that EPL had seen the gay community as such a drain on the campaign they hadn't even recognized them as potential donors until Sara came along and started calling them. Such good work! she reiterated. "Lewiston needs its own Avenger chapter."

Beware of what you wish for.

A couple of weeks before the election, Sara and the others sent the New York meeting a copy of a letter they'd finally given to EPL, very politely notifying them that while the Avengers continued to share their goals, their skills could only be used to their full advantage working independently. And frankly, Lewiston queers deserved action from people who weren't ashamed to be gay or lesbian. Their guts told them that a closeted, fearful campaign did more harm than good, and it was time to put it to the test.

I should have been glad, but I only felt anxious. Like we were going to get hauled to the principal's office. I'd temporarily run out of nerve. It was partly the thrashing we got at the hands of Barbara Smith. Partly the snotty reminders from EPL that the Avengers had to do what the locals wanted. My god, we were outsiders. There were questions of class to consider, over-entitlement. We couldn't deny how many Ivy Leaguers were in the room, how much accomplishment. Even if it wasn't mine. I didn't want to be cut off from the community that we were supposed to be working for. I forgot for a minute that EPL didn't represent all of gay Lewistonians, or even most of them. Just the ones who had the money and the press lists.

In reality, the Avengers entered more deeply into the city, advised by local students, members of ACT UP Portland, and

LGBT people too poor or queer to be poster children for EPL because they liked to hang out in bars, or were members of the Franco-American minority that maybe still had a French accent, or didn't look freshly scrubbed. Many were pissed that the poor neighborhoods they dared live in had been totally ignored by EPL.

Looking now at the reports in the archive, I can't believe how much the Avengers in Lewiston got done in the few weeks before the election. They helped churn out English–French literature, went door to door handing out pamphlets and registering voters, all as out queers. They hit low-income, high-crime areas that EPL had dismissed, and even their advisers warned against, shivered in front of literature tables, and found that the people who stopped to talk were surprisingly welcoming. Or maybe just surprised. Nobody ever went to their decaying neighborhoods, not liberals, not conservatives. Or fascists or commies. The Avengers were the first in decades to turn up and look them in the eyes.

Most important, they paid attention to local queers, taking voter registration forms to bars, persuading people to hold house parties where they showed the Avenger movie and talked about how Lewiston was part of something bigger, a national attack on LGBT people. They struck a chord, got kudos for standing up to EPL, which was widely resented. As one dyke told them, "You might be outsiders to Lewiston, but we're all from Queer." People from the community started getting involved, suggesting their own events, getting so excited they came out in front of TV cameras, even when they hadn't meant to.

Though strictly speaking, queers were defeated at the polls, the Avenger strategy worked. The *Lewiston Sun-Journal* reported that wherever Avengers and out queers had hit the streets, the gap narrowed substantially. We almost won. On the other hand, the areas that EPL thought they had in the bag, based on their "professional" polling data, actually did the worst. Equal Protection Lewiston was furious, spreading it around that the loss was the Avengers' fault, these New York dykes parachuting in and demanding to do things the way they did them in the big city. Know-it-alls. Outsiders. Egomaniacs. Irresponsible. Insensitive to local issues. Which locals? Which issues? Who gets to decide?

The Avengers came back to a hero's welcome. They'd even made the national press. The Avengers had helped plan a small demo for the day after the election, but so many people were angry after their defeat that a hundred protesters came out on the Lewiston streets, and the small die-in they'd planned was converted into a spontaneous march. Six people were arrested, including two Avengers and a lesbian teacher who picked that day to come out. The cops were awful, but the demonstrators scored a photo in the *New York Times.* Local queers felt energized. So did the roving Avengers.

Their faces positively glowed as they talked about their work. Laconic Sara Pursley actually seemed ready to burst. They'd learned a lot. Toughened up. It's easy enough to develop a stance against your enemies, but not against your "friends," who seemed to hate loudmouthed queers in the street even more than the homophobes in the state house.

It was a lesson we'd all have to learn. When the New Orleans Avengers publicized a photo of a lesbian couple kissing, the queer establishment there denounced the "radical" Avengers for undoing all their slow, patient (semi-closeted) work. There were also conflicts in New York where activists and lobbyists were duking it out over how to celebrate the twenty-fifth anniversary of Stonewall. The official organizers seemed to be turning it into a big, self-congratulatory celebration of how much they'd accomplished, and a chance to dress up in suits and ties and talk about their favorite word, *equality,* as if it solved everything. Others wanted confrontation. Queers were still dying of AIDS. We were still being beaten and raped and killed. For groups like the Avengers and ACT UP, the Stonewall anniversary was a call to remember our revolutionary roots as a *liberation* movement—the whole thing sparked by street kids, rent boys, and drag queens and butches who finally got sick of being hauled off by cops raiding gay bars and set the Village on fire.

Who was right? Could we coexist? Kafka thought activists were always doomed: "They rule the streets and that makes them think they rule the world. They are mistaken. Behind them stand the secretaries, officials, and professional politicians, all the modern sultans for whom they are preparing the way to power."

13.

December passed in an uneasy blur. For Christmas, Ana and I split town and went to Paris. God, it was dark. It was dark when we got up, dark when we went to bed in that apartment we'd borrowed from some of Ana's friends. It was partly jet lag, partly the medieval sun-deprived streets, mostly the endless rain. How it rained in Paris. Then rained some more. And after that it stormed. We'd eat breakfast in the afternoon, then venture outside in the streets where the sky was black, and the dark pavement streaked with water, though puddles reflected light from streetlights and headlamps and the yellow, steaming windows of bistros. I suppose there were holiday lights, too, but we couldn't see them from underneath our umbrellas.

With sopping feet, we went to cafés and galleries and museums. I tried to find some key to enter the place. Some crack to sneak through. In high school, I'd been routed to Spanish. Only snobs took French. The knee-jerk prejudice had stuck, even if I loved Marcel Duchamp, and had a thing for Gertrude Stein, who had a thing for the City of Light. I tried to chill out. France was Ana's second home, the place she'd lived after Cuba, where I'd probably never go, and didn't particularly want to.

I knew a little bit about pottery, anyway. At the Louvre, I drug Ana to the Islamic art wing and showed her *azulejos* tiles, with the same abstract designs they had all over Spain. It was a legacy from successive conquering Arab waves that I'd learned about in high school. I didn't think of them yet as Muslims but as *árabes* and *mozárabes*. I'd taken ceramics in college and blabbed to Ana about the composition of glazes and clays. When I had to piss, I discovered my French was as good as hers if I ignored everything people said and just followed their pointing fingers, "First go straight, then take a right, and you'll find the bathroom."

We went to the Picasso Museum. He was familiar, too. That balding, laughing man photographed on the beach. That earnest almond-eyed boy. I stared a long time at the sketches from *Guernica*. War seemed distant, but the agony and violence real, embodied in that lopped-off arm holding a sword. The wild-eyed horse.

Ana showed me all the places she lived and worked and studied, mapping the city with her life. From the movie theater where she took tickets to the place she lived during May '68— which she had to explain. How students and workers rose up, sent de Gaulle fleeing to Germany, while the cops sent protesters fleeing over garden walls.

I still couldn't overcome my aversion to what I thought was France. All that dark, monumental stone. The blackness of ages. Narrow suffocating streets. The horror of the Luxembourg Gardens where trees were manicured into careful, mathematical shapes. Across the river in the Tuileries, the arch lined up with the pyramid lined up with the other arch, and an obelisk. No wonder Duchamp had evolved here, inserting tendrils of ridiculousness to break apart the gray, gray stone. Give me Dada instead of the Enlightenment any day, I thought. Give me bicycle tires and broken nudes. No wonder the students had risen up. And before them the sansculottes. My god, I missed the wilderness of New York but tried not to show it.

Okay, so maybe I told Ana a little of what I felt.

Maybe after a couple days of gray stones and tidied gardens I ranted and raved and threw myself on the slippery cobblestones and foamed at the mouth. Until we went to that demo.

America had its David Duke; France had Jean-Marie Le Pen, lawyer, legislator, anti-Semitic, anti-immigrant Holocaust denier, ex-foreign legionnaire, and maybe a torturer. His rallying cry was "France for the French," and traditional values. Some lefty group was holding a protest against the racism he incited. Ana and I picked up a tube of white acrylic paint, a brush, and a dry black umbrella. Riding the metro, I painted a bomb in the center and lettered in French around it, Lesbian Avengers [Les Justicières Lesbiennes] Against Racism. It was the first thing that made me really happy in France, painting that umbrella on the subway while the riders looked on. At the demo, one or two nodded in acknowledgment, but nobody said anything. They're polite, those French people. So discreet.

Go to something about racism in New York, it's mostly people of color with a few whites tossed in. In Paris, there were black people, Asians, North Africans, plenty of whites. All speaking French like they owned the language. And I realized, like Le Pen, I'd thought of France as a white place, though it hadn't been since the Gauls painted their faces blue and greased their hair. It rained, of course. I held the umbrella high.

Afterwards, Ana took pity on me and booked two places to the Côte d'Azur, which was my first trip ever on a real train if you don't count those commuter things to Philly. There were bunk beds, like in the movies. Porters. Heading south, we shot through the damp countryside arriving in Nice after dark. Greeted by an enormous and terrifying dog, we slept that night in a small hotel, with thick moldy curtains, and the sound of waves crashing on an invisible beach. When we woke in the morning, and Ana pulled open the windows, we were blinded with light and ran outside like two mental patients. What an incredible and strange blue the sky was. What a strange green the sea. They were the colors of Matisse. Colors I thought were made up. How come no one had told me? Ana laughed when I grabbed her hand and didn't let go.

We moved to a hotel on the Promenade des Anglais that had a cut-rate Christmas special. Our new room had a balcony overlooking the bay, and a minibar, which I'd never seen before. Below, there was a fisherman among the enormous rocks in the crook of the bay. The waves would hit him and spray shoot up fifteen feet. A couple of people actually swam. There were others in chairs on a beach made only of pebbles, which I'd never seen before, either. We went down and slid around on the stones. Later, we walked up a path to a park where they had all these strange desert plants. Some had the smooth, thick leaves of aloe. Others were cactusy and prickly.

We stumbled over an old cemetery up there filled with Americans who'd come from Cincinnati when it was an important center of American culture, and San Francisco just a dirty little port town. There were worse places to die, I thought. Later, we found an enormous eternal market with fifty stalls selling masses of cut flowers, and dozens others with olives that were flavored with orange or garlic or burning peppers. At an outdoor restaurant, we ate *soupe au pistou,* which was full of vegetables and no meat. I could understand some of the French because they pronounced it more like Italian or Spanish. They also had their own Niçard dialect, which had outlasted the Genoese, Saracens, Sardinians, even the French kings.

I decided it was small-minded of me to despise a whole country and told Ana I wouldn't mind retiring there. She laughed, but I meant it, imagining a tiny room with a balcony, staring out at that sea and that sky. Reassured by my insignificance and yours. Christmas Eve we went to the fancy shopping street and bought a bottle of champagne and a little Cuban cigar, which I smoked, pretending to be Janet Flanner chatting with Gertrude Stein about her latest article in the *New Yorker.* At a bakery with an enormous line we got a *bûche de Noël,* a Christmas cake in the shape of a log and decorated with funny meringue mushrooms and a little sleigh. We took it all back to the hotel where the champagne went into the little minibar, and we squabbled over the mushrooms on the *bûche* because I had picked up some intestinal bug (wasn't it kind and generous of Ana to offer to eat them all, so I wouldn't have to?). And near midnight, we walked back into town where the cathedral was having a mass. It was too packed to go in, but you could hear the chants and carols in the square.

Afterwards at the hotel, I stood on the balcony for a long time, listening to the waves crash against the rocks, and trying to make out the line between the black sky and black sea.

Paris was okay after that, even if I was on a diet of Imodium. We got a dry day and saw other parts of the city where the architect Haussmann hadn't left his stamp. Montmartre was still villagey with steep winding streets and little human-sized buildings. In a different neighborhood we found African bazaars, Moroccan souks. With working-class people! Immigrants! We went to the Gobelin tapestry factory, and to the catacombs of Denfert-Rochereau where underground avenues were laid out in more straight lines, with bones neatly stacked along the walls mingling together millions of exhumed Parisians, tibias crossing each other, skulls aligned. I got the idea that the obsessive order of the formal French gardens must have been a sophisticated joke.

A day or two before we left, Ana's brother came up from the Loire Valley where he lives. They had a coffee at the café downstairs. He stuck his head in. I didn't do much but say hello before I had to go puke. Afterwards, Ana went to the pharmacy and described all my horrifying symptoms and came back with a bunch of drugs a pharmacist gave her, just like that.

I was sad to go. The place grows on you. Like a fungus, maybe. At the airport, I confessed France wasn't so bad. I wouldn't mind coming back. "We could stay for a year. Why not?" Ana bought chocolate truffles. On the plane, I stretched out on two empty seats and slept.

14.

Back in New York, I scrambled to pick up some cash to pay back Ana for our trip to Paris. I wasn't much good at it. I bussed for Kathryn sometimes when she worked the room upstairs at the restaurant, even though I was a total jinx for business, and all I did was refill two or three water glasses. I also cocktail-waitressed a couple times at Crazy Nannies, where one Avenger bartended on the top floor and another was go-go dancing. Later, I stuffed envelopes for Jennifer Monson about some dance thing, and for Eileen Myles about a poetry event, and typed a manuscript by Abe, this old ex-boxer guy who was sleeping with my former Bengali roommate. It was full of Rocky-like stories of pounding meat carcasses and old brick walls, and bloody sagas of the murderous Jewish mob, which he swore were true, and a love interest in the form of an Indian princess, not South Asian at all, but Native American. I charged too much, but he didn't care. It was going to be a best-seller.

And almost every Tuesday I was still off to the Avengers, who were in a state of perpetual fury at our new mayor, Rudolph Giuliani, who had messed-up ideas about law and order. As a candidate he joined this enormous mob of rioting cops protesting Dinkins' plan to improve the civilian complaint review board. And as mayor he quickly unleashed the Street Crime Unit, which seemed largely reserved for harassing African American and Latino kids and nailing squeegee men who swirled dirty water on car windows to scrounge a few tips.

It was a war zone around Tompkins Square Park, with banners hanging from windows. And cops in riot gear dragging away skinny white kids with dreads from their decaying squats. They shouted "Power to the People" and other retro slogans. If two activists got together over beers, they'd spit and curse Antonio Pagán, this gay Latino councilmember who used to be all about low-income housing and queer rights but had decided it was time to let the developers in. Besides the squatters under attack, you'd see clubs and bars shuttered for breaking obscure laws. And fences would appear overnight around public parks that would then get locked after dark, so there was nowhere free to sit.

On the West Side, where Ana and I had our first kiss, the crumbling piers were posted with warnings and barred off. Fags and drag queens were the casualties of plans to turn the place into a nice waterside park for the pricey neighbors. Only money talked. Giuliani dumped the liaison to the LGBT community, slashed AIDS funding and the budget for Housing Works, and installed notorious Rainbow Curriculum foe Ninfa Segarra not only as head of the Department of Education but also of Health and Human Services. Which meant the woman who told *New York* magazine that the Rainbow Curriculum made her want to throw up could torture queers from preschool straight to the grave, controlling half of the city's multibillion-dollar budget.

The Avengers tracked her down and serenaded her on Valentine's Day, but in that shabby room in the center we did more bitching than planning. I ranted with the best of them. That homophobe, Giuliani! That racist!

Ana and I were practically living together by then. The word *love* had been mentioned, but we weren't counting our chickens. What could be more unlikely than a dyke from Cuba, another from Kentucky? Though I'd joke sometimes we were both Southerners after all, both born below the Mason-Dixon line.

One day, after a meeting full of more Giuliani phobia, she started wondering aloud why none of the Avengers ever asked how New York ended up with the guy in the first place. Plenty of black and Hispanic voters pulled the lever for him. Others didn't bother to vote. Maybe it had something to do with the corrupt Democratic machine. Or their perpetual fear of taking on problems like crime, especially in minority neighborhoods. Were they afraid of getting called racist? Or was it because they preferred to see people of color always and only as victims, as clients of the Democratic Party and never agents of their own lives? She was fed up with white people defending drug dealers just because they were Hispanic—as if that made a difference. It was a disaster, the whole lefty tendency to make a cult of the victims of bigotry, exempting them from normal rules, keeping them not quite adult, not fully responsible. Still not equal.

The next time I launched into an anti-Giuliani diatribe, I heard the sound of my own smug voice and started to wonder at what was behind it. A privilege I didn't know I had. A self-indulgence.

I think it was around then that the Avengers got a call from the *Montel Williams Show,* and imagining it was cool to be on national TV, a bunch of us piled into the limo they sent and made spectacles of ourselves. Most of us were on stage. I ceded my place to Chanelle because she looked way better than me in her shades, and we needed a little diversity. Several years later, Ana and I were in a hotel room somewhere, Kentucky maybe, flipping through the cable, and I screamed. "Oh my god, look at that."

"What? Is that you?"

"Turn it off. Turn it off."

There I was, that worked-up dyke in the audience. That peculiar self. That ranting activist whom Ana knew and loved anyway.

On St. Paddy's Day, I crawled out of Ana's bed and met up with Cindra and Boy Kelly to take the train up to midtown. It was nice and sunny, but the crowd of queers was still smaller than the year before. ILGO was suffering from the activist curse of internal disputes that would soon strike the Avengers. And the rest of the community was already tired of fighting to be included in the cheesy het parade, even if other minority queers like South Asians and Poles were trying to get into their own. Al Sharpton was there, though, with his rock-star hair and retinue, courting the gay vote for the next mayoral election. There were also a few queer notables like Tom Duane, Tony Kushner, and the up-and-coming Christine Quinn. The Church Ladies For Choice serenaded us with the old standard "God Is A Lesbian," which was perfect, considering that the city's excuse to exclude us that year wasn't our personal safety but that the beer-swigging, step-dancing, baton-twirling St. Patrick's Day Parade was religious in nature, so organizers could ban whomever they wished.

A hundred and two got arrested that year after shouting, "We're Irish, we're queer, we'll be here every year." Increasingly, it looked as if we'd have to be. New Yorkers showed no signs of rising up to protest how stupid it was to define the beer-swigging, step-dancing parade as religious, especially when queers were marching in parades all over Ireland. So somebody had to protest. Somebody had to stand on their rights. Even if the parade *was* idiotic. Even if you didn't really want to go. Somebody had to remember who the streets belonged to. Especially when they were being tidied up. All the squeegee men gone. The homeless not housed, but shoved out of sight. The parks closed. And the music dimmed.

It was so depressing. It must have been a dream, lesbians on the covers of magazines. Twenty thousand dykes in the street in D.C. It all suddenly seemed like a hopeless fight, but so what? I told myself. What does it cost you to pretend that the world can change (for the better)? That history is an arc and it bends toward justice, even if it is long?

15.

A few weeks later, I was back on Fifth Avenue, this time with a genuine smile on my face, a silly hat on my head, and over a little black frock I borrowed from Ana a leather jacket I'd ripped off at a fancy *Out* magazine party that I'd decided was such a repulsive display of queer money it couldn't pass undisturbed. I was at the tail end of my Jean Genet phase that included appropriating Rennes' book *Journal du voleur* (The Thief's Journal), which gave me a lot of satisfaction when we found out that Rennes wasn't his real name. Neither was the moniker *Sontag* that he gave to Ingrid Roettele when he worked at her eponymous restaurant, or any of the other aliases we'd seen on his fistful of credit cards. Later on, though, I felt guilty about the jacket, mostly because it turned out to be from Sears, so probably the guy I stole it from wasn't much better off than me. When my experiment in class warfare was over, shame kicked in and I gave it away.

But back to Fifth Avenue. That time we were there for the Easter Parade, the only day of the year New York's women engage in extravagant frivolity, putting parrots on their heads, or whole flower gardens, erupting in kitsch. They reminded me of those old-fashioned drag queens who would throw on a girly frock, high heels, and wig but leave beard stubble or a mustache on their faces so you'd know they knew just how mostly artificial gender was. We waded into that, Ana, me, Chanelle, two Michelles, the architect Rebecca, who did the hat consults, and a freckly Italian photographer, Miriam, who took a picture of me as Atlas holding up the giant globe at Rockefeller Center while people spun around the ice rink.

Women in the crowd smiled at us almost uniformly when we gave them delicate Avenger eggs that Rebecca had emptied out and decorated with little painted bombs and bits of that nylony ribbon you wrap packages with. They were real works of art, those eggs. Ana and I saved one carefully wrapped with tissue paper.

You can't always go out there with your fist raised.

Half these Avengers were from InterAction, International Actions, a group I'd started at the Avengers to work on the international front. I was finally using my own brain, or at least my gut. I figured that if Avenger chapters had started to pop up all over the place, and if we were sending people across the country as reinforcements, and NAFTA was getting signed, and the EU taking wing, that the Avengers should start to think in global terms. Especially since it was in New York that the UN convened and consulates were housed. And if New York was handy for national media outlets to call attention to murders in Oregon, it was just as good to publicize how dykes were killed in Armenia or institutionalized and tortured with electric shock in China (or Cuba). Even Rudolph Giuliani declared in his inaugural speech that he wanted to make New York the capital of the world, once again.

I figured it was time to plant our own country's flag, and like the *Village Voice* writer Jill Johnston, to declare our own Dyke Nation.

InterAction's first action was ambitious, expensive, and relied on drag. On April 30, 1994, five or six of us slung on our best girl clothes, like skirts and blouses and dresses and shoes that weren't made of canvas and didn't have holes. Then we took a cab up to the UN Headquarters where they were holding a black-tie dinner for UNIFEM, the United Nations Development Fund for Women. There was no way we were going to be able to muscle our way in, so we'd bought hugely expensive tickets and crammed propaganda into our pantyhose. The security guys went through our purses and grabbed the pamphlets there, but didn't search anywhere else. We felt very clever as we climbed in the elevator.

Upstairs, in what looked like a made-over conference room, were elegant women in sequins and silk, saris and other kinds of fancy dress, accompanied mostly by men in tuxedos and smoking jackets. We looked like squatters next to them, and very white, but they let us in anyway and showed us to our table, which was just past the enormous dessert buffet. The women chefs preparing the dinner were all big deals, especially the one who did these outrageous sculptures with chocolate. There were also puff pastry things. I was sorry we were going to miss the grub and considered, just for a minute, forgetting the protest to stay there and stuff myself. But I didn't.

We were Avengers, after all. With a mission inspired by all those hundreds of pages of literature that UNIFEM put out without using the word *lesbian* once. Because the primary concerns of all women were birth control, violent husbands, and economic independence, and there wasn't this other category of female that on top of all that also had to deal with being considered criminals, or sinners, or sick, raped "correctively," or killed. No, they thought the solution to the problems of all the world's women was to teach them how to raise poultry.

Our response, "You can't raise chickens in jail."

The plan was pretty simple. Just making a quick speech at some point, speaking aloud the word they'd redacted out of their global vision, and reminding them we existed, ten fingers ten toes, with our own urgent concerns. We sipped ice water for a couple minutes and tried not to make eye contact, and when one of the elegant bejeweled women took the mike and welcomed everybody, we exchanged looks, took a deep breath, and stood up.

The good thing about this sort of event is that no one ever expects an interruption. The woman at the podium just stood there in shock as Michelle Cronk, a blonde massage student, approached and very politely said, "Excuse me. I'd like to say a few words." The woman stepped away from the mike and Michelle read our list of demands. Nothing outlandish. Just for UNIFEM to include lesbians in their basic calculations. Like when they talked about violence against women, they should acknowledge the doubled risk for dykes. While Michelle talked calmly, and eloquently, the rest of us went around the room and began to hand out pamphlets. A few of the stuffed shirts and fancy-dressed guests refused, outraged that their nice, self-congratulatory supper had been interrupted by the dykes. The rest took them out of politeness or curiosity, even asked a few questions. Then security arrived and all hell broke loose.

They were total storm troopers, six and half feet of muscle that picked us up like puppies by the scruffs of our necks and dragged us out. They tried to cover our mouths as we shouted, "Women won't thrive until lesbians survive." Or something like that. What I remember most was lying facedown on the scratchy carpet near the elevators with a beefy guard's knee on my neck and my hands behind my back, while a small Mary Lumetta jumped on the guy and shouted, "Get off of her, get off of her!" Which he eventually did. But not before I had to bear the weight of the two of them and wondered just how much my spine could take.

They hustled us all downstairs to a basement that looked a lot like a modern kitchen all gleaming white tile and steel and took mug shots and demanded ID, which they copied. They had actual cells down there, but they didn't lock us up, though some woman came and threatened to turn us over to the Seventeenth Precinct cops who were lurking outside and charge us with a federal offense. Yeah, us, the terrifying and ragtag bunch of revolutionaries who didn't have anything more harmful than a handful of Xeroxed pamphlets stuffed in our pantyhose. Then with a little smirk she tossed us out, warning, "Your mug shots will be up near all the entrances. So don't try this again." Then we took the elevators up to the surface where they released us like animals into the wild, and we joined the nearby demonstrators, who cheered when we appeared and demanded the news. "Hey, hey, ho ho, dykes are women, too, you know."

And right away Sarah Schulman came over and busted my balls. "We were worried. You were inside a long time. What if they'd kept you? You hadn't made any provision for someone to communicate. You were totally irresponsible. No exit strategy. No legal backup. The whole thing was shit." She was right, of course. On the other hand, it wasn't exactly the Bay of Pigs. "Chill out," I said. "Everything was fine. You should have seen Mary jump on the security guard's back and try to get him off me. She's a hero. And Michelle Cronk was so calm up there with the mike. We had a real impact."

Or so I hoped. We didn't get any media coverage at all. But we'd spoken a forbidden word into the silence. "Lesbian, lesbian, lesbian." And we would do our own PR where it counted, too, among queers.

While my organizing skills may have stunk compared to other superefficient Avengers (even Ana agreed I should have had a better exit strategy), I wasn't wrong about the timing. Queers from all over the world flooded the city during the Stonewall anniversary, and we met a bunch of them at a conference put on by the International Lesbian and Gay Human Rights Campaign. All we had to do was set up our table, and these girls would see the name there, Lesbian Avengers, or *Vengadoras lesbianas,* and they'd rush over to take the pamphlets, sign up on the mailing list, and beg to hear what we'd already done. They oohed and aahed when we described how we'd invaded the UNIFEM banquet. Like U.S. dykes, they were sick of asking politely for their rights like eternal beggars. You want to feel powerful? There's no better way than going out there and demanding stuff, toot sweet. Right now. They were ready to be heroes. Or at least party with them.

Dozens accepted the invitation to the Avenger fund-raiser at Ana's. We thought it would be a little cocktail party, but a good seventy or eighty dykes came, mobbing the place, and sucking down our liquor as fast as they could, demanding more and louder music—something you could dance to. You got salsa? And girls made out in the corners and twirled each other around, barely pausing when Ana's downstairs neighbor came up and knocked on the door, announcing she had to work the next day and if we could maybe keep it down a little...?

Too bad, darling. We were celebrating a revolution. Shouting over the music, the handful of Avengers who bothered to attend, tried to collect addresses and pitch the Dyke March coming up on Saturday. We were competing with the Gay Games, and when we pressed them, people were nervous. A Dyke March? "You're sure there won't be arrests?" "Haven't been so far." And they said they'd think about it, fetched another rum or scotch or beer. Then spun each other around some more.

When we ran out of ice, I made a run to Roger's deli over on First Avenue. It was a relief to get out of there, with all those voices, all those demands, though a couple of Latin American dykes came with me. They thought our lives were strange and asked about how we did things, even why we had to go out for ice. They were from different countries and argued about whether Ana and I were rich or poor. "The apartment is big." "No, it's small." "There's nothing in it." "There are paintings." They talked like I wasn't there at all, until they asked if I was a typical American, and I said I didn't know. "It's a big country. Lots of people. I don't know them all." And they thought that was hilarious, and I was incredibly witty. And complimented me on my Spanish like everyone did, as if Americans were such barbarians that knowing even a few words redeemed you.

The party seemed like it would never end. Then suddenly,

a few decided they wanted to go to a real lesbian club, word spread, and then, like a plague of locusts, they departed the ravaged field, leaving little shed skins of empty cups behind. You could hear them buzzing in the street, their voices fading. What energy! So much it scared me. Imagine if we recognized it ourselves. If it could be harvested.

The only peculiar thing was that a few people asked us if we did our actions topless, like the one at the elementary school. With children. "No. Are you kidding? Who told you that?" But nobody could ever say.

16.

We were calling it the International Dyke March and figured it would be big, but how big? Pride Week that year was marking the twenty-fifth anniversary of the Stonewall riots when queers at the Stonewall Inn in the Village refused to submit to one more night of beatings and arrests and threw themselves a riot, which bloomed unexpectedly into a full-fledged liberation movement. Celebrating it, the city embraced us, at least temporarily. Couples that usually kept themselves at arm's length walked the streets holding hands. Gay-friendly stores flew rainbow flags. We filled hotels with fancy dress balls, and trashy private parties overflowed onto fire escapes where no one cared that the only things holding us in the air were a few pieces of rusty metal that had already started to separate from the brick. We were already so unlikely. Never meant to survive, as Audre Lorde said. So we swapped spit on street corners, in trains, waiting for restaurants, just like annoying straights.

While even we could see the benefits of incremental progress and long-term thinking, the official events still seemed just a little too full of lobbyists in suits and ties. A little too self-congratulatory as long as Christian extremists still portrayed us as monsters, and gay men died by the tens of thousands as Americans muttered, "Good riddance." It was still too early for polite politics. At the International Dyke March in New York, the Avengers called on lesbians to Incite the Riot. As in D.C., we handed out thousands of palm cards, and a new manifesto, OUT AGAINST THE RIGHT, written by the newly christened Lesbian Avenger Civil Rights Organizing Project (LACROP). In it we proclaimed that "Butch, femme and androgynous dykes, leather queers, drag kings and queens, transsexuals and trans-genders will not be thrown to the wolves so that straight-acting 'gay people' can beg for acceptance at our expense." "We have to respond on our terms, not theirs." "1,000S OF ANGRY DYKES CAN'T BE WRONG—AND WON'T GIVE IN. EVER."

I thought the manifesto was great, an important call to action. But its earnest, angry tone also signaled a huge shift in Avenger sensibility. I didn't really notice its importance at the time, just recoiled a little when somebody said they were glad to dump the old one. "I never was comfortable with it," she said. "It was silly."

"Yes," seconded somebody else. "I expected something more serious."

Several Avengers exchanged knowing nods, and I wondered why they hadn't said anything before. I'd thought it was so beautiful, so funny, joking, "subversion is our perversion." I felt absolutely mortified. I often did. Like during that discussion over the final "Sally" press release. For months, the Ministry of Propaganda had been working to get coverage for the International Dyke March. Besides doing the usual, they decided to also use teasers featuring a character called Sally. I wrote the copy for the final, thinking of all the dykes I'd been reading about or working with as part of the international group, and wrote, "SALLY wears saris and Doc Martens…SALLY speaks all the best languages…SALLY says, I shouted loudest at Tiananmen Square."

When the text was presented to the meeting, I remember expecting kudos for inclusiveness, or at the worst a criticism that it was an annoyingly poetic laundry list. But somebody said, "I'd like to know why there's no images here of African Americans. Did you do it on purpose?"

"I'm deeply offended," said somebody else.

Then it was open season on my "insensitivity," with plenty of attacks from young white women burnishing their antiracist credentials, and afterwards a big gaping silence that I was supposed to fill with a commie-style self-criticism or cheap Freudian analysis, confessing, I suppose, an unconscious desire for the erasure of black America. But I didn't. Because I didn't. I kept my mouth shut and my eyes blank in the face of all those death rays until Marlene finally said, "I don't think it was intentional. Let's just add a phrase or two. All right, Kelly?"

"Perfect," I said. And cheerfully scribbled down their suggestions, like it was water off a duck's back and my hands weren't shaking. Fucking activists.

Internal squabbles didn't paralyze me yet. Not when I saw how many dykes were pouring into Bryant Park, dragging their new friends from Brazil or Spain or India or South Africa, and marching even without guarantees of safety, I remembered why I put up with the nonsense. After a brief confab with the cops at the beginning, we took Fifth Avenue with an enormous banner, a marching band, and huge inflatable globes bouncing through the crowd. Our own Irish dykes Anne Maguire and Marie Honan were at the front, at least briefly, before others took their place. There were tons of New Yorkers, and international dykes, plus Avengers from all over the States who had come in an ambitious caravan that they'd called a Pride Ride so as not to offend anybody. Doing actions along the way, one group set off from Austin, Texas, and took a route that went through KKK country, including Vidor, Texas, and Ovett, Mississippi. Another group began in Minneapolis, passed through Lansing, Michigan, and Pittsburgh, and converged with the southern group in Philly. Canadian Avengers turned up, too.

At Twenty-third Street, I climbed a lamppost and looked back. The march was as big as D.C., and we filled the Avenue like twenty thousand dyke ants waving Avenger signs and homemade poster boards, blowing whistles, shaking noisemakers, bellowing, ripping our shirts off. It was our street. Our city. For a couple of hours, it was our world. At Washington Square Park, the Avengers gathered around the fountain, displaying banners from all over the country. And after making a short speech and consecrating the moment by eating fire, they joined the cheering crowd, plunging into the water with dogs and backpacks and lovers and best friends.

With twenty thousand dykes, the march should have made the cover of every rag in the city, with all the work we'd done offering press releases and photos. And follow-up calls. But out of the fifty articles covering the Stonewall anniversary celebrations in the *New York Times,* we only scored nine lines. Nine lines. Ana counted. She bought the papers and smeared her fingers with ink going through them line by line. We didn't make it at all into the *Washington Post,* the *Chicago Tribune,* or the *Los Angeles Times,* though the *San Francisco Chronicle* published a nice photo of the Dyke March there. Nope, in New York, all we got was a little radio and TV coverage. It was like it never happened.

Worse, GLAAD, the Gay and Lesbian Alliance Against Defamation, which was supposed to be the media watchdog, gave the *New York Times* "top honors for outstanding national coverage of Stonewall history, culture, and events." When we sent them a two-page report proving that the International Dyke March was virtually ignored, GLAAD awarded us one pathetic line in a second press release, as if the Dyke March was just a minor event and even they didn't think twenty thousand dykes in the street was particularly newsworthy.

I remember Maxine Woolf, with her lifetime in radical lefty movements, asking, "What do you expect from an institution?" And I partly agreed but also thought it was a bad sign when stuff like this ceases to surprise you, and all you do is shrug. Wasn't it outrage that pushed them to create the Avengers? Later on, Ana told me how before she helped start the Avengers she walked around like a ticking bomb, sick of being invisible, of how dykes blabbed in conference rooms while fags took to the streets. Finally she told her friend Sarah, "We should do it, start our own direct-action group," who sent her to Maxine, who wasn't as phlegmatic as she pretended, already mulling over her own idea that there should at least be a hotline or something that dykes could dial up for an instant action. Together, they drew in the rest.

After the International Dyke March, it was Ana going ballistic by herself over the coverage, because she was convinced media was the key to any power at all. If you weren't seen, you weren't heard, simple as that. She found out that GLAAD, which was supposed to be standing outside of things with their watchdog teeth bared, had actually been hired to run the PR campaigns of several LGBT organizations and had done it out of their official offices. Their reviews of the media had a direct correlation with how well the rags had covered their clients—international focus (International Lesbian and Gay Association), fight the right (National Gay and Lesbian Task Force), historical perspective (Stonewall 25), and AIDS (Gay Men's Health Crisis).

It was the first time I realized just how smart Ana was, how relentless. She buried GLAAD in paper. Faxes, letters, memos denounced their conflict of interest, how they'd ignored dykes and, for that matter, people of color. Because Ana started counting how many times they were mentioned, too. And her tactics worked. Kind of. GLAAD was a media operation, after all, used to damage control. They arranged phone calls and meetings, offering tight, polite smiles and promises to do better, though denying the conflict of interest. They blamed funding for everything. "Our monitors are volunteers, after all. After all, we have such limited resources," they claimed, though they picked their teeth with gold toothpicks compared to groups like the Avengers that were funded with house parties and kissing booths.

Ana stewed in her own juices. Made me stew in mine. Wondering what the Avengers could do to bust through that glass ceiling. Wondering what I'd gotten into with Ana. I was a lump next to her, even if I hated restraint as much. Being erased. Being confined to our little corners. Even when I was a toddler and my aunt Connie tried to stuff my chubby legs into itchy white tights, I wriggled and fought. Then there was that time at the swimming pool with my sisters when the bigger kids grabbed me like they always did, dunked my head under the water, and I kicked out with all my force, elbowed, threw my head back, writhed, bit. Left them bloody and bruised and shouting, "What the heck?! It's just a game. Vikki! Kim! Your brat sister's nuts!"

Ana was me times ten. Times a hundred. She was Avenger concentrate, and starting to simmer. I tried to hypnotize her to sleep. "Imagine we're back in Nice, sitting on the beach. There are all the pebbles. The waves are pounding. The sky is blue. The air is soft..." And she'd get all relaxed, then irritated. "I'm almost asleep. Would you quit talking, please?"

17.

It wasn't quite true we were invisible. Lesbians were always a staple of straight guy porn, the butt of their jokes. Especially in New York's Hispanic media. When Ana stopped by a group of Latina lesbians, Las Buenas Amigas, to pitch the International Dyke March, she met Carmen, a high-priced Cuban lawyer who'd been keeping tabs on Spanish-language media, taping radio and TV shows on Telemundo and Univisión. Their comedy skits were all stereotypes, all the time. And not just with queers. White Hispanic guys in shoe-polish blackface played these stupid *negritos,* then came back to do a scene as stupid Mexicans in enormous sombreros. Sometimes it was stupid women with enormous tits, or stupid *mariposas* homos stuffed into tiny ridiculous pants. I was shocked, along with Ana, even if I knew people of color weren't immune to bigotry after hearing a Bengali immigrant going on about how lazy American blacks were.

The radio station Mega KQ 97.9 FM was among the worst. Their morning shock jocks had a repertoire of jokes about raping fags, with plenty of elaborate pranks like the one calling people up to tell them they had HIV, then laughing at their horror and humiliation, before announcing, "Jes' joking!" They sneered at Indian cab drivers and weird disgusting dykes, and didn't even bother coming up with punch lines to skewer black people, just came right out and said they were stupid and had bad hair. They were more offensive than Howard Stern, just as popular, and way more powerful if you figure that for the two million Hispanics in New York this was often their introduction to America. It wasn't just bad for the objects of their scorn, it saddled them with a bigotry that made them unfit to succeed in a city where their coworkers or bosses might be Jews or queers, Pakistanis, or African Americans.

Hitting la Mega was a no-brainer when Ana decided to head up an action herself. Especially because the Spanish Broadcasting System that owned the station was a national force and was being used as a model across the United States. The trick was to find the right angle. If we held a picket, they'd just poke fun at us on the air, "Oh, those ridiculous dykes. They have no sense of humor. We're not bigots. We're equal opportunity offenders." Naw, we had to do something bold, something dramatic, something worthy of the name Lesbian Avengers.

Our house became a vortex of planning for one of the Avengers' most daring actions. The small group included Melanie Fallon, the Scottish girl, along with the Irish dyke Sheila Quinn, and a couple of others. Embroiled in fund-raising for InterAction, I mostly just watched it unfold. Ana and Melanie got their seed of an idea from watching a Costa-Gavras movie, *State of Siege,* in which leftist militants in Uruguay kidnapped an American "advisor" of the repressive right-wing regime. When the group went to the Avenger meeting, they only reported it was something ambitious and risky and important. They didn't want the news to leak. We'd imagined the Avengers would leap at the chance for a new project, some real excitement, but the response was lukewarm at best. Most were far more interested in preparations for an action at the Alice Austen house in Staten Island. They were going to infiltrate a reception dressed as lifeguards to "rescue" this photographer's lesbian history.

We didn't worry about it then. The Mega action was for a small group anyway, a tactical strike force, though we also organized a public demo.

The group prepared as carefully as characters in *The Dirty Half-Dozen* or *Ocean's Not Nearly Eleven*—getting ready to knock over a bank or casino, or kill Nazis. Celinés, a cute Latina student, volunteered to be the scout. She went to our target and begged for a tour. Pretending to be enthralled, she made notes the whole time about where the security guards were, the elevators and stairs, and how many steps it took to get from place to place. She came back with a detailed map, and they blocked out their route on our living room floor using masking tape. The door is here. Security there. Rehearsing it again and again, the conspirators all contributed to refinements in their plan. I watched green with envy, because I was stuck doing legal support and had to stay safely at home with a list of phone numbers.

It was impressive watching them work. They thought things through, came up with contingencies, exit strategies, feared the worst. Ana pushed hardest, standing there with a stopwatch and rehearsing her Avengers like a theater director. Until they quit giggling and, blindfolded, knew which way to turn.

On August 17, 1994, they went up to the glass and brick high rises of midtown and invaded the Spanish Broadcasting System. One persuaded the guard to let her in, then held the door open for the others to enter. In moments, they were on the floor of the broadcast booths. Melanie and Sheila blocked the stairwell and controlled the elevator. Ana, Harriet, and Celinés took over the sound booth and studio broadcasting *el Vacilón de la Manaña*. They had an easy time of it, surprising the techies and DJs, replacing the usual blather of sick, bigoted jokes with demands for an end to hate radio. When their calculated minutes had ticked to an end, they beat a quick retreat, taking the elevator down, as security pounded on the stairwell door and the cop sirens got nearer. They separated on the street, fleeing to assigned locations. Phyllis Lutsky was the getaway driver, careening full speed in midtown traffic to retrieve them from their hidey holes.

While this was going on, there was a small Avenger demo outside with only twenty or so dykes, though they made a lot of noise and had good signs. Raúl Alarcón Jr. was the president of the Spanish Broadcasting System, so they had placards we'd made with his photo reading "WANTED: For inciting hatred against Latina lesbians" and shouted, "Boycott la Mega." "Mega KQ is hate radio." And "Mega KQ es Mega Caca [shit]." My contribution. They handed out hundreds of bilingual flyers.

I arrived late, stuck at home and waiting for word until Ana reported from a hotel bar, absolutely breathless, "We pulled it off."

We were so excited, going back to the main Avenger meeting. My god, we'd invaded a radio station. Broadcasted our own message. Were excited to do more about hate radio. Everybody clapped and cheered, but that was about it. The radio action group only picked up a couple more people. A lot of new members seemed content to just sit there, applauding when Marlene Colburn or Max would report how the new group in London had invaded the Queen Victoria monument near Buckingham Palace. Or Sara Pursley announced that LACROP had gotten a grant or a major contribution. Maybe that's what they thought activism was.

That was about the time that Sara went to Idaho to work with four other LACROP members. There was yet another statewide antigay amendment in the works, and they were going to work with members of a tiny Avenger chapter in Palouse. New York meetings would be launched with tales from the land of Ruby Ridge and the Aryan Nation in which the Lesbian Avengers were heroes. The foes weren't always skinheads or homophobes pushing antigay legislation, but bureaucrats from the national LGBT organizations. They were playing the same closeted game in Idaho as they had in Maine, framing their campaign as a question of abstract equality and civil rights, and not about those creepy flesh-and-blood homos. We heard they made volunteers sign releases promising to refer any questions to designated spokespeople—as if the ordinary worker couldn't be trusted to hold the party line. They also warned local activists not to work with the Avengers, those out-of-control, irresponsible activists who demonstrated naked in front of schoolchildren.

We booed and stomped when we heard they ripped down signs that local queers put up. And laughed when Sheila Quinn arrived one Tuesday with a story of how she'd flown out to support the Avengers for a couple of days and joined a meeting of some local lesbian business people who were sitting on the fence about working with them. She'd done her best to convince them to participate. And when Sheila got back to her job at Astraea, a national lesbian foundation, she got a phone call from one of the same dykes who was trying to check on the Avengers. Are they reliable? Are they competent, serious, worth working with? "I believe I was one of those you met," Sheila told her, in her charming Irish accent. "And yes, we're all those things."

LACROP persisted anyway, making alliances with progressive straights in local churches if the national groups had scared off queers. They stuck to the tactics that had worked in Lewiston, canvassing as out queers, reminding people that they had their whole lives at stake.

I talked to Elizabeth Meister not long ago, a thin, long-haired Avenger who said working in Idaho wasn't at all what she expected as an East Coast activist. Like that time going house to house, or more accurately, farm to farm, she'd knocked on a door that was answered by this big scary burly guy. When she'd choked it out that they were there about Proposition 1, he said, "What kind of person do you think I am?" And she said, "Ummm…" And he said, "I'd never support that kind of discriminatory crap." That was traditional grassroots organizing at its best. Enlightening everybody all around.

LACROP deserved all the credit they got. More, in fact. They worked 24/7. Smoked too much, drank too much. Ate take-out as they organized speak-outs and designed flyers. Maxine, who'd cut her teeth on grassroots organizing, was their mentor. She visited awhile and reminded them to breathe. "Sit down together, eat a meal," she counseled. Their work was hugely important, and the group back in New York realized it.

Ana got Sara to take video for Dyke TV. If they had the time or money, people like Sheila even flew out there for a few days.

At the same time, the radio action group could barely persuade anybody to participate. Only a handful, mostly Latina, would volunteer. We stank at raising money, while funds seemed to be pouring in for LACROP. We started to feel at odds with them, as if the whole thing was a popularity contest in high school, and we'd lost.

We didn't really understand what was going on. Were newer Avengers afraid of crossing cultural and linguistic lines? Were they just at the meetings to cruise girls? After all, we'd already done the heavy lifting. The Avengers existed. We'd accomplished things. These new dykes had already seen images of Lesbian Avengers eating fire in front of the White House. Out singer k.d. lang got shaved by that model Cindy Crawford on the cover of *Vanity Fair.* Bi comedian Sandra Bernhard played a lesbian on *Roseanne.* We even seemed to have our dyke Toni Morrison in Dorothy Allison, whose *Bastard Out of Carolina* had hit the best-seller lists. Lesbians were goddamn fucking chic, at least briefly. Nothing was urgent. Nobody was desperate. Alone, the name *Lesbian Avengers* gave them a bold identity. They didn't have to shape their own.

Or maybe their problem was the project. Did they see it as just some marginal, city thing, while LACROP was national, out there fighting the Christian Right with their important, serious manifesto? Was it us? We didn't think about how to incorporate newbies. The first wave of Avengers had gotten to know each other by doing actions, and at the time we hadn't had too many in New York. Some of our most experienced activists like Maxine were focused on Idaho. Sarah Schulman was off on another book tour. Anne and Marie were increasingly besieged with ILGO infighting. And Ana wasn't much of an advocate. She's too earnest. Never learned the trick of leaning back in her chair, smiling, and pontificating in a persuasive way.

The whole group started to feel unbalanced, off-center, like in action films when you see a stunt guy straddling two speeding cars.

I didn't want to think about it, skipped meetings, and went to the Greenwich House Pottery for classes. It was very soothing, mucking around in the clay, and I'd daydream a life in which I could set up a little shop somewhere and spend my days throwing bowls that people would beat down the door to buy. How exquisite. Let me shower you with money for this chunk of mud. Bette Midler turned up at a class one day. She was smaller than I imagined. With thin, bleached hair. We were all so cool ignoring her that it started to get weird, too, nobody helping her when she started struggling to get the round wooden bat off the wheel. I finally said something idiotic, "Yeah, that thing can have you in tears." And she shot back, "I hardly think it's worth that." And I slunk away in humiliation.

There was no escaping it. Not at the pottery. Not at the Avengers. The center of operations for the Radio Mega actions was still our apartment, even if we weren't planning anything as exciting as an invasion. After Ana's son moved out, Melanie became our new roommate, and I teased her like a younger sister. It felt like a clubhouse, all girls all the time. Especially once we put together the coalition.

18.

Ana prodded Carmen, the Cuban American lawyer, to get Las Buenas Amigas more involved in the Radio Mega campaign. She was one of their co-chairs, and Ana had already pushed her to meet with GLAAD to reiterate the facts of New York life—that Hispanics made up a huge part of the city and that Spanish-language media was a cesspool. Plus antigay Hispanic fundamentalism was beginning to explode. They had to act quickly, recruit more Spanish-speaking volunteers, get Latino spokespeople.

After the action, Ana met with Carmen and pitched the idea of a coalition to dive deeper into the issue. She came home talking about how smart Carmen was, how exciting it was to find somebody so brilliant, who could maybe become a partner in this work, maybe eventually a friend. Carmen had a more mixed response. She wanted to work with Ana but was wary of the Avengers. She sent a fax saying every mixed project she'd worked on had ended up being dominated by white Americans imposing their language and culture. At the same time, she thought it was an important venture, and that it would be good for the girls, *las muchachas,* to work with Ana in particular. She was a great role model for Latina lesbians.

Ana didn't notice that part, or she might have been reluctant herself. She didn't want to be anybody's role model, or mentor, no matter how much she liked them.

By early fall the Avengers had established a formal coalition with Las Buenas Amigas (LBA), and also with another group called African Ancestral Lesbians United for Societal Change

(AALUFSC). We'd approached BLUS, Bronx Lesbians United in Sisterhood, but the white woman running the thing told us street activism wasn't culturally appropriate for her group, which was mostly black and Latina lesbians. "Who does she think started the Avengers?" Ana asked. "Or, for that matter, took to the streets with King?"

We offered our house as a meeting place. It was free and centrally located, with a bathroom right there, a stereo, and flexible hours. It was fun at first, a great big party, even if not many Avengers participated. The LBA dykes were a lot more social than Latina Avengers like Ana, Susana Cook, or Lidia. They had to have music all the time, and beer and food. I got to know Carmen and her girlfriend, Patricia, the two LBA heads. Carmen had close-cropped hair and bright red lipstick. Patricia had long wavy hair, a grad student's slouch. I've never been looked at with such interest and delight. They absolutely cooed when I mumbled something in Spanish, complimented my appearance, my intelligence, my dedication to lesbians. They congratulated Ana on having found such a prize and told me how lucky I was to be with such a saint, an icon. "You're a million times blessed." Ana shrank from it a little, but I ate it all up after getting attacked by the Avengers at least once a month.

In those days, being the Good American was my specialty. It had started in college on that trip to Spain when I'd agreed with the locals when they criticized U.S. foreign policy even if I didn't know what they were talking about. Living in Harlem, I'd eat as many hot peppers as any of the Bengalis and nod promptly when they condemned the Gulf War or American militarism, keeping to myself the dirty secret I had cousins in the service. And when the Irish girls poked fun at their hyphenated colleagues for appropriating an Irish identity when they were clearly American, I laughed as hard as them, desperate to be on the right side of things.

No wonder I kept mum when Carmen stared at Ana with awe, asked me questions about this person she'd only seen in that 1984 documentary by Néstor Almendros, *Mauvaise conduite* (Improper Conduct), about what happened to queers in Castro's Cuba—the concentration camps, the prisons, the endless harassment while the global Left turned a blind eye, denouncing homosexuality as a bourgeois phenomenon. I didn't wonder at her motives when she interrogated Ana about why she didn't do the interview in Spanish. "Because the film was for a French audience, and I spoke French." And why did she write in English? "Because I live in the United States and I feel freer in it." Her curiosity extended to Ana's books and CDs. She and Patricia approvingly pulled out Gloria Estefan and Albita but laughed at Beny Moré and Bola de Nieve. "What are you, an anthropologist? A scholar? A snob?" As if one weren't a Wall Street lawyer, the other an academic in an ivory tower.

After that first meeting, the LBA dykes brought their own music to the house, and it was nonstop salsa and merengue, their culture dominating the group. They also had a lot of parties themselves, and Ana and I went to a few where there were enormous spreads of food, lots of drinks, and dancing, also party games that involved people scribbling things on Post-its. Ana wasn't very comfortable. It was even worse for me. All that cuteness. The demands that everyone participate. I spent a lot of time hiding in the bathroom.

Kim and Keisha and the other African American dykes were lucky. Nobody expected them to party with LBA. They were there to work toward the demo. We started painting banners and made a huge radio out of cardboard, with the three monster heads of homophobia, racism, and sexism coming out of it. I was obsessed with chicken wire and papier-mâché at the time and used them at every opportunity. It was a good chance to meet girls from the other groups while we glued bits of paper to the frame, then painted it. I admit that, like with the Avengers in the beginning, it took a while for me to separate out individuals from the smiling, chattering mass.

Melanie did media with Ana and Carmen and Anne d'Adesky,

when she wasn't working the counter at Casa Linga, a restaurant we called cunnilingus for fun. Ana and Carmen in particular exchanged a million faxes. Ana sending short ones, Carmen the lawyer responding with pages and pages of notes. I'd tease Ana sometimes, say her beau had sent another love letter. I recently found some going through Ana's old folders. They're like tissue paper now, and the words have faded almost to illegibility. Some are written with a scrawling hand. Others are typed. Some are in Spanish. Others in English, depending on Carmen's mood and the subject matter. The indistinct words almost seem like a sign to let sleeping dogs lie. What will they howl when they wake? That words like *Cuban* are meaningless? Identity a sham? Hope always burns?

There's that early fax about Carmen's reluctance to collaborate with the Avengers, her fear of integrated groups, her hopes Ana will be a role model. Then there's one about broadcasting regulations and how the FCC worked, the background that would shape our strategy, and tacked on at the end a faux humble invitation to a little party with "cheap" merengue. Later, personal concerns began to dominate. They show not just admiration or interest but flat-out need as she looks for affirmation in the words of this Cuban dyke who was older and more experienced, who was a kind of icon for her.

Though what did they have in common, really? Ana came of age in Cuba, and became an immigrant in France, then the United States, her national identity already formed. Carmen mostly grew up in Anglo America as a mixed-race Hispanic. For her I was white. For Ana, American.

The expectation of sameness was a disaster. Carmen wanted to know what that change in commas meant. Why did you delete the one thing and add another? She analyzed Ana's tone of voice on the phone. Pleaded with her, accused. Felt rebuked. She reminded me of a lover I had once who would dissect every move I made, every word I spoke in fits of rage and jealousy. I'm sure Carmen would think it presumptuous, racist, even, but I try now to imagine what she felt, faced with Ana. Who didn't really notice all that, just kept making more and more demands of Las Buenas Amigas without giving Carmen what she needed or expected in return.

Ana will admit it herself. If she was a flawed advocate for the project in front of a bunch of Anglos, she was worse with Carmen, because she's a rotten Latina. Ana doesn't open up. Is not particularly effusive. Hates chitchat. It's why she adopted New York as her home. You can make a call, get right to the point without inquiring politely into what the other person did last night, or is going to do tomorrow, or how she felt about it all.

Carmen took it personally, Ana's New York abruptness. Perceived it as rejection, which made her more obsessed than ever. Patricia made an appointment with Ana and came over to the house, hinting around at something, but never getting to the point, like a girlfriend who'd discovered an affair and was trying to tell the other woman to back off. She already rubbed us wrong since that moment early on at the Sunshine Diner when the four of us were bonding over coffee, and Carmen told us how difficult things had been for her growing up as a mixed-race dyke, caught between the rock of an America that preferred things in black and white, and the hard place of a gay-hating, racist, macho Cuban community. Thinking of it, she got upset, pushed her cup around the sticky table.

Patricia's response was to snicker, tell a story of her own about growing up in Costa Rica and hating the foreign kids who had arrived from Cuba with their parents. All the local children threw rocks at them or chased them with sticks. Sitting next to her Cuban girlfriend, Patricia laughed as if she still thought it was hilarious, attacking these little Cuban kids. I figured I misunderstood the Spanish, but when I asked Ana later, she confirmed it.

I began to avoid them, spent more time with the other members of Las Buenas Amigas. Like Adriana, a funny butch Colombian dyke who wanted to be a cop when she finished up at CUNY. Or her pal Diana, a photographer and another Colombian Amazon. There was also Cathy Chang, an Ecuadorian dyke who poked fun at everyone, including herself. She knew Ana from way back and treated her like a normal person, and not some luminary. Without her, things may have collapsed even before the first joint demo.

We did an enormous workshop beforehand, explaining our legal rights. A lot of Latina dykes were worried, even if they were legal U.S. residents. Some of the African American dykes were also plain nervous about Giuliani's cops. Still, a huge crowd turned out at the Spanish Broadcasting System on November 17, a few days after the midterm elections when Clinton's Democrats got dumped. It was all the dykes from the working group plus hundreds more, this whole enormous sea of black and Latina faces that at first were tentative in the twilight, surrounded by the huge buildings of midtown. They were more and more happy as they brandished their signs, and chanted in English and Spanish, and pounded drums. Spanish-speaking Latinas giggled trying to chant in English. African Americans and the few white dykes did their best in Spanish. For many of the dykes of color, it was their first time on the street as themselves. They looked at each other and smiled. Their voices got louder and louder. They shouted, transformed with joy, cheering when the beast of homophobia, racism, and misogyny was slain with a giant sword.

When demos click like that they're incredible. What amazing energy. Unified, what potential to transform a divided city, lead a divided country. For once a huge campaign of phone calls and press releases paid off, and we actually made it into the Spanish press. New York's *El Diario,* the biggest Spanish-language newspaper in the country published a photo with a long caption. Ana was thrilled. On behalf of the three groups she sent out press releases about the successful rally, announcing an awareness campaign in New York Latino neighborhoods and trumpeting our achievement. In a fax cover to Colleen

Marzec at the *Washington Blade,* she wrote, "Never has there been a coalition of this kind: for the first time in history, ethnic-based lesbian groups are doing *direct-action* in their own ethnic communities. We think this is a turning point for lesbian activism in this country."

19.

It was a turning point, all right, but not for the better. Things got more and more weird between Carmen and Ana. I kept to the role of Ana's delightful white girlfriend who miraculously spoke Spanish. They weren't interested in seeing beyond the mask. Maybe they didn't realize it was one. In the early fall, I'd disappeared for a few days on a trip to Louisville. Took a Greyhound down, saw the seasons change in reverse, yellowed shrunken leaves plumping out, turning green again. The highway cut through the crumbling, shale hills and ended in a generic decaying sprawl of a modern metropolis that had all these separate little pockets, from white-trash rural exiles and crumbling black slums, to an aspiring middle-class and a genteel, Gentile upper class.

My grandmother was dying. I can't remember who called to tell me. My mother never spent a dollar on a phone call when a seventeen-cent stamp would do. My sister Kim picked me up at the bus station and took me straight to the yellow-brick Suburban Hospital where I had volunteered when I thought I was going to be a doctor. My grandmother was in a private room and didn't look human anymore. She'd been plump and pretty with black hair streaked with grey that she kept in an old-lady perm. All the color and curls had drained away. The roundness of her face was gone, leaving just skull and the whiskers she'd grown on her chin. She looked like a primate. That's where we come from. That's what we all become. Graying apes among the white sheets and tubes. Only her belly was rounded. Later, the nurse said the morphine made it impossible for her to shit.

They had to go in there with their fingers and dig it out when enemas didn't work anymore.

She kind of recognized me—or pretended to. Or maybe it was just the enthusiasm from my aunts and uncles in the room. Cancer had eaten away at her bones until they were like Swiss cheese. She'd complained for years that they hurt, but all old ladies complain, right? And she'd had shingles just a year or two before, and the pain often lingers.

My mother shrieked loudly with false joy at what the cat drug in and gave me uncomfortable pats while she looked me up and down for traces of the monster I'd become, and any weight gained, which would make me like my lazy no-good father. She also worked in a surreptitious sniff to see if I stank, which I did, perfumed with diesel and sweat and disinfectant after twenty-four hours on the bus. And she said, "Shooey. They don't let you bathe up there? No wonder you can't get a man. Haw haw." All grinning and laughing hysterically.

Then my aunts and uncles asked what I had been up to with that peculiar mix of curiosity and disdain that forces you to respond as vaguely as possible. "Still writing?" "Uh huh. Poems mostly." "Any money in it?" "Well." My face turned green under the fluorescent lights, the distance imposed by their old-fashioned twanging speech, and what everybody knew now and didn't say. Maybe because it was just as strange to be a writer up north as it was to be a lesbian.

And I imagined trying to translate that room, those people with their homemade clothes and union cards, to the folks in New York and couldn't bridge that gap either. My grandmother, who had considered it an accomplishment to complete fifth grade, which she had gone to on a pony through twelve feet of snow. Who had moved back and forth from the dirt-poor country to the city where she'd worked in a factory, raised kids, saved money, bought the house there on Dundee Road. Owned it outright. Her husband sometimes worked, sometimes not. He was

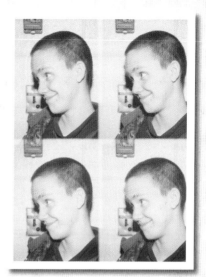

Born to be bald.

Giggling in the center of my first girl gang.

Athletic at twelve,
artsy at twenty-one.

So that's Gloria Steinem. March for Women's Lives, my first demo, 1989.
PHOTOGRAPH BY KELLY COGSWELL.

WE WANT REVENGE AND WE WANT IT
NOW!

LESBIANS!   DYKES!
GAY WOMEN!

There are many more lesbians in this world than men
like George Bush. But cold-blooded liars like him
have all the power.
Let's face it:
Government, Media, Entertainment, The Money
System, School, Religion, Politeness ... are irrelevant
to our lives as dykes. We're wasting our lives being
careful. Imagine what your life could be. Aren't you
ready to make it happen? <u>WE ARE.</u> If you don't
want to take it anymore and are ready to strike, call
us now at (718) 499-3802. We'll call you back.
Think about it,

What have you got to lose?

 The Lesbian Avengers
(ove)

The club card that launched it
all. Text by Sarah Schulman.
*FROM THE LESBIAN AVENGER
COLLECTION, LESBIAN HERSTORY
ARCHIVES.*

the LESBIAN AVENGERS

WE RECRUIT

PARTY & FUNDRAISER
GO-GO GIRLS   MUSIC
MEDIA INSTALLATION
SAT, OCT 24
9PM-4AM
119 AVE D, 2nd FLR
$5 AT THE DOOR
The LESBIAN AVENGERS is a direct-
action group focused on issues vital
to lesbian survival and viability.
We meet every Tuesday at 8PM at
the Lesbian & Gay Community
Services Center, 208 W 13 St, NYC.
For info: (212) 967-7711 ext. 3204

THE LESBIAN AVENGERS ARE COMING TO MAKE THE WORLD SAFE FOR BABY DYKES EVERYWHERE

Who knew dykes were superheroes!? *DESIGNS BY CARRIE MOYER.*

DYKE MANIFESTO

CALLING ALL LESBIANS!

WAKE UP!

IT'S TIME TO GET OUT OF THE BEDS, OUT OF THE BARS AND INTO THE STREETS.
IT'S TIME TO SEIZE THE POWER OF DYKE LOVE, DYKE VISION, DYKE ANGER, DYKE INTELLIGENCE, DYKE STRATEGY.
IT'S TIME TO ORGANIZE AND INCITE. IT'S TIME TO GET TOGETHER AND FIGHT.
WE'RE INVISIBLE, SISTERS, AND IT'S NOT SAFE—NOT IN OUR HOMES, NOT IN THE STREETS, NOT ON THE JOB, NOT IN THE COURTS.
WHERE ARE THE OUT LESBIAN LEADERS? IT'S TIME FOR A FIERCE LESBIAN MOVEMENT AND THAT'S YOU: THE ROLE MODEL, THE VISION, THE DESIRE.

WE NEED YOU.

BECAUSE: WE'RE NOT WAITING FOR THE RAPTURE. WE ARE THE APOCALYPSE. *We'll be your dream and their nightmare.*

LESBIAN POWER

LESBIAN AVENGERS BELIEVE IN CREATIVE ACTIVISM: LOUD, BOLD, SEXY, SILLY, FIERCE, TASTY AND DRAMATIC. ARREST OPTIONAL.
THINK DEMONSTRATIONS ARE A GOOD TIME AND A GREAT PLACE TO CRUISE WOMEN.
LESBIAN AVENGERS DON'T HAVE PATIENCE FOR POLITE POLITICS, ARE BORED WITH THE BOYS.
THINK OF STINK BOMBS AS ALL-SEASON ACCESSORIES. DON'T HAVE A POSITION ON FUR.
LESBIAN AVENGERS BELIEVE CONFRONTATION FOSTERS GROWTH AND STRONG BONES.
BELIEVE IN RECRUITMENT. NOT BY THE ARMY; NOT OF STRAIGHT WOMEN. DON'T MIND HANDCUFFS AT ALL.
LESBIAN AVENGERS DO BELIEVE HOMOPHOBIA IS A FORM OF MISOGYNY.
LESBIAN AVENGERS ARE NOT CONTENT WITH GHETTOES: WE WANT YOUR HOUSE, YOUR JOB, YOUR FREQUENT FLYER MILES.
WE'LL SELL YOUR JEWELRY TO SUBSIDIZE OUR MOVEMENT.
LESBIAN AVENGERS DON'T BELIEVE IN THE FEMINIZATION OF POVERTY. WE DEMAND UNIVERSAL HEALTH INSURANCE AND HOUSING.
WE DEMAND FOOD AND SHELTER FOR ALL HOMELESS LESBIANS.
LESBIAN AVENGERS ARE THE 13TH STEP. LESBIAN AVENGERS THINK GIRL GANGS ARE THE WAVE OF THE FUTURE.

LESBIAN SEX

BELIEVE IN TRANSCENDENCE IN ALL STATES, INCLUDING COLORADO AND OREGON.
THINK SEX IS A DAILY LIBATION. GOOD ENERGY FOR ACTIONS.
LESBIAN AVENGERS CRAVE, ENJOY, EXPLORE, SUFFER FROM NEW IDEAS ABOUT RELATIONSHIPS:
SLUMBER PARTIES. POLYGAMY (WHY GET MARRIED ONLY ONCE?). PERSONAL ADS. AFFINITY GROUPS.
ARE OLD FASHIONED: PINE, LONG, WHINE, STAY IN BAD RELATIONSHIPS.
GET MARRIED BUT DON'T WANT TO DOMESTICATE OUR PARTNERS.
LESBIAN AVENGERS LIKE THE SONG "MORE MADONNA, LESS JESUS"
USE LIVE ACTION WORDS: *lick, waltz, eat, fuck, kiss, play, bite, give it up.*
LESBIAN AVENGERS LIKE JINGLES: SUBVERSION IS OUR PERVERSION.

LESBIAN ACTIVISM

LESBIAN AVENGERS SCHEME AND SCREAM.
THINK ACTIONS MUST BE LOCAL, REGIONAL, NATIONAL, GLOBAL, COSMIC.
LESBIAN AVENGERS THINK CLOSETED LESBIANS, QUEER BOYS AND SYMPATHETIC STRAIGHTS SHOULD SEND US MONEY.
BELIEVE DIRECT ACTION IS A KICK IN THE FACE.
LESBIAN AVENGERS PLAN TO TARGET HOMOPHOBES OF EVERY STRIPE AND INFILTRATE THE CHRISTIAN RIGHT.
LESBIAN AVENGERS ENJOY LITIGATION. *Class action suits fit us very well.*

TOP 10 AVENGER QUALITIES

(IN DESCENDING ORDER)

10. COMPASSION
9. LEADERSHIP
8. NO BIG EGO
7. INFORMED
6. FEARLESSNESS
5. RIGHTEOUS ANGER
4. FIGHTING SPIRIT
3. PRO SEX
2. GOOD DANCER
1. ACCESS TO RESOURCES (XEROX MACHINES)

THE LESBIAN AVENGERS. WE RECRUIT.

Yeah, I helped write this, with Activism 101 on the back of the manifesto. We handed out thousands of these at the D.C. march to spark a worldwide lesbian movement. *DESIGN BY CARRIE MOYER.*

Frozen but cheerful at the shrine to Hattie Mae Cohens and Brian Mock, which also became a shrine for Marsha P. Johnson, trans activist and drag queen. Center foreground, Marlene; from left, Pat, me, Jennifer, Andrea, and Lysander. *PHOTOGRAPH COPYRIGHT CAROLINA KROON.*

Lesbian Avengers eat fire in front of the White House in the first-ever Dyke March. *PHOTOGRAPH COPYRIGHT CAROLINA KROON.*

The Thespian Avengers getting laughs at the Gertrude Stein action: "Pussy, how pretty you are." *Photograph copyright Carolina Kroon.*

the LESBIAN AVENGERS

Media Contacts: Michelle Cronk (212)795-3106 & Rebecca Uss (212)995-0862

THE LESBIAN AVENGERS DEMAND THAT UNIFEM (the United Nations Development Fund for Women) END THEIR LONG SILENCE ON LESBIAN ISSUES.

What: The Lesbian Avengers will stage a fiery action in front of the UN while UNIFEM holds a fancy black-tie benefit dinner inside.

When: **Saturday April 30 8:30 pm**

Where: UN visitors' entrance at **46th Street and 1st Avenue.**

Why: UNIFEM, which claims to work to improve the situation of women worldwide never includes lesbians in their economic, human rights, and refugee programs for women. **NONE** of these programs even footnotes lesbians even though lesbians are among the world's impoverished women, even though lesbians across the world are brutalized, tortured, jailed, encarcerated in mental hospitals and electroshocked, harassed and killed. The lesbians of the world need economic programs, advocates for human rights and programs for refugees from lesbophobic violence, and we need them now!

THE LESBIAN AVENGERS DEMAND THAT UNIFEM

1) Put lesbians at the top of their human rights agenda.
2) Develop special services for lesbian refugees, especially those fleeing from lesbophobic persecution.
3) Discuss lesbianism when they teach about female sexuality and safe sex.
4) Include discussions of violence against lesbians in programs combatting violence against women.
5) Research the special economic and development needs of lesbians. Lesbians often do not not have the same access to economic programs as heterosexual women.
6) Consider the different roles of lesbians in the family structure. For instance, care of the elderly is often left to lesbians.
7) Develop programs for survivors of lesbophobic torture, harassment and abuse.
8) Develop lesbian-specific health programs and give lesbian-awareness training to all UNIFEM health professionals.

IT IS TIME FOR LESBIANS TO DEMAND INCLUSION IN THE GLOBAL FEMINIST AGENDA.

The LESBIAN AVENGERS is a direct-action group focused on issues vital to lesbian survival and visibility.

We meet every Tuesday at 8PM at the Lesbian & Gay Community Services Center, 208 W 13 Street, New York. 10011
For information: (212) 967-7711 ext. 3204

You think you can ignore lesbians? Not on our watch.

Cathy Chang leads the Radio Mega action. Melanie (peeking from behind), then Anne-christine d'Adesky, Belkis, Ana, and me. *PHOTOGRAPH COPYRIGHT MORGAN GWENWALD.*

"Prohibido Olvidar" (Forbidden to Forget) in Puerto Rico, 1998. *PHOTOGRAPH COPYRIGHT ANA SIMO.*

Stunned on our roof with my neighbor, Sally. Soon to be frantic about Ana, who had gone downtown to cover the story for our zine, *The Gully*. *PHOTOGRAPH COPYRIGHT LISA KAPLAN.*

On the job photographing La Barbe, after they beard Marianne one Fourteenth of July. *PHOTOGRAPH COPYRIGHT KELLY COGSWELL.*

Sneaking a kiss from Ana at the 2010 NYC Dyke March. *PHOTOGRAPH COPYRIGHT MORGAN GWENWALD.*

one of a dozen or so kids, and the Pierces always were as lazy as sin. The old man married one woman after another to raise the new baby that had killed the last wife. My grandmother confessed to me once how happy she was after her fourth baby, when the doctor told her that it would kill her to have more and tied her tubes. She whispered that she understood those women "who, you know..." We were looking at knitting needles at the time. The wooden ones her father had whittled for her not long before he died, leaving her at the mercy of her relations.

Or maybe there was no gap at all. New York's all surface. Half the closets, even of Ivy Leaguers, are stuffed with a dirt-poor grandma from somewhere, a granddad planted in the living room watching football in silence and occasionally teasing the kids, "Pull my finger." We didn't leave them behind. My uncle Bill, who brought us biscuits and cinnamon rolls in tubes from the Pillsbury factory. My uncle Phil, who aspired to own a camper and do cross-country trips with his wife when he retired. The mysterious women sitting around the tiny kitchen table talking about their blood sugar and cholesterol as the ham cooled on the counter and the corn boiled.

My grandmother would pour me a glass of iced tea, ask if I wanted it sweet, and when I said yes, would stick her finger in it, and laugh while I howled, explaining, "That should be enough, sweet as I am."

The last time I'd seen her, she'd been in a retirement complex, handing me bits of old lace she'd hooked when she could still see properly. She patted me on the back and told me that she had a relation like me, who'd lived with a friend all her life. She called them both "aunt."

And there she was in the hospital bed, changed utterly.

My sister wanted me to go home with her, but I kept vigil with Nana, one night, anyway. It was the least I could do. She dozed off, then hallucinated, and spent a couple of hours threading the needle of a vast factory sewing machine. And then it was a water pump. She was pissed off at someone for not fetching a bucket like she asked. "I'll get it for you," I offered. But she didn't hear. And later, she came to her senses and wept a little.

I held her thin, cold hand and asked if she was hurting bad and needed more meds. Or if she was afraid. And she said, "Yes." It was God and his judgment that terrified her. And I told her she had nothing to worry about, but she wasn't convinced. And I got in deeper and promised that God was merciful, and all she had to do was let go, and then the pain and suffering would be over, and she'd sit on those cool, green banks of flowing rivers that I used to imagine when I'd walk my old neighborhood, pause at the football fields, watch a sunset and pray, or compose a poem like I'd read in the Billy Graham newsletter. I stroked the greasy gray wisps of hair across my grandmother's forehead. I held her hand. She seemed calmer, for a minute, as I kept mouthing the words I'd believed once, and she fell into a true sleep. I made a bed of the extra chairs the nurse brought me and curled up in the twilight of the monitors and buttons and bells.

I wanted her passing to be easy, but I only relieved her for a few hours. It took her another three weeks to die. I was back in New York by then and told Ana when we were up at the cabin.

I stayed with Nana all morning, drinking decaf, eating leftover breakfast from the patients. Kim came in the afternoon and we went to Taco Bell, where the colors were too bright and there was sauce on the counter. The server had a big accent, like Ana, and Kim twanged, "I don't know why they cain't speak English right. If they're going to come here . . ." She sounded just like my mom who locked the car door with her elbow when she saw a black person, not at all like the older sister I'd admired, tried to be, stealing her T-shirts. I think that was just after Kim had created a family scandal by marrying a black man, then divorcing him when he tried to kill her. She'd already been married once, had a kid and a dog that she locked in the bathroom with her, while her new husband screamed outside with a knife. I wonder what kind of blonde, blue-eyed devil he imagined cowering behind the door. I wonder what she thought when she married him, what he meant to her. Was he himself, or just a little bomb she wanted to set off among the hicks?

I hung around a day or two, visiting my grandmother, holding her hand, smiling at the relations. My mother's anyway. My dad's parents, the ones who paid to have my tumor removed, sent the message through my mother that I was absolutely not to visit or call. When I asked why, she smiled smugly, "They hated those pictures you sent. Said you looked like a refugee. What's the point? You being what you are." I probably ignored my dad, even if he lived in town with his second wife and young daughter, still humiliated that I had competed with his dog— and lost.

God, I was happy to take the bus back home. That's what New York was. My mother, as much as I sickened her, recoiled when she heard it, "Home. I'm going home." And when I got to that filthy chaotic terminal at Port Authority after almost a night and day, I nearly bent down and kissed the dirty linoleum. Though it didn't quite end there. I'd been infected, you see, by her eyes. And when I stopped by my own room on Avenue B it suddenly seemed shabby. And my clothes were ugly. And I stank. And the people I knew had no direction. And there was no music to their voices. I was wasting my life. Even Ana's accent seemed briefly obscene. The Irish girls had each other. There were Cubans everywhere I looked. But girls from Kentucky? None. Nowhere. I was adrift, unmoored, again. At the loft, Amy tried to console me, but when she got out her banjo, I had to leave.

20.

When I wasn't working on the radio project, I tried to write a poem about my grandmother, describe how it felt to live exiled in a place where people from Kentucky were sometimes subtitled on TV, if they appeared at all. I'd stare ambivalently at the weather map and point it out to Ana. "There, right there. That's where I'm from." And she'd look, searching for a minute, then turn back to her work.

The coalition was pushing forward despite the weirdness between Ana and Carmen. They wrote letters and faxes pressuring the sponsors to complain to the station, tried to get the mainstream press to cover bigotry in the Spanish media (even Anglos should have noticed the blackface when they were channel surfing), and asked the FCC why they didn't enforce the same rules governing obscenity in the Spanish-language press as in the mainstream. Were they American or not?

The videomaker Janet Baus, who had Cuban roots herself, held a fund-raising party at her house for Latina lesbians, and Ana got a friend of hers, Carmelita Tropicana, to do a benefit show of her new performance, *Milk of Amnesia*. It was a hit with Las Buenas Amigas even though Carmen and Patricia seemed doubtful about such a highbrow event. "Half the members have never even been to the theater!" But everybody laughed at the jokes and practically fell on the floor in hysterics when Carmelita appeared in man drag as Pingalito, "Little Dick."

We organized a flyering campaign for several neighborhoods including Bushwick and Spanish Harlem, and Ana and Melanie and I went to the Avengers and tried once again to pitch the project: "It's historic." "It'll have an incredible impact in a city wracked not only by homophobia but color lines." But we only picked up a few including a white girl, Kristen, and a young black woman called Yancey. And we were back to wondering why almost no white Avengers came to the demo, and why the group was unaffected by our excitement even though we'd taken over a fucking radio station and mobilized all these new activists. Was it straight-up bigotry? A demographic shift? It seemed to us the Avengers were more and more full of dykes that had come from the Midwest to go to Barnard or NYU and had remained isolated and fresh-faced in their dorms. Flatbush and El Barrio were like foreign territories to them. They sweated hearing anything but standard white English. Is alienation, or cowardice, the same thing as racism?

I was nervous myself when we had the very first meeting of the coalition. I smiled and smiled as I played hostess and opened the door, asking people to remove their shoes to save the floor, and would they like a drink? A snack? There was beer in the fridge. Food on the counter. Most of the black women were bigger than me and made me feel like a dwarf. The Latina dykes were louder, chattered, came in gaggles. Way in the back of my mind was getting called honkey in high school, and that time on the train when the young black men surrounded me and my shaved head. Or later, when I was living in Harlem and had just bought these amazingly shiny caramel-colored boots, and these two black Latino kids on a stoop called out, "Look at those shoes." "I can't. They're blinding." And when I turned to roll my eyes at them, the girl nudged the boy, calling out, "He likes you." "No, she does," he said. I never wore those shoes again.

Yeah, I was aware of my whiteness. Probably why I grinned like an idiot.

But it goes the other way, too, that fear of what difference will bring. Adriana later told me that Melanie and I were the first white girls she'd ever really sat down and talked to. She grew up in Queens, and while her schools were more or less integrated, students' social lives weren't. She'd been nervous about getting to know us and was surprised at just how like regular people the two *blanquitas* were. Shee-it. I punched her in the arm when she confessed. And we both laughed. It *is* a big deal to work with people who are different from you. And if you're white or of a higher class, no matter what race you are, you'll probably mess up. Maybe get yelled at. But there are worse things. Like keeping your dignity safe at home, while the world goes to hell.

I can't remember what the rest of the Avengers were doing. The November election was over. And in Idaho, the LACROP strategy had helped defeat the proposition. They were back home in New York, toting a remarkable string of testimonials from the folks of rural Idaho about how great LACROP was to work with, how inspiring, how much everybody had learned. Maybe they were researching other places to go, other targets. Or they were raising money. Or were sitting at home burned out and staring at the walls. Even without their competition, we couldn't get the group behind us. Maybe because the radio project seemed so much more vague than a referendum. Come fight racism. Fight homophobia.

Maybe that was when the bisexuals came to the group and took up weeks and weeks demanding we include bi issues and call ourselves the Les-BI-an Avengers, because apparently a group focused exclusively on lesbian issues had no right to exist. And they accused us of bi-phobia or something, even if we actually had a bunch of bi members. And nobody cared as long as they were okay working on lesbian issues. You knew what the deal was, joining the *Lesbian* Avengers. Or we were already wandering through the minefield of discussions about race. The only thing that's certain is that in New York nobody was planning actions. Pretty soon, even we wouldn't be doing that.

A day or two before everything exploded with the coalition, there was an uncomfortable meeting at the apartment as we tried to finalize a flyer. It was just the heads of the three groups. I was in the back bedroom at the computer, making each change as fast as I could in English and Spanish. It went on for hours, with Patricia and Carmen asserting their control by making suggestions on every line, which then had to be revised by Ana, who brought them back to me in the bedroom. Kim and Keisha agreed with everything. At midnight or so, I announced I had to go to bed if I was going to be able to get up early the next morning and get the thing Xeroxed and distributed to the groups that were flyering later in the day. "C'mon. The flyer's fine. And I'm totally exhausted. No more revisions, please."

Kim and Keisha were thrilled to agree and get out of there. Carmen and Patricia muttered, then shrugged, so I thought it wasn't that big a deal. We were friends, right? And all I was thinking about was crawling into bed so I could crawl out of it again way too soon, make Xeroxes, and hand them out to people who were my enemies at school board meetings but there on the street might even smile at me curiously, or ask a question. Force me to speak in Spanish. While I grinned and grinned like the Good American I still was.

And even afterwards, I exchanged a perfectly polite fax with Carmen about changes to the flyer that had been suggested by the people handing them out on the street. And she didn't give me a hard time or anything. But at the meeting a few days later, Carmen exploded, accusing Ana and the Avengers of trying to control the coalition by holding the meetings in her apartment and facilitating them herself, then demanded a meeting in neutral territory to rebuild the coalition's decision-making structure from the ground up.

At the time, it seemed to come out of nowhere. Kim and Keisha got on the phone with Ana and Cathy Chang, the dyke from Las Buenas Amigas, who said not to worry, it was all about the relationship between Carmen and Ana, and it would blow over. So we set up a meeting at the Sunshine Diner. The neutral parties, Cathy Chang, and Kim and Keisha, recommended that Ana stay at home, so she wouldn't be the lightning rod.

But "Where's Ana?" was the first thing Carmen said when she walked into the room and just saw me, Melanie, and Yancey representing the Avengers. Kim and Keisha had brought a few older members of African Ancestral, and maybe there were a few other Buenas Amigas, too.

In practically an act of repudiation, a furious Carmen read a detailed indictment of the racist plot for Avenger supremacy. We were guilty of censorship (when I refused to accept more comments?), secret meetings (Ana coming into the bedroom to bring me revisions?), control of the meeting place (a large, free apartment with stereo and bathroom?), forgetting or confusing names with bigoted intent (definitely me). While Patricia smirked next to her, egging her on, Melanie and I shrank in our seats from Carmen's lifetime of anger, all this talk of racism that seemed directed at us since there were so few white girls among the dozen or so Avengers who regularly participated in the coalition, unless Yancey and Ana and all the other Avengers of color were counted as white, especially Ana, who was too much of an egghead to be a Latina, too horribly direct, too pale.

After Carmen was done, Cathy said that while she appreciated her feelings, she didn't necessarily interpret things in the same way and said we should all cool down. Kim and Keisha didn't say much at all, because their mouths were hanging open in shock. When it was all over, Candice Boyce, one of the older African Ancestral Lesbians, saw my gray face and went out of her way to pat me on the shoulder and say not to worry, it would be okay. Which was really nice of her, even if it wasn't true. Because Carmen and Patricia ignored Cathy Chang and all the other members of Las Buenas Amigas, went home, and prepared a letter as heads of their board and officially denounced the Avengers as racist, itemizing our sins, which they'd knitted up in a damning scarf like a couple of Madames Defarge. Carmen even gave a couple of damning interviews to gay rags.

It was tough coming up with a report to the Avengers. We couldn't tell the truth without getting personal, and Ana didn't want to attack Carmen. "Why not?" I asked. "The bitch's lost her fucking mind."

"She's hurting."

"She's a nut, and her girlfriend is the devil."

"I shouldn't have pushed so hard. Besides, that would let the Avengers off the hook. We do have a problem with race."

So we went to the center and delivered some sanitized version of the whole thing, only to have the room fall totally silent until some white girl pointed her finger at Ana and said, "You've offended people of color. How could you? That's horrible. You're racist." Maxine broke out with a kind of cackle in the corner, which could have meant anything but was interpreted by the room as approval, giving license for the rest of the Avengers to join in with snickers or nod in agreement. "That's horrible. You're racist." And Melanie went all ashen. And Ana sat down with the room spinning around her in humiliation.

Now, students visit the Lesbian Herstory Archives and dig up Carmen's damning letter and our mealy-mouthed response, which seems to give her credence. And when they write about the end of the Avengers, they quote all these fragments of truth, half-truths, and lies. Some written out of hate, some out of kindness and shame.

Afterwards, some of the older members from Las Buenas Amigas tried to get Ana to sit down at the table with them so they could apologize for the two ill-mannered pups who didn't last much longer in the group. Still, Carmen and Patricia got their last shots in, purging a few members like Adriana who were perceived as being too cozy with the Avengers, especially white ones. What a cesspool.

If I hold a grudge against someone, though, it's Patricia. Provoking Carmen, sneering in the corner. When I see her out, I still want to spit in her face and pull her hair, though maybe she's not as bad as I think. Maybe it was the alchemy between her and Carmen that made her so malevolent. But who cares, really? It's been two decades. Awww, let it go.

21.

Are flies smarter than bees? It's a relevant question. Trap a bunch of flies in a clear glass bottle with its base to a bright shining window and watch what happens. The flies will find the opening after a couple of minutes of banging around randomly. Do the same with bees, the industrious little things will be stuck forever, always heading toward the window's light where the escape should be, wondering why they've been betrayed. Maeterlinck finds the beauty in it, and an almost mystical sign of the bees' intelligence:

> They evidently imagine that the issue from every prison must be there where the light shines clearest; and they act in accordance, and persist in too logical action. To them glass is a supernatural mystery they never have met with in nature; they have had no experience of this suddenly impenetrable atmosphere; and, the greater their intelligence, the more inadmissible, more incomprehensible, will the strange obstacle appear.

I'm not sure he's wrong, but the bees end up dead, after all, if you leave them in the bottle with the wrong end facing the light. They'll die of hope, persistence, and their idée fixe that because light once meant an exit from a hive, it would always get them out. They're not quitters, those bees. No sirree. They pursued. They're rationalists. Like the French. Like Ana, who believed, at the time, that every problem had its solution. And that there was still some way to work with the Avengers. I guess we all believed it. She and I, Melanie, Yance, along with Gail, and Lidia who'd also been there from the start. We'd invested too much to cut and run, allow the group to get further and further from the city. Nothing to do with the larger questions facing us. So we plunged back in, throwing ourselves against the glass again.

To start over, we had to face facts. The group had gotten younger and whiter, with a whiteness more freshly scrubbed, less and less diverse (where were the cab drivers and teachers?), though there were also some young dykes of color appearing. We were back to questions Barbara Smith raised. Was the Avengers a white group or not? Were we racist? If, in the days of slavery, it only took a few drops of African blood to define a person as black, how many lesbians of color did it take to define a group as mixed? One? Ten? Thirty? To be legitimate, did you have to reflect the demographics of the entire city? Was America a "white" nation?

In meetings, one or two young black women said the Avengers should set percentages. But that would mean recruiting women specifically for their race. Hey, you're black. Wanna come to an Avenger meeting and integrate our asses? Marlene Colburn tugged down her baseball cap over her black face and disagreed, said plainly that the Avengers was the most mixed lesbian group she'd ever been in, in New York, and she'd been in plenty. It couldn't happen quite like that. Once again, nobody talked about differences of culture. Or how power should be factored in. Ana's role, and Marlene's. By then Chanelle Mathews, another black woman, was hugely important to LACROP. Gail Dottin was a fixture at almost every demo. And what about members, like Valarie Walker, an aspiring stand-up comic, who helped shape the tone of the meetings? Or Lidia Medina who did the banners, mild-mannered Valerie Kamaya who did a lot of shitwork? Did they count or not?

And was the solution necessarily just about the membership, something tough to control in an open group, rather than our actions? We actually had a good history when it came to race. We'd spent almost a year supporting the Rainbow Curriculum. Had been among the few to call attention to the deaths of Hattie Mae Cohens and Brian Mock. The ex–Radio Mega working group had the intuition that a city-focused project evolving from the radio actions would solve a lot of problems, though we felt we had to talk things out, too.

I don't know why we thought we could pull it off. Solve the problems of race and class, when Americans have been stymied by them for centuries, were burning up with them. The Klan was resurging, all those skinheads. The Pat Buchanans of the world were setting us against each other. But I guess you have to try. Sitting around that wooden table, prodded by nails, Ana started to think it was time to round up the Avengers of color and brainstorm about constructive ways to change the Avengers.

Ana really sweated it. She'd never wanted to be in a racially segregated group. One that would exclude her own girlfriend. But there didn't seem any other way to get people to talk freely. I told her I didn't mind, and I didn't. Who needed more meetings, anyway? Ana got Chanelle on board, and they decided to throw a party at Marlene's out in Brooklyn.

I offered to make enchiladas, help do the invites. There had been so much talk of race and percentages we did cards with green cows, asking mysteriously, "Is it skim milk?" Or 6%, 4%, 2%, or 1%? When March 6 rolled around, I sent Ana off with enchiladas, pots of rice, and enormous bags of chips and jars of salsa. And waited back at the ranch. For hours and hours. I even watched the news, Governor Pataki blabbing about something, then a piece on a federal decision to let idiots carry concealed guns and a spot on Greg Louganis coming out as having HIV.

Ana finally came back moved and excited and a little disturbed at how these seventeen dykes greeted each other with a kind of freedom that she'd never seen at Avenger meetings.

It was a kind of epiphany, realizing that the dykes of color in the Avengers never did what she'd seen elsewhere, chattering in corners, drawing attention to themselves as Latina or black. There at Marlene's, they laughed a little louder, smiled more broadly. And god, how they talked. They talked and planned and plotted for seven full hours, drinking beer and eating enchiladas and chips, filling little note cards with their thoughts.

They are yellowing now, the rubber band that held them together turned to a strange hard brittle substance that breaks apart like a strand of dried, whole wheat linguini. A lot of their criticism affected everybody. The group may have been open, but its cliquish nature put off newcomers and made it hard for people to speak, especially if they thought their voices weren't welcome. There was a lack of basic courtesy. A need for a formal orientation telling people what the group was about—a question that was getting more and more urgent.

At the next meeting, Marlene passed around a press release about a great zap the San Francisco Avengers had done. They'd released "locusts" at the offices of Exodus International, which ran a bunch of programs to "cure" queers of homosexuality. And for the first time they'd posted the press release online. The problem was they'd also changed the tag line of the group, redefining the Lesbian Avengers as "a direct-action group of lesbian, bisexual, and transgendered women focused on issues vital to our survival and visibility." They'd both redefined the membership and dumped the whole focus on "issues vital to *lesbian* survival and visibility." Once again, *lesbian* was turned into a simple modifier for women along with many others. We had no specific issues, no culture, community, or visions. No right, or need, to organize by ourselves.

Ana went insane for a couple of days. Laundry lists were part of what she'd been fighting against when she'd begun imagining the group. She asked why diversity almost always meant including bi, transgender, often straight females—mostly white. "If we keep this up," she said, "the Avengers are never going to be able to recruit dykes of color. Do they think we're morons? We know they don't care." She wrote a whole furious letter. Spent hours revising. Then shoved it into a file. We began to admit that the group was slipping away. All that work down the toilet trying to establish once and for all that lesbians had the right to exist and to organize. That she had a right to exist. This Latina lesbian.

Though she still beat against the glass. It made a horrible sound. The whole rest of the story is horrible. Hope is always horrible, when you know it's going to be smashed.

Skim Milk decided to organize formally as a caucus for Lesbian Avengers of Color and held a bunch more meetings, while the remnants of the Radio Mega group outlined the plans for a project dedicated to city actions to counterbalance the group's focus on national issues. The first meeting was March 10. I think it was me who came up with the name CITYAXE, which annoyed Ana because it didn't have lesbian in it, but everyone else thought it was okay. And we spent several days drafting a huge working paper that talked a lot about how issues intersected: class, race, homophobia. Banking on the idea that logic and reason and more hard work were going to save the day, we outlined strategies about how to insert ourselves as out lesbians into existing issues, from the battle over community gardens to school board policies.

If announcements from the Lesbian Avengers of Color caucus were met with silence, CITYAXE was met with resentment and disdain. Maybe it was the sound of our voices. They were too shrill, too emotional at that point. Maybe we shouldn't have gone into detail with all this theory. The strength of the Avengers was action, not blab. But I'm not sure it would have been much different if we'd just come up with some actions and pitched them. Probably we would have been hung out to dry again, like we were with the Radio Mega thing, where the group approved the action but a handful of us did all the work, almost no one came to the demos, and when things finally went sour, we took all the blame.

We tried appealing to the masses with a big mailing meant to bring some of the old-timers back. Sitting around the table at Ana's, avoiding protruding nails, we came up with a letter that was somewhat critical of the group but still hopeful for our prospects.

We were optimists to expect that all right-thinking people would rally around us, shouting, "You go, girls. How can I help?" Instead, they asked to be removed from the mailing list. Anne and Marie, who were embroiled in their own fights with ILGO, sent me an irate, insulting letter demanding I explain why we were attacking them. Thinking of Las Buenas Amigas and AALUFSC, we'd put something in our own mailing about avoiding arrests, trying to minimize danger so as many people as possible would feel welcome, but they'd taken it as a direct rebuke to their efforts. And if it wasn't an attack, they said, it was badly written. I sent a letter back on my high-flying horse, explaining we had no such intention. It was not badly written. They were just insane, etc.

God, I hope they threw it away.

All the pressure from CITYAXE started to strain the Lesbian Avengers of Color group. There were older alliances than ethnicity or race. Like sex. Plenty of dykes of color had white girlfriends. There were even more important ties. Maxine Wolfe, one of the oldest, most experienced Avengers, had been an important mentor to the members of LACROP, particularly Chanelle. Maxine and Marlene had also become good friends. We heard she was pressuring them both to back off. "All these discussions are tearing the group apart." Maxine wasn't wrong, but there was no easy way to move on. It wasn't that we wanted to just highlight issues of dykes of color, but that we wanted "lesbian" visibility to reflect us all.

Sometimes I wonder what would have happened if, instead

of fighting with the group, we had founded an East Village Avengers chapter, for instance, or a Queens Avengers, and sent a letter to LACROP asking them to help us organize in the region. Would they have sent help, then? Would the room have opened their hearts? I shouldn't joke. Poor LACROP. They came back from Idaho to this shit storm, already worn out and having trouble readjusting to their New York lives.

Maybe that was part of it. We were all very tired, worn out, running on nerves. You can't live the way we did with ten meetings every week, trying to save the world, which, guided by entropy, was falling apart anyway.

On April 19, 1995, the Federal Building in Oklahoma City was attacked. When all the people were finally pulled from the wreckage, the dead tallied 168, including 19 kids. Almost seven hundred had been injured. For a couple of days, everybody was looking under their beds for Arab terrorists, but the culprits ended up being a couple of American men, Timothy McVeigh and Terry Nichols, with a grudge against the government for the deaths at Ruby Ridge, and Waco, Texas, exactly two years before.

CITYAXE held a meeting and decided that if we were going to do anything at all, we'd have to do it outside the group. On May 2, we went to the meeting and read our letters resigning from the Avengers. It was all very heartfelt, dramatic, and useless. Because alone, we only stumbled on a few more months before the whole thing collapsed. And even our dramatic departure fizzled, because afterwards Lidia, who had been part of CITYAXE, sent her own letter agreeing with some of what we said but denouncing us for being on high horses, emoting rather than offering solutions.

There's a word for that Buddhist moment when you no longer perceive the separation between the object and mind that's observing it. All is unity. All enlightenment. Wikipedia says it's *Bodhi*. Well, what I felt was the opposite of that. I walked around seeing the world all splintered and fractured, and me separate even from the shards. Every night I relived those horrible Avengers meetings with white and black faces glaring at each other. Replayed Carmen's and Patricia's attack, trying to work my way to a different ending. I experienced again how the Avengers sneered at us there on the ground with our pants pulled down.

I shrank from the world. I'd hear J-Lo singing from a radio in the street and turn away. I cringed at the sound of Albita. Was conscious of my skin, that impermeable membrane bound by words. I wanted to drag them all out, flay us all, destroy all the artificial separations of history. You'd merely done what I had, after all—split from two cells into four then eight then sixteen until you'd accumulated all your arms and legs and organs and pushed yourself into the world—so fucking what? You honkey, nigger, spic, dyke, cunt. If I cry out, who will hear me?

But I didn't call anybody anything, or even say much to Ana, who was chewing over her own role, believing that she had killed the Avengers, or at least hastened their death. It was around then that she left Dyke TV, having similar fights there. Her grandmother died, and we suddenly had to deal with her mother, and all that brutal Cuban history. Our house was full of anger and grief.

Back at Avenue B, one of the actresses from that film *Go Fish* moved into the loft. The one with the name of a Russian princess, Anastasia. Anne d'Adesky moved there, too, with her girlfriend, Cindra. Everybody in those days was consolidating or moving to Williamsburg. Or fleeing the gentrifying city altogether.

No more Mister Nice Gal, I decided to start eating meat again, took a bite of Amy's bacon at Odessa's, then moved on to the Filet-O-Fish at McDonald's. I needed to toughen up. It wasn't like fish were particularly sentient, anyway. A pig had them beat. Hell, a pig had most humans beat, smarter than small children, and we didn't eat those but maybe should.

I unwrapped the pale blue paper and stared at the sandwich a long time. That little square of deep-fried flesh gloppy with tartar sauce and cheese. The stale white bun. I took a bite. Then another. I felt queasy but kept on going, right until the end.

III. A LABORATORY OF IDENTITY

Now I am ready to say how bodies
are changed into other bodies.

—OVID, *THE METAMORPHOSIS*

22.

Melanie moved out, fleeing the former activist den, and we turned her bedroom into an office with a desk for each of us. I was done as an activist, I declared. Done as a poet. I didn't do another performance until long after we moved to Paris. My lofty thoughts were all about money. I decided to try my hand at the voodoo of fiction. First, a screenplay set at the New York headquarters of a tobacco company with a cast of interracial queers solving a murder. See how easy it is to get along if you just know your lines. Next was a mystery set in Gertrude Stein's Paris, called *The Clever American*. The sleuth was a Janet Flanner–type journalist before I ever thought of being one. A dyke from Kentucky, less virtuous than anybody in my Benetton cast.

I was sure it would be a gold mine. Amy's shelves were full of dyke mysteries. Somebody was writing them. Others were buying. Not at all like sonnets. I really churned it out, typing a couple thousand words a day on Ana's old PC, giving people their comeuppance, organizing a world that resisted order. It was avenging by proxy, now that I think of it. I envied Marlowe his fedora, the dirty glass in his drawer, wanted desperately to be him taking a punch, and still cracking wise though the city burned.

In New York, like old LA, the fat cats were still obese. Cops rousted black and Latino kids who harassed each other and any white dyke at hand, while ordinary people stood on dignity they didn't have. Life was a morality play, all the old noirs said. This is the rich guy's role. This belongs to the poor. Or the white or the black. Here's the tragic outsider. At night we'd rent movies from Kim's Video, with gangsters in black and white talking out of the sides of their mouths, going soft on tough-talking dames, and everybody ending up dead. On the way back and forth to the Catskills, we'd discuss the best ways to kill somebody. We were eating French fries on the road once, and when I fed Ana a sharp one, she nearly choked. "Perfect," I said. "You eat the evidence afterwards." Icicles seemed clever, too. You stab somebody with one, the evidence melts. Though you might leave traces of fiber if you were wearing gloves.

Around then I had the idea we should start doing the holidays with Ana's mother and middle brother, Carlos, an unknown blustery man. Faustina was alone, after all, this older lady rattling around an empty apartment out there in Queens. She had nothing to look at but the car wash across Queens Boulevard and a White Castle. The trick, I figured, was to keep everybody's mouth so full they couldn't fight. For Thanksgiving I made salmon and couscous and this enormous chocolate Sachertorte. For Christmas Eve, I did a cod dish of *bacalao a la vizcaína* and snuck in Kentucky ham, and made pecan pie with blackstrap molasses and Kentucky bourbon just to keep my equilibrium, so outnumbered by Cubans.

In the spring, I drug Ana down south, aiming to show her where I was from. We broke the drive in Gettysburg, where farmers still dug up bones. In Louisville, we zipped past the little brick houses in the suburbs, the patches of grass, the highways dividing them all. I was an awful guide. "There's the church. There's the school. There's the house I grew up in. Speed up for fuck's sake." Ana demanded to go in the church, found the sanctuary full of light and oddly peaceful. Said my old high school looked like a jail. The big cinderblocks. The chain-link fence.

We got out of the car and we walked through the sports fields around it. One for practicing field hockey. "Watch for the crawdad holes. The creek's back there." Another for football. "I used to sit there, watch the sunset, and pray." I could hardly remember what for. My mother probably. My angry sisters. My dad hardly figured in, usually working out of town. Them I omitted from the tour. For their own good, really. If they were mean to Ana, sneered at her accent or beige skin, if they turned up their noses at our relationship, I would've had to kill them. Downtown, the guidebook directed us to buildings with cast-iron facades like in New York. Artists were taking over old factories.

We went to the mountains afterwards, lifting up our mining eyes to the hills. Went to a national park my family used to visit as a kid. We saw the blooming dogwoods, cinderblock houses built by the Army Corp of Engineers, big muddy scars from strip mining, and played chicken with fat coal trucks barreling down the middle of the road. Sinking Spring Farm, where Abraham Lincoln was born, smelled cool and minerally and as familiar as the dust in my grandmother's attic. I was moved and tried to cover it with jokes. Asked Ana to take a picture of me in front of the log cabin replica. "I'll tell 'em I was born here. That's what everybody up in New York imagines anyway." But I forgot to take my shoes off. And when I had my fill of the accents, and dry counties, and Taco Bells, we bolted straight east across two or three states until we got to the ocean. And ended up in this strip of North Carolina sand that has since been eaten away by the rising seas.

It was that June, I think, that Ana pestered her mom until she agreed to walk with PFLAG in the Gay Pride Parade. "It's the least you can do." "I'm too old." "I don't care." Faustina probably would have refused if she didn't depend so much on us. She began the morning sullen as a teenager but was reassured when she saw that the other parents looked like ordinary heterosexual people. When we started walking and the crowd cheered to see somebody's, anybody's, parents out there in support, I swear I saw a tear in Faustina's eye. She wiped it away quickly, but it was there.

It was a kind of landmark. As big for her as Ellen's big coming out a few months earlier in April '97. Ana and I watched at Crazy Nannies. When the bumbling character of Ellen Morgan managed to declare, "I'm gay," over the airport's loudspeaker, we all cheered, white and black and Latina alike. And when the ultrafamous Oprah Winfrey, playing Ellen's shrink, said, "Good for you. You're gay," the whole house came down. It was like we'd finally gotten our green cards, been admitted to the Union, even if only until the next commercial break.

Lesbian chic was long gone, along with the Lesbian Avengers and ACT UP, which had lost its urgency since protease inhibitors started saving lives the year before. Around then was also when Clinton had caved to the Right and signed the Defense of Marriage Act. He was up for reelection and had to buy a few votes after the mudslinging of Whitewater and the early fiasco of health care reform. It worked, feeding us to the howling Christian Right, feeding hate. He got a second term.

On August 9, 1997, Haitian immigrant Abner Louima was picked up by cops after a fight outside a club in Brooklyn. He got smacked around in the cop car, inside the precinct, drug to the bathroom, and raped with the handle of a toilet plunger, while the cops shouted the usual slurs, plus, "This is Giuliani time, not Dinkins time!" He started hemorrhaging in the holding cell, his intestines all ripped up, and barely got to the hospital in time. His face was on the newsstands for weeks, the half-closed eyes and swollen lips. The hospital gown.

When the blue wall of silence went up, thousands of protesters took to the streets, waving Haitian flags and plungers, and calling the NYPD just another version of Haiti's brutal Tontons Macoutes. But then the crowd started to chant, "Sodomites, sodomites," etc., etc. Like an antigay lynch mob. Which it would have been in Haiti. Nobody's moral ground is as high as you'd wish.

A year later, in June 1998, three white guys in Texas grabbed a middle-aged black man walking home from a party. They wrapped a logging chain around his ankles and dragged him behind their pickup truck hooting and hollering with joy with every bump, every scream. James Byrd Jr. finally died when a culvert sliced off his right arm and head. They dumped his torso in front of an African American cemetery. In October, two white guys picked up a young gay student in a bar in Laramie, Wyoming, beat the faggot to a pulp, and tied him to a fence like a dead coyote or bloody Christ. Matthew Shepard was awake, too. Conscious of his own slow death while his attackers went looking for more fun, tried to beat up a couple of Hispanic guys, but got a taste of their own medicine, and one ended up in the hospital himself, where he was arrested.

That image of a thin, white gay kid tied to a fence and left for dead finally woke queers up again and we remembered the street. Ana and I ventured to the center when a couple of people put out a call for action, a political funeral. It was one of the first times that the rabble was roused by e-mail instead of mobilizing phone trees or wheat pasting. We expected a couple hundred protesters, got five thousand confronting hate in the vulnerable flesh. There were almost as many cops as demonstrators. It was a mess. Police trying to barricade the way. Protesters trying to go around. I was carrying a kind of symbolic coffin with a bunch of kids from the Hetrick-Martin Institute for queer youth when police blocked the street, and the sidewalk, too. One officer went nuts, and I almost got guillotined when he shoved the two by fours and barbed wire against my neck. Thank god none of the kids let go.

After that, cops on horseback charged the crowd. I got smashed up against a car by a fat haunch. Most people ran away, but pretty soon some started running back toward the police, throwing the pathetic candles we'd meant to light for Matthew Shepard. Bystanders got arrested. Along with all the marshals. It was the lead story in every rag the next day; even

El Diario called up Ana for info, her number still on speed dial from the Avenger days, the Hate Radio fiasco good for something. In every article, at least one participant hailed the protest as the beginning of a new LGBT movement. As if it just took one death, one demo.

I was torn by what happened, excited at how many people had come out, a real mixed crowd in terms of races and ages, but furious at the organizers. At least some of the mess was our fault. I wrote a long letter trying to assess everything that had gone wrong from the minute the first meeting was called rounding up the usual suspects (white) and omitting the rest, to the casual attitude toward marshaling. No training sessions, no scoping out either the beginning or ending sites to make sure they could accommodate a large crowd. Just relying on experience.

And probably my rage was all out of proportion, but I finally understood why Sarah Schulman blew her top at me at the UN action when I hadn't done nearly enough prep. So much could go wrong. People could have been hurt. Somebody could have been killed. We'd acted like amateurs. Which I suppose we were. Because we sacrificed a lot and didn't get paid. But to be so nonchalant. Calling people into the streets to play at revolution. When we were taking on a state that doesn't want to be reengineered, not by you, not by anybody.

The race stuff got me especially. When we'd gone to the center for the organizing meeting, there were almost all white faces, maybe a third of them former Avengers. And while you shouldn't worry about who your friends are, what does it cost you, really, to look around and see who's missing? Reach out beyond the magic circle? Especially in the case of Matthew Shepard, when the connections were so clear with James Byrd and Abner Louima, and the rise of violence and beatings and deaths. Bigots hated us in our very bodies, wanted not just to kill but to obliterate us all.

Sometimes I'd look over at Ana and wonder why. I'd caress the soft curve of her neck, her cheek. Press my face against the tender flesh of her belly, which I love, along with her strong, small delicate hands that somehow manage to capture octaves on the piano. Her taut narrow back. Her eyebrows that oddly remain black. The gray-green eyes that even strangers fall in love with. Her skin the color of Earl Grey with milk until she's been in the sun, and then it turns to toast. Her bones, her nerves. Those ears she thinks protrude. Yes, I love her body, every cell of it, that you would like to destroy.

I was remorseful after sending the strident, chiding letter, even if I wasn't wrong. Fuck me and the high horse I rode on. Better something than nothing. Maybe. I resolved again to retire from activism. I was too burnt out, too sensitive, too shrill. Let me work out my life in print. One good thing, though, that came of the demo was that Ana got a tearful call from her mother, who had been following the story, gone to the march herself, and taken another step toward understanding what she'd done to Ana in Cuba.

23.

We got offered a free apartment for a couple of months in Puerto Rico, packed our bags, and fled an America that let black men and queers die in the streets while they discussed the really important things, like stains on a blue dress and blow jobs in the Oval Office. The taxi driver who took us to the airport in New York was an old Puerto Rican guy with salsa on the radio, a crucifix, and limp P.R. flag on the dash. When he found out we spoke Spanish, he slammed the latest referendum on statehood, along with everybody who bothered to cast a ballot. "All the votes get used as toilet paper, you know, because the place is a U.S. colony, and only the Feds can make it a state. Or anything else, for that matter, since they snatched the island in 1898. The Spanish-American War, you know."

When we got to San Juan, it seemed the same driver waited for us, with salsa on the radio, curses for the referendum, and a battered flag. Like only *independentistas* drove cabs, or we hadn't really gone anywhere. I was still an Anglo surrounded by Latinos, beginning to grapple with my role in the world. Did I participate? Resist? What did it mean to be an American?

I looked for signs and saw them literally on the billboards painted that pale swimming-pool American green, in the streets filled with Fords and Chevys, in rust seeping from every building on Condado Avenue. Iron railings dripped onto the cement plastering below. The rebar of skyscrapers still under construction with American dollars trailed a lovely brownish red onto their foundation. Even new cars grew a crop of corrosion in the arc over their tires, or around the doors, as if the very land rebelled against the colonizing presence.

The apartment itself was a history lesson. Just down from the Walgreens, and sandwiched between a Haitian trinket and art gallery and a Condomania, the white gay American owner had decorated it in a squalid fantasia of Early Spanish Inquisition and late Americana complete with sharp black metal pikes, carved virgins, dripping red and black candles, crucifixes, and a fuzzy green La-Z-Boy. The couch was a stained brown velvet. The red shag carpet under it had roaches, sand, and rot. We scrubbed a lot and went to the beach, where I got to know the sand, surf, and the angry volcanic rocks called *dientes de perros*, dogs' teeth, that rip the crap out of your feet, though the sea was a refuge, indifferent to everything. I threw myself in.

We fell into a routine. In the morning, Ana sent her translations using the miracle of e-mail. I wrote poems and took notes for articles I was sure to sell. During the day, we walked on the beach. I observed everything. The air thick with salt and the scent of ravenous plants. Bats dive-bombing our heads after dark. I had nightmares in the strange bed, surrounded by papier-mâchéd mangoes and pineapples from the Haitian trinket shop. Creatures crept from the roof through the open back door. A woman floated through the grill above the air conditioner, a lost blonde tennis-racqueted American who disappeared when I screamed, then came back, retreating again when Ana woke up to save me. She was my alter ego. The gringa. What people always thought Americans were.

The old Spanish city was full of narrow climbing streets, cats, old colonial buildings that were built with a mix of local woods that resisted insects and rot, and nearly eternal stone. The Plaza de Armas was decorated for Christmas and featured the city's other giant Walgreens, along with Americans disgorged from big cruise ships. I stared at them, too, to see what we shared as they wandered up and down looking for tax-free bathing suits in the Speedo outlet store, or shorts at Banana Republic, cigars, rum, postcards, cheap traditional shirts embroidered with parrots.

In a greasy spoon off the Plaza de Colón, we ran into some Hoosiers who had stopped to eat across from a statue of Columbus. The TV was turned to CNN and announced that the United States was bombing Iraq again. A fat man in an NYPD T-shirt slapped his pal on the shoulder, "About time," while his wife scratched swollen red mosquito bites on her white legs. During a brief update on the Clinton impeachment trial, but before the TV went back to the Puerto Rican variety show, the tourists ordered fish with big sides of French fries, which they washed down with jumbo Cokes and Coors, just like at home.

More than once we saw a whole horde of red-faced, white-tennis-shoed screaming Americans descend on a local pizzeria with an outdoor terrace that the local intelligentsia used as a café. It was interesting how the waiter would cram them inside in a far corner, containing their screams for ketchup and Coca-Cola. The regulars didn't even look around, refusing to hear or see them, continuing with their conversations about something at the university, or a book they'd read, while inside the Americans honked at each other over their air conditioning and Cokes and sloppy fries. Nobody was shooting up a Capitol building like Lolita Lebrón, or even eating fire, but erasing the Yanks was a form of Puerto Rican resistance. There was also this bagel place that sold "cappuccino" for almost four bucks but would give you the same thing for two if you asked in Spanish for *café con leche.* I wondered if these were small nonviolent victories of passive resistance, or the mass delusion of colonial subjects.

Even the Puerto Rican media put the United States in its place. Venezuela got more airtime than Kenneth Starr and his vendetta. The TV ran a whole uninterrupted speech by Hugo

Chávez, who'd beaten the elite for the first time in decades. The guy could talk without notes for an hour, had so much promise. Even if it turned sour later. Successive failures are par for the course for young democracies. His voice seemed loud in Puerto Rico, compared to its muted sound in the States.

Now and then we'd break our routine with a car trip across the island, or a visit to something like the Christmas festival at the Bacardi Artisans Fair. They had piña coladas and cod fritters, roughly stitched leather hats, and photos of the smiling patriot Albizu Campos before Americans drug him to jail. We were roasted and drenched a couple of times, before a handful of musicians crept on stage for the finals of the *décimas* competition. They had guitars, four-stringed *cuatros,* and *güiros,* gourds ribbed like washboards. Once the musicians had scooted their chairs into a comfortable arrangement, the competition's rules were explained.

It amounted to this: the singers had to quickly improvise what amounted to a Petrarchan sonnet to a familiar tune, using as chorus a line that the judges gave them on a scrap of paper just seconds before the first chord was struck. Points were knocked off for faulty rhyme schemes, meter, meaning, diction, intonation, lengthy intervals between verses, and whatever else the judges thought of. The first few singers were amazing, but unsurprising.

The guy that won, Victor Manuel Reyes, pushed things a lot, at least formally. He was a thin young man with a baseball cap jammed on backwards. He nailed every rhyme and arrived at the chorus with flair. While the band played a quick interlude, young Reyes stalked the second verse. It was another crucial moment. Even a mediocre poet could manage one good verse, but the second was key. Beyond the rhyme scheme and chorus, there was development and meaning. The best singers to that point had developed their thoughts like salt water taffy, pulling meaning both toward and away from the repeated chorus like masters of the villanelle.

The audience was shocked when the iconoclast Reyes seemed to ignore his first verse, going in a different direction entirely. We held our breath. The structures began unraveling. He didn't end thoughts at the end of the proper lines. The rhymes jarred. But the final chorus, in a dangerous straining leap, pulled it all together. I couldn't say exactly how. The audience found itself both dazzled and uneasy. In the space of three or four singers we had grown used to conventions. Reyes had wrenched them to the breaking point. The judges, after much murmuring, gave him the top prize for it.

I thought it was a good omen, how a radical act was rewarded, even if it was just symbolic. It takes more guts than you think to break conventions, like bursting into the middle of a power breakfast: "We're here, we're queer, we're not going skiing." And Puerto Rico was a conventional, even traditional place. Which meant Ana stuck out with her short red hair and light eyes, her dykeliness in a place where most women still wore long hair, either the original brown or bleached blonde. Even the taxi drivers challenged her, "You're from Cuba? Really? I would never have guessed." While if I only said a few words, or none at all, they'd assume I was Puerto Rican, with my brown hair grown out, brown eyes. My adequate Spanish.

Before I left, I got into an argument with a girl at a dyke bar who asked where I was from. She had these blue eyes, naturally blonde curly hair, and should have been open-minded, but when I said I came from the United States, she repeated, "But you're Puerto Rican, right?" "No. I'm from Kentucky." "But you speak Spanish." "I learned it in school." A few years before, I might have tried to pass. But not anymore. I had decided to be what I was, an American, a dyke American from Louisville, whatever that meant.

I told her the girl that Kentucky wasn't very different from Puerto Rico. When Ana and I had taken that road trip across the island, we'd seen the same cinderblock houses on muddy hills as in Appalachia. The same trucks barreling down mountains, though carrying pineapples instead of coal. The nostalgic *décimas* spoke always of exile and home like bluegrass. We even shared the legacy of slavery. There was that time at the Plaza de Armas when we saw a bunch of women in Scarlett O'Hara hooped dresses that I suppose dated from Spanish colonial times when corkscrew curls were burned into "white" ladies' hair by slaves. And my god, how the mostly beige people there treated black Puerto Ricans and Dominicans. And everything was just as McDonaldized, so there was nothing good for visitors to eat. Calderón de la Barca was right. With a few little adjustments, we could swap places, easy. *La vida es sueño.* Life is a dream.

On the way back, at the San Juan airport, I spoke Spanish with an accent that was a little too Castilian, and the easy-going immigration officer who had joked with all the other passengers as he peeked at their driver's licenses demanded to know where I was from. I said Kentucky, which seemed like a lie if I spoke Spanish, so he actually demanded a passport. I had a couple of bad moments before I found the thing. He examined it for a long time with narrowed eyes before declaring me an American, and letting me get on the plane to the gray forbidding city of New York, where nothing had changed either, not even us.

Ana retreated to her desk where she'd surf for hours and days at a time. At 1 or 2 or 3 A.M., I'd bitch at her to come to bed, and she would, all red-eyed. On February 4, 1999, just a few weeks after we got home, Amadou Diallo, a twenty-three-year-old Guinean immigrant, got gunned down in the Bronx by four members of the Giuliani's Street Crimes Unit. They fired forty-one rounds, mistaking a wallet for a gun.

Ana and I went to a demo with buttons and T-shirts that made it clear we were dykes. We got a few curious looks, one or two hostile ones. Either because we were pale for the crowd or because we were homos. It didn't matter. We were all in it together. We blew our whistles. Waved our sign declaring, "NYC cops give pigs a bad name." With an illustration. It was a nice pig. Pink and snuffly. I drew it myself.

24.

Fast-forward a little. It's 11:58:25 P.M., December 31, 1999. Ana's off at a party. I'm home restless with a Y2K bug that has nothing to do with computers. I quickly make the gesture of mopping the apartment, then throw the dirty water out the front window at exactly 00:00:00 to rid the house of all last year's residual spiritual and physical crap. It's a *brujería* thing I don't quite believe, but why not? It's an annual reminder that some things end. Others begin. Might as well let go and hope for the best. It's less trouble than shaving your head, anyway. The water splatters on the fire escape, then the sidewalk. Somebody below screams. I didn't hit them, but in New York, everybody screams at midnight on New Year's Eve. Cars honk their horns. Illegal fireworks shoot up from the roofs.

Afterwards, I take some aspirin and tidy up the bubble wrap from my new enormous pink iMac that looks more like an alien space invader than a computer.

It was an extravagance, bought when we got paid for the translating–typesetting gig Cathy Chang sent our way. I plugged the pink, bubble-headed thing into the wall jack and followed instructions, setting up my own e-mail and everything. Or trying to. Ana came home and put me to bed with a raging fever. I was beginning the new millennium with the flu. To be companionable, she caught it, too. Even sick, Ana crawled to her computer and slumped in front of it, following all the stories about that skinny little boy pulled wide-eyed from the ocean in November, then tossed right in the Miami shark tank. His father in Cuba demanded his lawful return. His Miami relatives refused to give him up in the name of democracy and freedom, and the right to denounce that tyrant Castro and wax lyrical about that tyrant Batista. Too bad about the peasants starving at the side of the road. Too bad about the dissidents screaming in the police stations or rotting in a ditch.

Ana simmered and steamed as photographers shot the kid on the jungle gym in a leather jacket and shades. He was following in his thug uncles' footsteps like a baby Patty Hearst. Poor kid, she'd say about Elián. What assholes, she'd say about the Cubes, burning tires again in Miami. "They're making Castro look good."

She'd follow me into the kitchen where I was mincing garlic and tell me that, above all, she felt sorry for the father whose only crime was wanting his child back and wanting, too, to stay in the country of his birth. Didn't that ring a bell? Ana asked, still coughing up a lung. Wasn't he the same as a Native American parent whose kid was snatched and trapped in a right-thinking, English-speaking, white Christ-worshipping orphanage? Or like a dyke who lost her child because of who she was?

Yeah, I heard about it all, in triplicate, until the day I stared at the screen of the monstrous pink iMac and the solution became self-evident. Pure Hollywood, really, like a backyard musical that Judy Garland could have starred in with Mickey Rooney. "C'mon guys, let's put on a magazine." Once, I'd asked Ana what she'd do if she won the lottery. "Buy out Murdock." As a little girl she dreamed of battered beige raincoats and fedoras, filing stories on the wire. After the revolution, and during that project *El Puente,* she was a cub reporter at a daily newspaper. In the Avengers, when she couldn't get press coverage, she helped start Dyke TV.

So when she couldn't stop blabbing about Elián and the lack of rational Cuban voices, I knew what I had to do. I roped in my friend Amy who was working at an Internet start-up, and she bought me a book on HTML and walked me through a basic design. A couple of weeks later, on February 6, 2000, we brought out our first issue of *The Gully* online magazine. It was so immediate. You wrote an article, or edited it, slapped it into code that looked like garbage scrolling across the page, but when you opened it in Netscape or Explorer it looked as real as anybody else's site. And anybody anywhere with an Internet connection could read it. Free. No more of the begging and pleading I'd seen from the Avengers' Ministry of Propaganda. Oh, please write an article, run this press release, pay attention to my dyke point of view. The best thing was that every reader was a link away from activism. Click here for more info. Click here to get involved. Where do you live? Here's the number for your rep or senator. Or local troublemakers.

As Su Friedrich would tell me later, "Nobody really quits being a Lesbian Avenger." It's a habit. An autonomic function. And our first readers came from an e-mail list of activists we knew. But I also submitted articles to search engines and sites here and there that did roundups of news. It felt like dropping pamphlets from a plane. Or panning for gold. Every now and then we'd hit pay dirt when Yahoo News or *Mother Jones* online listed an article, sandwiching it between tidbits from the *Christian Science Monitor* or the *Miami Herald*. We'd suddenly get hundreds or thousands of hits, and I'd do a little butt-wagging happy dance, even if half sent hate mail, especially about the Cuban stuff. And because it wasn't only paper and ink that were gone, but the traditional distance, their complaints didn't go to a secretary in an office somewhere but directly into the vile pink monster.

I'd approach it warily. Take a couple of deep breaths. Fortify myself with coffee. Because checking my e-mail was like having a community board meeting for the Rainbow Curriculum suddenly appear in our apartment with all of the bigots shouting, "You Commie faggots should get your repulsive asses to Cuba if you love it so much." "I hope you all get AIDS." Weirdly, they'd toss in a few heartfelt pleas to understand the Cuban American community that was so easy to bash, and then start in again hating on the fucking faggots, our miserable homo flesh.

I begged Ana to shut them up, come out as Cuban, play the jail card. But she refused to claim that authority. "It will mean you, as a Kentucky girl, have nothing valuable to say about Cuba. And Cubans have nothing to say about the rest of the world." So their vomit kept pouring into my computer.

It wasn't all bad, that closeness. When we covered Puerto Rican activists trying to get the U.S. Navy to quit bombing their island of Vieques, a gay man with a guest house a few minutes from the range got in touch and contributed a couple of stories. Ana swapped e-mails with journalists in Namibia who were trying to keep their newspaper alive, under pressure to quit writing about government abuses, which included attacks on queers. They seemed a lot like us. Modest, but determined. Flying by the seat of their pants. In 2002, a guy wrote us from Venezuela to say there was a coup going on there, largely backed by U.S. interests. Could you please cover it? With his help, we ended up publishing a story before the *New York Times*. Now, he'd be using Twitter or posting on his own blog or Facebook. But then, small as we were, it was often just us looking so far outward and welcoming people in. We made a new kind of community online, defined partly by identity and issues, but above all a certain rebellion against meanness, stupidity, and hate.

We took things personally, wrote so intimately about our new friends that many readers decided we were neighbors, and once we had the Spanish-language section going, we'd get these letters from Guatemala or Mexico wanting advice on local gay stuff. In truth, problems weren't much different from place to place, especially when it came to queers. Time itself seemed to stick and repeat like Gertrude Stein or Mozart or mountain ranges. History, like nature, wasn't based on arcs but fractals. When Namibia's Sam Nujoma declared homos "un-African and unnatural," "European," and a national threat to independence, he was just repeating variations on a theme begun by the Cuban government of the 1960s and '70s that used to accuse people like José Mario, like Ana, of perverting the revolution, being a foreign influence. They goaded citizens to violence, sent us fleeing in droves.

This time, though, it was harder to isolate us. Squash the facts. The Internet gave new people access to that rusty old battleground, the media.

I named our zine *The Gully* because water can carve a mark in the landscape drip by drip if it persists long enough. The first tag line was "Digested news, raw opinion, from the queer edge of America," which I shortened pretty quickly to "Digested news, raw opinion, queer edge." We ended up a couple of years later with "Queer views on everything," refusing to fill a tiny niche or restrict ourselves. The world was large. I designed *The Gully* as a major daily, inserting us everywhere. My ambition was in the nav bar itself. Gaymundo. Asia. Americas. Africa. Europe. Race/class. And Art. For a while, the U.S. coverage was submerged in the Americas. I put my country back in its place, at least until Bush came.

I connected the dots. Seeded the "mainstream" channel pages like Africa with tons of queer stories and links from places like *Behind the Mask,* a gay African site. Then I'd stuff the Gaymundo page with stories about free speech or the right to assemble that affected LGBT activists all over the world. I'd use an article on Taiwan, which was having elections after a long dictatorship, to throw Cuban issues into relief. Like how do you forge a democracy with a colonial giant (China) breathing down your neck? How do you build a viable economy when you're so small? Where did queers fit in to the national picture? Taiwan also had its own racial and ethnic minorities, an indigenous people that were overrun by colonizers that were in turn colonized, like in the Caribbean. It wasn't just The West guilty of an ugly colonial past. *The Gully* was like the backside of the tapestry where all the threads of human striving were tangled up and knotted together. Returning the world to its unity. Pissing everybody off.

Straight readers subscribing after reading an article on police brutality would flee after seeing the word *gay*. A gay

Webmaster in Kentucky refused to list *The Gully* because we used the word *queer*. Didn't I know it was offensive?! And there was that time I was at a party telling some dyke art dealer about the magazine, and her face got all contorted with disgust, "What do you mean, gay point of view? There's no such thing!" She stormed off raging that sexual orientation meant nothing beyond who you went to bed with. She was right, in a way. In fact, that was the whole conundrum of identity politics. There was no single gay point of view. Like skin color or gender or any of those arbitrary, sometimes artificial, differences, sexual orientation didn't make us all the same. But it did affect us. It had to. Being pointed south while everybody else was pointed north. Being a cuckoo in heterosexual nests. Maybe it was even our contribution to society, that difference. Our lives making the radical point—things don't have to be the way they are.

I also did what I preached and looked to see who was missing. We featured writers of color or interviewed international LGBT activists. I'd put their photos up, or some video, and there'd be an Argentinian transgender woman online for maybe the first time ever. We'd feature Guatemalan dykes holding kiss-ins, and black South African lesbians marching against violence. Straight Taiwanese women were getting their riot on. An Iranian dyke risked her life to express herself in a blog post. No single group could ever plant a flag in that word *freedom*.

When St. Paddy's Day rolled around again, I interviewed Anne Maguire at the Mission Café on Second Avenue. I'd run into her in the street. Pretended everything was back to normal, post-Avengers, and it mostly was. It had been ten years since ILGO had begun the struggle to march in the damn parade. Ten years since we got clobbered with Dinkins. We talked about immigration, how it made some people more conservative, like the Hibernians, who clung to the past. How others embraced the chance to reinvent themselves and became radical forces.

Thinking about it now, I realize that's how the Avengers began. As a kind of radical immigrant project. Anne and Marie from Ireland. Ana from Cuba via France. Anne d'Adesky's mom was French, her father Haitian. Maxine Wolfe and Sarah Schulman were children and grandchildren of the Jewish Diaspora. Even most of the other American Avengers were far from their homes in Idaho. Alaska. Kentucky. All of us trying to claim a place in our own country. Be *citizens,* though I didn't grasp the word yet.

For a while the Internet seemed to offer us endless possibilities to participate. But not long after we published "South Africa: Apartheid Military Forced Gay Troops Into Sex-Change Operations," I turned on my computer and found a scary e-mail from a cabal of Canadian lawyers. They were suing *The Gully* and everyone involved with it for defaming the respected doctor Aubrey Levin, formerly Colonel Levin of South Africa, who'd reportedly performed forced sex changes on queers in the apartheid army. Better a female than a fag. A gay group had published a huge scholarly report on it in which he admitted a hell of a lot of ugly things. Afterwards, articles appeared in big publications like the *Daily Mail & Guardian.* At least until Levin got busy with his lawsuits, and all the South African and British rags pulled their stuff.

The First Amendment gives U.S. journalists more protection, so his lawyers were just blowing smoke at us, hoping we'd get scared and cave, but *The Gully* ended up having the last article standing. It was weird how quickly the story disappeared from the Web. That last chance for justice.

It was the first hint I had of some limits to the Web. Lawyers could force journalists to yank stories even if they believed they were true. Writers could change their minds and delete pages themselves, pretending they'd never said or done that, calling into question the legitimacy of bloggers, who were beginning to be called citizen journalists. We'd even find governments could filter, block, just pull the plug. And not just the ones you'd think.

25.

Much of that was later. At the end of June 2000, we were just waving farewell to Elián, the kid we'd followed as closely as OJ and his bloody glove, Clinton and that damn blue dress. In April, there'd been a big raid to get him out of the relatives' house and reunited with his dad. Photographers emerged with a snap of an INS storm trooper yanking open a closet to find a man holding a wide-eyed, terrified Elián. Miami Cubans played it up like it was another Waco. And it wasn't pretty, but it was right. The law held up. Which is nice if you care about things like that, and I was beginning to. I thought I might need it myself someday, believed law was the glue that kept all these fifty states from flying apart.

It wouldn't be long until it was tested again in the 2000 election. I couldn't watch the campaign, their smug faces. Clinton's uptight Ivy League Vice President Albert Gore, who pandered to the most extreme of the Miami Cubans and got photographed in front of stained-glass windows every chance he got. George W. Bush, the silver-spooned, down-home, Ivy League kid of the ex-President who himself had prayed away an addiction to alcohol and would open the door even further than Gore to gay-bashing, women-hating Christian fundamentalists.

Half the people we knew said there was no difference at all between the two corporate sell-outs. Their man was Saint Nader, the Ivy League Independent, consumer advocate, and environmentalist who called on the antiglobalization movement as his own higher power, eight months after the Battle of Seattle nearly paralyzed a big meeting of the WTO.

I'd watched Seattle with mixed feelings. Do you applaud them or kick them in the nuts, these guys who looked so middle-class and white? Who seemed to think it was enough to slap a bandana over their faces and wear T-shirts of that fag-bashing, middle-class bastard Che. Oh, and raise the solitary fist in the air before the baton came down. I'd made the gesture myself in the Avengers. You can see it in the documentary. My hand bunched in the air. If you watch carefully, I give a sideways glance, wondering if I'm ridiculous because I'm borrowing somebody else's pose. Hadn't figured out what mine should be, though I was making progress.

I wondered if the Seattle protesters would ever get beyond it. Maybe look around the room and see who wasn't there. Envision something more radical than their mantra "Local," which seemed to translate into women from Appalachia to Ecuador trapped weaving baskets and stitching quilts and popping babies, while the world went by and menfolk served as enforcers.

What about girls who wanted to learn computers? What about the urban poor? Or queer homeless kids? What about me? When we wrote about police brutality and race, I'd started to look closer at my own life. I realized I'd overemphasized the whole hickster-farmer's-granddaughter thing ever since college, when all that stuff about cultivating your mother's gardens was pushed so hard it made the whole impoverished rural thing seem more authentic than my life growing up on the margins of suburbia, not just praying in football fields but hanging out occasionally at the mall where I'd get followed around by security because I looked too poor. Too alone. My dykeliness showing. Too smart and sullen, they said, for a job at Mickey D's.

There was the time I was out with my sister Kim and her boyfriend, and the cops put on their big flashing light and pulled us over because the car was a beater, the tape deck blasting Kiss, and the boy's hair too long. He got frisked by the pigs. We didn't tell my mother. It was so white trash. Later, it helped me imagine what black kids went through. My humiliation squared. Along with the anger and fear. Education could give you a step up, but not much more, unless you acquired that veneer of entitlement. That gloss.

Nothing was separate, class or race. Gender. Sexual identity. Even place. And when it came to social policy, the Nader campaign pretty much ignored all that. When *The Gully* insisted that all these things were related, you should have seen the screaming all-caps e-mails including, "NOTHING is as important as class." "NOTHING is as important as the environment." "Even to mention such differences is an attack on a more egalitarian, color-blind world." There was a contest of oppression, and they used every old lefty excuse in the book to silence people of color and women and queers. They hated *The Gully*. Wanted to reach across cyberspace, rip our hearts out. They imagined we were the forces of evil.

I supposed that was progress, having the power to incite such fury with each article we published, declaring that class was intertwined with other issues. I wonder who they thought we were. Probably not these two dykes, one white, one Latina, sitting in the East Village all alone in front of their computers.

When I'd stumble out into the street, I was as insignificant and inoffensive as ever, awkward in the air. I'd go to the Fourteenth Street Y, enter the locker room, and the aging ladies would scream, "A man, a man. This is the women's locker room." And I'd shrink and sigh and say, "I know this is the women's," and let them mutter among themselves until they figured it out. I'd do laundry at that place on First Avenue and Second Street where you had to fight for a dryer with the little rich kids taking over the neighborhood. They came in and out between errands, trusting nobody would steal their stuff, while the old-timers sat around watching their machines and complaining about their diabetes in raspy voices like my aunts and uncles back home. They were too fat or too skinny. They downed sweet tea and soda pop and smoked. I drank diet Orange Crush and ate Cheetos where Ana couldn't see me. If I wasn't careful, I'd smear neon orange from my fingers onto the clothes.

That was my real life, wasn't it? Off-line. It was the place I felt attacked when George W. Bush seemed to squeak past Gore in the November election, and my lefty pals lit up the bulletin boards with a surge of posts hating on those inbred HILLBILLY MORONS from the red states, even if they'd wasted their own votes on Nader or shared real estate with the likes of Cardinal O'Connor or Mary Cummins. Some even mentioned Kentucky. People whose names I recognized, and I thought knew me from the Avengers or ILGO. Who knew where I was from. And for that matter, where bell hooks was from. I wanted to explode. Got enraged again. Seethed. I can call myself a stupid hick if I want to, but not you, you snide fucking fucker. Maybe it's your arrogance, like Gore's, that lost you the working class, and what's left of rural America. I felt more and more alien. Only Ana, maybe, was from a nearby planet.

Meanwhile in Florida, Secretary of State Katherine Harris was busy using Democratic ballots to wipe her Republican ass. And probably Puerto Rican cab drivers made jokes that Jimmy Carter should be down there instead of wherever, overseeing the election. And the same Cuban Americans who said they wanted Elián to grow up in a glorious democracy held violent demos attacking the recount. Poor George W. Bush retreated to his ranch and suffering greatly from the stress, appeared in photos with enormous swelling boils on his face under big cowboy hats. And Gore with his fleshy red face just smirked and shrugged and let things take their course.

Ana was online 24/7. Only making brief forays to her own gym, where nobody shouted at her to get out of the women's locker room, but did sometimes ask her as a short brownish woman for fresh towels. I wrote sneering articles but suffered a lot. It felt like our democracy was at stake. The rule of law. That web that had a harsh beauty to it, and was tested but held when Elían was returned to his father. No matter that he was Cuban or his opponents had powerful friends. The law was the law. Even imperfect, it held the promise of justice. It fed us our lines as activists. Offered ways to settle differences, be together.

You could almost see it rip as the Florida election was rushed to the U.S. Supreme Court and they decided it was more important to hand over power on schedule than to respect each American voice.

Nobody remembers now, just how it was. But that was the real moment the country shifted, weakening the ground on which the two towers stood. Making their fall more awful. Paving the way for Bush to ignore international treaties, dash into Iraq after imaginary foes. Everything was set up like dominoes, and the last nudge was the certification of the vote in Congress when not one single senator out of the hundred stood up to protest the widespread fraud and the disenfranchisement of black voters. As Clinton's vice president, Al Gore was still presiding. He could have acted to slow things down, but he just grinned and shrugged at the protesting Rep. Jesse Jackson Jr. "The Chair thanks the gentleman from Illinois, but, hey…" Let's just get this thing over with. As if the consequences of racism didn't poison us all.

The Gully stepped up efforts offering resources for activists and encouraging people to get involved, write e-mails and letters, hold demos protesting the election, and helped people network. When I posted a link to the Lesbian Avenger handbook, some helpful soul wrote in to say that he was sure our hearts were in the right place and all, but probably some people would be put off by the source, and maybe it would be better if we found one that was, you know, more mainstream. And I responded that I thought it would do hets good to know who their allies were. We were in it together like a bad marriage.

And there *was* a small protest movement. Mostly online, though thousands got on buses and turned up at Bush's inaugural, where network TV carefully framed them out of the picture like they didn't exist. Luckily, there were alternative media sites that posted photos and showed video. Every week hundreds of Oral Majority activists denounced Bush from the sidelines of some Republican event. Planes with banners questioning Bush's victory flew over opening-day baseball at Cincinnati's Synergy Field and circled Churchill Downs during the Kentucky Derby.

But we didn't push back hard enough to count. And the mainstream media, those protectors of democracy, characterized us all as loudmouthed freaks. Silence, apparently, was for the good of the country. When the Supreme Court ended the Florida recount, the big dogs of the *New York Times* and network TV hysterically howled that anything short of public unity would end with heads in baskets and mobs at the palace gates. Not to mention the ejection of reporters from the inner circle of the irritable White House.

When Bastille Day came, celebrating the bloody end of kings, Ana and I threw a party with lots of red wine and Bush's head in a basket. The day after, the *New York Times* very nearly acknowledged that the election was a fraud; the Florida vote was dirty. So Gore should have had the state and the election. But as Bush's spokesman Ari Fleischer said, "The nation, the president and all but the most partisan Americans have moved on."

Nobody wondered what a scam like that would give birth to. Maybe a president who thought he was above the law whether it came to environmental treaties or launching wars. Maybe a timid opposition so demoralized they'd cave in to his every high-handed demand.

I started hanging out in front of the laundry, even when I didn't have any. I'd met Al Baltrop, this black gay guy who'd sit in a chair in front with this incredible walking stick by his side. He dressed in a mix of Africana and Blaxploitation gear, knuckledusters on his hands. A camera usually, stuffed into his bag. He was a photographer. And a dirty dog. He'd freak out the skinny white and Asian women folding their clothes by loudly declaring that what he liked were fat boys, with some meat on their bones. Something to hang on to. Make a meal. "I don't understand skinny. All that bone. You can hurt yourself," he cackled. I nodded my head, played the role of choir. "Uh huh. Exactly. Preach on." He'd show pictures of how fat he was before the chemo. "Look at me now. Terrible."

He reminded me of home. For better and worse. His mother was from the South like a lot of black New Yorkers. Serving up Southern fried homophobia along with biscuits with sausage gravy. Fried ham. Pie. My god, pie. Pecan pie. With molasses. We'd groan at the thought. He'd learned to cook from the women at her church. That was before she'd kicked him out and ripped up his photos when she found out he was a fag. He'd had some good shots, too. Of the Black Panthers in New York. Later, he caught all these beautiful men living and dead against the backdrop of the piers. I posted some in *The Gully* along with an interview.

He was our biggest fan, thought it was cool that you didn't have to rely on galleries and museums or newspapers anymore. They never supported people like us until we were dead. And I'd tell him about the stuff we wrote about Namibia or Zimbabwe, where Mugabe sponsored ferocious antigay campaigns and burned his opponents alive. I'd gripe, "At least people there are fighting back, resisting." And Al would tell me what was going on in the neighborhood. This little girl on the street that was going to be a dyke. How he told her parents to lay off when they tried to force her into dresses and bows. There was another kid, a boy thrown out by his West Indian preacher father. Al let him sleep on his floor a couple nights. "I make it clear there'll be no favors exchanged. So he feels safe." We talked about whether or not the down low was just a sexy term for the closet (Al thought it was).

I invited him over for dinner once, made jambalaya with big fat shrimp and the tastiest pie. Ana's mom, Faustina, came over, too, and her eyes got all wide at his stories. I sent them both home with leftovers, and woke up in the middle of the night, puking my guts out, terrified I'd poisoned them both. The guy with cancer. The old lady. And when Ana woke up I had her call and check they were both alive. And order them, if they were, to toss out the stew. Al thought it was hilarious. Told everybody at the laundromat what a killer jambalaya I made.

26.

It woke me up, a man's voice from the building behind us, screaming, "Holy shit! Holy shit!" A minute later a woman echoed, "Holy shit!" before giggling hysterically. We thought it was the usual New York farce until we turned on the TV and saw flames coming out of the top of one of the Twin Towers. It seemed like a movie and any second they were going to switch back to the news and Alan Hevesi's fleshy red face, and Mark Green's smarmy one, or the earnest flip-flopper Fernando Ferrer, and the mayoral primary. Except then the second plane hit. Ana threw on some clothes, grabbed a notebook, and dashed downtown to cover the story for *The Gully*. I went up on the roof with all my neighbors and just stared downtown. The sky was blue, like the one Icarus fell out of in that Brueghel painting. Sunny and blue. There were ragged plane-shaped gashes in both towers with smoke trailing from them. Everybody had cameras. I reminded myself I was a journalist and went back down to get my own.

When the first one collapsed, it seemed to come down slowly, almost gracefully. Shiny things flew into the air. Karen from next door screamed a little self-consciously. Neighbors asked each other how many were inside. Somebody asked me where Ana was. "Down there," I said. "Getting the story." A couple of minutes later the other tower went. Karen screamed some more, then stopped when we ignored her. I took more pictures that I didn't develop for months. I stood there for a long time, until I had to pee, then stayed in the apartment and stayed watching it replay in slow motion. It seemed hours before Ana came back covered in ashes and dust, and we churned out some of the first stories.

I kept my distance from that word *terrorism*. Though the attacks were meant to inspire fear, like a series of gay bashing or pogroms, it felt more like a natural disaster. An earthquake. Maybe an industrial accident. Ana and I had just been down there two days before, walking south along the East River toward the tip of Manhattan, accompanied by the smell of muddy water and burnt sugar. We passed the enormous feet of the Williamsburg Bridge, the Manhattan, the Brooklyn. There were old Latino men with their lines in the water, then Asian ones with their Styrofoam coolers and poles. The sidewalks around Fulton Street Fish Market were slippery and rank. We cut in, heard the big vents of the Towers as they breathed in and out.

Geopolitics wasn't enough to explain the two plumes of smoke, all the dead, what came after. Later, I'd try to write a poem comparing it to a fire that started at a garbage heap in Centralia, Pennsylvania, "that dove underground and found the seam of coal and burns still, buckling highways, gulping down towns, gathering violence to itself because the only art of fire is to burn." I could see what was coming. The bloody tide of patriots and martyrs on all sides. I wondered if that was what he expected, Mohamed Atta, when he climbed into the cockpit and set the course on the Tower. Or did he think it was a tactical strike that would punish the United States for meddling in the Middle East, supporting dictators? Somehow force us to withdraw? So many deaths and voilá. Just like that. Like Bush and Cheney who thought they were in control when they responded in kind.

There were little shock waves. One of them erased the local politicians and city news anchors, often black and brown and female, the other usual suspects on TV. Gone were black activist Al Sharpton and dyke councilwoman Margarita López. Plus no more mediocre politicians duking it out for the Democratic spot on the mayoral ticket. We had Giuliani 24/7 in firemen's or NYPD ball caps. There were white male congressmen with the occasional shot of Bush Jr. trying to look presidential, the rare glimpse of New York Senator Hillary Clinton. An upswing in New York of white masculine power.

Our neighborhood was also transformed. With all the barricades, it was as deserted as a movie set, or an abandoned town in Spain with only a few people out in the dust and sun. One afternoon, on Second Avenue, I saw a solitary figure, an old man, suddenly fall down dead. It was like he was supposed to have died in the Towers, but Death hadn't caught up with him until then. Two or three people rushed over, then an ambulance came, but he was already gone.

Telephone poles grew faces of the dead. HAVE YOU SEEN THIS PERSON? Flags sprouted like kudzu, colonizing car bumpers, windowsills, T-shirts. Hardware stores sold out of them. Somebody, maybe from the Chinese Merchants Association, Xeroxed a couple thousand in color and taped them to all the doors in Chinatown like a smear of blood beseeching angry gods, Please pass over. We're one of you. The image was backwards, but I doubted anybody noticed. Some of the bodegas, too, put up flags, and once Al Qaeda was confirmed, all the Middle Eastern and North African employees suddenly spoke stilted English to each other and didn't joke any more in Arabic with their taxi driving compatriots who came in.

Here and there, white guys started beating up Muslims and Indian Sikhs who weren't Muslim but had turbans, and what difference did it make, right? When cops responded to a complaint from a guy out in Brooklyn, whose apartment had been graffitied, they yanked *him* in for questioning. He was a member of a gay Muslim group, Al-Fatiha, which had been working to free the Cairo 52, these gay men grabbed at a dance and tortured until they confessed to a whole slew of crimes. They were being tried in Egypt's special emergency court, set up to deal with their own Islamic terrorists. Apparently, they thought, like so many U.S. preachers, that two men screwing can bring down a nation like an H-bomb.

Most New Yorkers, though, chose a different road. The white bourgeoisie kept popping by their delis to ask the Arab guys how things were going, keeping an eye on them. Al said he used his walking stick to beat the crap out of a guy who was making towelhead jokes and sneering at the dead. In the supermarket, blacks and whites and Latinos were so kind to each other, it was a little disturbing. Newspapers were printing half-page ads from community groups expressing their shared grief with the city we all loved, despite its problems.

Three or four days after the Towers fell, Ana got herself to the LGBT Community Center to ask if we were going to do the same. At least have a memorial service or something, so we could grieve together as New Yorkers and as queers, sharing our anger and loss. Shouldn't queer citizens express themselves, too? The receptionist just stared at her like it was a ridiculous idea and sent her to the administration office. The functionaries there asked her to repeat, explain, and elaborate the question like it was in a foreign language, then showed her the door.

Even after our institutions recovered from the initial shock and started providing services to the community, making sure queers got disaster benefits or grief counseling, there wasn't any sense that we were a part of the nation's civic life or public discourse, unless you count the preachers blaming us for the attacks. There was no sense that the silent masses of ordinary LGBT folks might want to merge two identities and grieve as queer New Yorkers. No sense of a broader connection to the larger society, the possibility of integration, without complete assimilation.

When Ana wrote an article lamenting our community's lack of vision, queers blasted *The Gully*. It wasn't the moment to call attention to our difference. As if we alone had to choose in times of crisis. Love it or leave it. As if gayness were like a limb available to be amputated from ourselves and from society. And when, in the future, that troublesome bit was firmly reattached by enough legal change, nothing would distinguish us. We will forget the Avengers, the irritating indigestible likes of David Wojnarowicz, Audre Lorde, Valerie Solanas. We will become honorary straights with just a few seams showing.

When some fool started to send little envelopes of anthrax around the week after the attacks, the Bush team capitalized, keeping their citizens busy with a bunch of color-coded threat levels, and daily press releases about the imminent dangers of dirty bombs in Grand Central Station. In the mayhem, Bush declared a War on Terror, issuing an executive order legalizing kidnappings, indefinite detention, secret military tribunals, and hidden prisons for any suspect. He cooked up a new program called TIPS that would have had us spying on each other, and encouraging cable and telephone repair guys to snoop around and look for anything suspicious. Books in foreign languages? Porn? The Koran? No matter what it was, your name could end up in a big government database forever. He tried to get permanent exemptions from bodies like the International Criminal Court, which prosecuted things like war crimes and torture. And he bombed Afghanistan and split, leaving behind not much more than a skeleton crew.

They entered my nightmares, the civilians that got hit. Along with giant fireballs, I dreamt of limbs missing. Bodies buried under rubble like a continuation of the other bombing.

Iraq was already on the drawing board. From the beginning, Rumsfeld pushed the CIA to blame Saddam for it all. After the first Gulf War, the Bush family had unfinished business there, and George Jr. had found a reason to go back. And aimed also at Iran, and North Korea. Bush burned with a religious mission. Every day there was a new enemy in his Axis of Evil. Somebody else that had to be punished. Reined in, destroyed. When Undersecretary of State John Bolton offered dark suggestions that something would have to be done about rogue states like Cuba, Ana and I decided it was time to make a trip. She hadn't been back since she left the place. And didn't want to wait until it was all rubble. Like Kabul.

I wasn't thrilled about going. The idea was kind of horrible and interesting at the same time. Like meeting someone's parents. Ana's mom, Faustina, asked if I thought I'd like it, Cuba. "Maybe," I told her.

"Everyone likes it . . ."

"I guess so."

"I've never known anyone not to like it." She pursed her lips in outrage.

I bit back all my rude responses.

27.

I'm not sure how to describe the trip. It wasn't a vacation, and I wasn't your average tourist out for mojitos or mambo or some revolutionary thrill. Call it a visit to an alternative dimension, with a hint of what we'd become if we embraced programs like TIPS or fear-mongering politicians. If the full weight of state homophobia was allowed to come down on queers, or any group, like they'd pushed for in Oregon and Colorado.

Cuba. I thought it should have been bigger. At least as big as Texas for all the room it took up in my skull. But coming in on the plane you could see it was just this ordinary island of brown and green. The same size as Kentucky. My first glimpse was weeds sprouting from cracked tarmac and soldiers every-where in their olive-drab fatigues. One by one, we entered into little plexiglass cubicles where the door slammed behind us, and a boy with a skimpy beard and AK47 demanded to know why we were there. There was so much I was tempted to say, but the little guy with the wispy beard offered, "¿Familia?" And I said, "Yes, family." And that was that. I was through. They didn't even check my luggage where Ana had asked me to stash a VHS of *Lesbian Avengers Eat Fire Too*.

Gerardo and Nancy were waiting at the gate in coats and scarves, the only dark faces in the crowd. These were Ana's teenage friends. Gerardo Fulleda León, the playwright now with his own modest theater company. Nancy Morejón, the poet who hobnobbed at the Casa de las Américas. I thought I should get it on video. I had our new camera there in my hand but didn't raise it to catch the awkward hugs. They were Ana's first gestures on the island after thirty-five years. It felt wrong to film. Too voyeuristic.

They had a gypsy cab with a pink rhino dangling from the rearview mirror instead of a flag. Right away the cops stopped us, because visitors are supposed to use official taxis, but Gerardo told them we were relatives, all of us. And they let us through. We took a long decaying highway. There weren't any golden arches or Speedo stores, but there was plenty of advertising if you count the building sketching Che in broad strokes, along with *¡Hasta la victoria siempre!* Always, until victory. The apartment we'd rented in Vedado was surprisingly big and clean, with a balcony that gave you a view of the crumbling Malecón and the ocean if you craned your head a little, though you didn't want to linger. There were cracks running up and down that building, too, and iron railing on the stairs that formed new piles of rust every day.

Conversation was awkward. Gerardo would start sentences, shrug, and say, "You know . . . ," leaving a big ellipse, as if the words had decayed in his mouth. Then Nancy said some vague thing to Ana about "what happened to you" and seemed to be giving her smarmy absolution for getting the hell out. And when he saw my eyebrows go up, because Ana didn't have to apologize for anything, Gerardo changed the subject with a funny story about Ana's departing words—or was it a letter from Paris in which she proclaimed that she was leaving to join another revolution? And when the '68 student revolution happened in France, he imagined her there in the center of it, manning the barricades and throwing stones.

Ana blushed twelve shades of red. "Did I really?"

And we all laughed like it was a joke, though of course it was true. Afterwards, she'd organized Parisian dykes—or tried to. In New York, she helped birth other little smoldering revolutions like the Lesbian Avengers, though we didn't talk about that or even acknowledge we were all queer. In fact, when Nancy talked about a young interviewer asking her about the members of *El Puente,* if they were gay, she proudly said, "I threw them out by their ears." I looked at Ana and she looked at her shoes. It was the first time I'd seen her back away from a fight, maybe because I'd stuffed her full of Xanax to get her on the plane.

Nancy asked something about September 11, but her eyes glazed over as soon as Ana started to talk about what it was like. In Cuba then, the outside world was nothing more than a dream shaped by the official media. Even Nancy only had brief glimpses during her trips abroad for poetry readings and academic conferences. And if you hadn't grasped the world before the attacks, afterwards you missed the huge global shifts. They'd missed a lot of them. Four decades' worth. Couldn't conceive of what it was like to sit in a chair in front of the computer and gather the world in your arms like sea foam, let it go.

Ana herself was just a ghost for them, despite her short scarlet 'do. She was still some teenage prodigy with dark hair and a pressed white blouse, whom the government had targeted by mistake. Who later rose like Santa Barbara with her sword to publicly defend *El Puente* when the group itself was attacked. Though Ana had confided to me her act was less than heroic: "After jail, I was numb. I just didn't care."

I didn't say a lot. Ana had told me to keep my trap shut because they'd probably have to report our conversation. Instead, I grinned too much, showing my straight, white American teeth. I laughed inappropriately. Then Ana suddenly started on a rant about Bush the warmonger, stripper of civil liberties, the go-it-alone guy.

Light was fading when we were finally alone in the apartment. We didn't talk too much between us, just tried to unpack and arrange things. I jumped like a cat at little sounds. The worried-looking woman who rented the place told us not to answer the door if anybody knocked. Everything was legal, but members of the *comité de defensa* liked to harass her, sometimes press for bribes.

When we got hungry, we grabbed a flashlight and ventured out on our own.

There wasn't any light at all except a few bright squares coming from windows and a faint veiled moon. The sidewalks were a ravaged mess. The concrete would sometimes rise six inches, sometimes eighteen. We fell into holes even with the flashlight, stepping around piles of dog shit and rubble from buildings that had collapsed from hurricanes, but mostly malign neglect. *Take that, you shimmering city of degenerate capitalists!* No need for bombs: it already looked like Kabul, or the Bronx circa 1970. And like the Bronx at night, there weren't any humans in the street until we got to Calle something or other where Ana began to murmur the refrain that would accompany us through the trip, "This used to be, this used to be." This used to be a club. *El Puente* held a reading there. This used to be a bar where La Lupe sang. This is the corner I stood on during the October crisis in 1962 when American bombers were circling overhead, and an oblivious José Mario was babbling on about some boy he'd just met.

At a café, we planted ourselves at a table and tried not to breathe. The diesel fumes blocked out the sea. We ordered a couple of ham and cheese sandwiches, and beer for Ana, Malta for me. You could pay in pesos if you were Cuban, dollars for foreigners—my god, how they hopped for greenbacks, clearing away the Cuban riffraff to make more room for us tourists. At the next table, a Canadian guy made a complicated deal with two sleazy gray-skinned hustlers that involved a couple of bottles of rum and a blowjob. Behold the Revolution's New Man.

I wrote down that the beer was named Hatuey for an Indian chief barbequed by the Spanish Inquisition.

We had a guidebook and played at being tourists. We hit ancient convents and museums and art galleries and spent an awful lot of time running away. There was the day we dropped off medicine and videotapes at a government AIDS clinic, and I was so impressed by how clean and cheerful it was that I asked them if I could do a video for *The Gully*. The woman's face contorted in horror and she sent us to the subdirector, who sent us to the director, who said nobody could say a word unless we went through official channels. "Here's the address and phone of the government's press office. Should I call for you?"

"No, that's fine. We'll be in touch later." And we fled the premises, only stopping when we got to a park near the old Writer's Union, and Ana's old high school where the student militia had marched around a statue of Antonio Maceo's mother. Not far away, baby Pioneers piled onto buses with their little red handkerchiefs. Later, we spotted them at a demo in the center of town. They cheered speeches at the appropriate moments and got snickered at by tourists. There was a local election coming up, and they offered all the usual pageantry, speeches, and ballots just like in Florida. Or Puerto Rico.

Once a guy screamed at me when I videotaped laundry hanging in the ruins of a collapsed building with vines curling up the rubble. "It's not picturesque. Go away." The streets were full of simmering people, most of them men, and hissing air like leaky tires. "Hey mama, mamacita. Psst. Psst!" In Havana, they tended to be poor and white. Elsewhere, poor and black. "Hey mamacita, hey." I finally shouted back in Cienfuegos where Ana showed me her childhood home, the school she went to.

We were followed around by a young black kid who must've been all of ten years old. He was trying to hustle Ana, telling her how beautiful she was: "Hey mama, mamacita. I'm sure there's something I can do for you tonight." After him was the gauntlet of a dozen large hissing men, "Oye mama, hey mamacita, pssst, pssst." When a few grabbed their dicks, I screamed at the whole gang of them to shut up and leave us alone, "Enough already!

I'm not your mother" (in Spanish). Then this one guy, after consulting with his buddies, charged forward to chase us down the street, screaming in English, "Fuck you, you bitches!" He was dressed all in white, a recent initiate in Santería, and must've thought he was Changó.

That was the day we realized we'd rarely seen women in the Havana streets alone after dark. None at all in Cienfuegos. Even during the day, they didn't linger but marched purposefully. We also started noticing the "Fuck you's" in English scrawled almost everywhere. All that free-floating inarticulate rage. Directed at surrogates mostly, instead of the people in charge.

There was also that mob that we ran into in Santiago de Cuba. We'd spent a dozen hours in a tourist bus inhaling stinking fumes and cataloguing all the downed telephone lines and rusting metal of the glorious projects in the countryside that Havana had been defunded for. And when we arrived at the bus station in the Santiago twilight, we were engulfed by a crowd of gypsy cab drivers all reaching for our arms, our bags. Groping our shoulders. Sniffing after dollars with bared fangs. It was like hell. We didn't want to be swallowed up and forced into an illegal cab. What if the cops stopped us and Gerardo wasn't there to smile and lie?

The rejected cabbies sneered at us, got ugly. "Where are you from?" "Here, Cuba. Born and bred," Ana told them. "No, señora. There's nothing Cuban about you." Or maybe that came from the mob of women in Trinidad. Banishing Ana for what? Her red hair? Her new shorts? Her dykeliness, again? Palish skin? In Santiago, a bus station employee had to extract us. She took us around the back way and explained they'd lost control of the place a long time ago. When things got really bad, they'd call the cops who would come and break a few heads, but nothing really changed.

The Santiago hotel was its own separate inferno. The terrace a mix of drunken elderhostelers and scrawny little European men with these beautiful mixed-race Cuban women, not yet allowed there on their own. The day after we arrived, a couple of snaggle-toothed Swiss bastards started eying us. Got more and more aggressive with each polite rejection until it was Ana's turn to go berserk and scream, "Not all Cuban women are whores! Fuck off!" And the waiters came and couldn't decide which of us to throw out. And Ana let them have it, too, these shitty little Cuban pimps who did nothing but whore women out or reduce us to beggars. Like that older black woman we'd seen earlier in the day who trailed us begging for "Savon, savon." Soap. Soap. Too old to offer herself. Too black.

The revolution was mostly a bust for her, too, even if the government had legislated an end to racism. And as beautiful as the law can be, it has to have roots in society and requires activists for a cultural shift to be enforced. At home, Ana has this mushy, rotting little book called *Cómo surgió la cultura nacional* (How the National Culture Arose), centering Afro-Cubans in the heart of Cuban history. The author, Walterio Carbonell, didn't fare well. He was on the verge of launching a negritude movement, a kind of Black Power thing like they'd had in the French Caribbean, when he got dragged off to jail, along with all his papers, even his typewriter, as if it could write by itself. Afterwards, the renaissance of black culture was carefully controlled.

One Sunday afternoon in Havana, we went to a community center to watch a rumba group. The audience was mostly Afro-Cubans dressed in their Sunday best with a few white tourists. The patio was shabby and hot with broken concrete. Two young black men tried to do rap, dressed all gangbanger with new jeans from somewhere and do-rags. But it was hard to pull off. The sound from the mike cut in and out as they worked their arms and rhymed about Antonio Maceo, Cuba's one black hero from the nineteenth century. The middle-aged black audience stared at them in amazement, waited for the rumba group. It turned out to be a mediocre band plastered with Adidas and Nike logos. They barely went through the motions. Two or three white tourists squealed and applauded.

After a couple more Hatuey beers, a few locals joined in with an equal lack of enthusiasm.

We visited a black writer friend of Gerardo who had this enormous two-bedroom apartment with a fabulous view that was absolutely great if you didn't mind that the woman running the elevator was a stone-faced capo keeping track of your comings and goings. But your status didn't always protect you. Even Nancy who could get an exit visa whenever she wanted, got detained by the cops for being a hooker when she was showing around a foreign white male writer. "I told them, 'You can take me in if you want to, but you're going to be sorry.'"

28.

We wondered what would happen next. If the Communists would perpetuate themselves like in China. If they would collapse like the former Soviets into corruption and crime. Civil society was as rusty as our balcony. There were a few hopeful signs—rappers who didn't bother with official gigs, doing protest songs about cops profiling black kids, tyranny passed off as revolution. Sometimes these *raperos* got pulled in by the police when their impromptu concerts got too big, or by security when the content was too hot, but they kept it up. There was a Cuban metal scene, too, radically raunchy in a place were the bureaucrats still pretended they were as pure as the Holy Virgin, while regular people fucked tourists to survive. Later on, bloggers like Yoani Sánchez would emerge, bothering the government merely by refusing the ellipse and writing honestly about their lives.

Before we left, Gerardo borrowed an apartment and organized a party for a bunch of lesbians and gay men. They mostly didn't know each other, but rum flowed like water so it didn't matter. When everybody's eyes got bright and shiny, we turned on the VHS and slipped in *The Lesbian Avengers Eat Fire Too*.

I'd avoided seeing it until then, and felt weird, watching my younger doppelgänger talking about lesbian visibility and activism, while I was standing right there in Cuba where so much was forbidden. Queer parties got busted sometimes. A visiting Pedro Almodóvar got arrested once. Every now and then, somebody would get four or five people to hold a demo, and they'd all end up in jail. Not that you didn't see queers.

Our first night there, we'd passed a cinema with a huge chic gayboy crowd outside, socializing and cruising. They even had their own Elton John reigning over the space with his sparkling glasses, though the cops could have chased them off at any time. The only protected queers were organized by Castro's straight niece who promoted such a medicalized understanding of LGBT people you felt like Ike was still in the White House.

But the Avengers was their history, too, with a Cuban dyke as the cofounder, and Cuban Americans like Janet and Lidia and Belkis.

I don't know what they expected in the video. To Cuban ears, *Vengadoras Lesbianas* sounded more like the Baader-Meinhof Gang than a bunch of superheroes or crafty British spies, images the founders had been thinking of when they sat around Ana's table in prickly chairs and tried to come up with the first action and a name. The Cuban audience actually sighed with relief when they saw the marching band enter the screen and got the idea. We paused now and then to translate the interviews or speeches and explain all the black and brown faces. U.S. TV hadn't been widely pirated yet, and they'd assumed all Americans were white, or most of them anyway. At the very least, they were sure we were still segregated, kept apart by water hoses and police dogs and hate.

They giggled nervously when they saw me scuffle with cops on Fifth Avenue. And were horrified to hear of queers getting killed in Oregon. A young dyke murmured, "At least that doesn't happen here. We're very tolerant." But another rebuked her in quiet outrage. They were impressed with the fire-eating, and chuckled at my shaved head. And oohed and aahed at the massive Dyke March in Washington, and the sight of us, there, in front of the White House, which even they recognized. And laughed out loud at waltzing dykes.

Afterwards, something weird happened. Arguments broke out. People started completing their sentences. The young commissar-type who declared that Cuba was tolerant, and went on to explain how it was no big deal when she took her girlfriend to office parties, had to listen to an older dyke tell her what happened when she and her girlfriend had tried to rent a hotel room with only one bed. And somebody else told one of their stories. And somebody else told one of theirs. It seemed to be the first time most of them had talked openly about their lives as queers and this thing called homophobia. I told the baby commissar that there were still antigay laws on Cuba's books, like the one from 1971 that prevented queers from teaching.

"But they're surely not enforced?"

"Yes." I should have told her about Josefina Suárez. About Lina and her sister as well, but I would have had to start so many decades before. And do it all in Spanish. And Gerardo himself had warned us about talking openly. I thought about those Polish journalists who got busted for not having the right visa, remembered we were trapped on the island. And in a couple of days, I'd be sealed again in a bulletproof cubicle. I kept mum.

We'd been encouraged to see Lina. "Things had happened to her." Ana didn't know her well, though they'd roomed together briefly when Lina had arrived in Havana from the provinces, a cardboard suitcase full of poems. It was the tail end of *El Puente*. Ana left soon afterwards.

Two women answered the door. They looked like poor rural whitish Americans with too-tight polyester clothes and bad hair and broad smiles featuring decaying teeth. We handed over some real coffee that we'd bought at the dollar store and exchanged a few pleasantries with Lina and her sister before the poet launched into her story.

I'd been all ready with my dyke sympathy, but what she talked about were the black feet, dangling from the bunk above, like two dead crows. In the cell, there was nothing else to look at, she said. If she sat up, they were inches from her face, scaly, dark, and rotten. She shivered like my mother did at interracial couples or a dyke holding a coffee cup. Lina hated their pale soles more than the stench from the slop bucket, unwashed cunt, the old rags they used for menstrual blood, the iron bars, the stone walls. Hour after hour, day after day, they hung unguarded and black in her space. If she had a knife she'd cut them off. Or kill herself.

We didn't know what to say. Couldn't even exchange glances. "Why were you in jail?" Ana asked.

"I'd been asked to direct the big Communist Youth literary magazine. I guess because I'd won a big prize for my first poetry book." (It helped that her parents were fixtures in the Party, Ana told me later.) "It went fine until they asked me to quit publishing homosexual writers, and I asked why. 'Their writing was the best around,' I said, 'and none were enemies of the revolution.'"

The answer launched her into *inzilio*. "You get it, right?" she asked. "Not exile, but inzile." Afterwards, people would cross the street to avoid her. Nobody would give her work or touch her poems. Finally, she couldn't take it and went to the Spanish embassy, demanding that the guards kill her before she did something. They didn't. They took her to the authorities. And even though one of the Cuban guards testified on her behalf, they convicted her of actually attacking the place. It was payback for publishing queers.

She got sick in jail, couldn't stand at attention, and got dragged from the cell by her hair and tossed into solitary. "They thought I was faking."

When her family got her out of there a couple of years later, her hair fell from her head in chunks. She was covered in rashes and filth, could barely tolerate water or raise the weight of her head. She showed us a picture of herself the day she was released. "Ninety pounds." They fed her with IVs, and a shrink diagnosed her with paranoid schizophrenia.

Ana and I looked at each other. "Of course," said Ana, rolling her eyes.

Lina pooh-poohed Ana's mild suggestion that the diagnosis

had something to do with politics. All the best poets were mentally ill. She told us a little proudly how bad she still felt, the pills she had to take. Then she read aloud a poem she composed for the mysterious beautiful Ana, while my flesh crawled. Then tried to sell us some books.

Her sister had her own stories. Girlfriends who killed themselves, mostly after getting denounced in school auditoriums.

"Ladykiller," Lina taunted her. "Ladykiller."

Her sister's eyes teared up. I had the camera there at my side but didn't bring it out, afraid it would stop the flow of their stories, afraid to have them there on tape.

Lina didn't tell the whole story. Like how she embroiled Josefina in her troubles. Ratted her out as a dyke. Got her inziled, too. We went to see Josefina a day or two afterwards. She would have been a good New Yorker—stubborn, opinionated, relentless, talked a mile a fucking minute. Made us feel oddly ourselves. She lived in this big apartment taking care of a father that she'd stashed in a back room for our visit. There was dog hair everywhere, and piles of mildewed paper and books. "You brought coffee. Great. I need something since I quit smoking, and you can't get pills. I don't know how people work." She dumped filthy cushions off something for me and settled Ana in the chair previously protected from dog hair by the stacks and stacks of papers she removed to the floor. She herself perched on a hairy sofa with an enormous poster of Che behind her. She kissed and patted the dog as she talked and talked, explaining how she'd probably have been left alone except that Lina embroiled her in everything.

Hours after Lina was arrested, Josefina was called into the office of the philosophy department and asked to resign. The department head was waving a statement from Lina detailing how she and Josefina had been lovers. That Lina had gone over to Josefina's that day, quarreled with her, then taken a knife from the drawer, before going to the embassy where she attacked the guard.

"Was it written in her own hand? Not just something typed and signed?" Ana asked, finally talking.

"Yes, I think so," said Josefina, a little irritated that we upset the rhythm of her story.

"Did they force her? During interrogation?"

"Had she actually been at your house?" I asked.

"Yes."

"And did you fight?"

"No, of course not. She'd been there, but I didn't notice anything in particular. We'd broken up months before..."

"How long were you all together?" Ana asked.

Josefina counted out the years.

"Was it your knife?"

"Apparently." The dog ran to the door and barked madly. "Come back here, sit down, be quiet," she yelled. Howl, howl. "Be quiet!"

Josefina wasn't interested in the details, just what came next. They wanted her to sign some mea culpa, breast-beating letter resigning because of her degeneracy, but she wouldn't. "Because what does sex have to do with anything?" And after she was fired and entered her own *inzilio*, there were pleas from her friends to make some conciliating, self-deprecating gesture so that they could give her some related, nonteaching job. But she refused. And had been fighting the bastards ever since. Writing letters, haranguing officials, quoting Marx at them. In daily, weekly, monthly, yearly letters analyzing their false dialectics.

Somehow she stayed out of jail. Maybe because she bent over backwards to show her loyalty to the regime. She told us that after a trip to Paris in which she had shown up unannounced on Ana's doorstep, she'd gone straight to state security to tell them all about her visit when she got back to Cuba. She didn't even give them a chance to call her in.

I don't know what my face showed, but Ana's mouth was hanging open. What could you possibly say to that? What could you say to anyone about anything in that strange fucking country where you had to contort yourself into unrecognizable shapes to survive?

And Josefina talked about *El Puente,* digging out the broadsheet they circulated establishing the group, a few old diary entries describing their nefarious, degenerate activities that largely consisted of talking, drinking, bumming money, reading, walking, eating pizza, drinking beer, swilling rum, sitting on the beach, and talking, talking, talking.

She had a photo of Ana in the "psychiatric clinic" after her own stint in jail. Ana asked about the other queers purged at the same time. Plenty ended locked up in concentration camps, jailed, suicided. Had she seen it coming? Josefina waved her hand dismissively. "Not my department," while Che stared meaningfully into the middle distance, a few dog hairs clinging to his face.

I should have said all that when I talked to the young communist at the party, plant more seeds of information. Already, you could see her worldview shifting. At least a little. But I didn't. And Ana kept her own trap shut, was just a friend of Gerardo's, though every now and then I could see him pointing at Ana and telling somebody, "I told you about her." And they'd get a disturbingly reverent expression on their faces.

I felt like a traitor, like a coward sitting in the room with all these queer Cubans, knowing more about their own history than them. More about their present. We informed a lesbian in gender studies at the university that there was going to be an LGBT conference in Havana. She hadn't heard about it. And probably wouldn't unless she was handpicked for it. Later on, though, outside queers would tout Cuba's openness, never asking if it was largely for external consumption, like the restaurants, like the hotels. Never wondering if you can have social change at all with proxy organizing. Whites organizing blacks. Straights representing queers. There was stuff even Gerardo didn't know. Ana never told him that when she was interrogated by state security all their questions were about *El Puente*. Who was gay? Who had degenerate counterrevolutionary tendencies?

No, I chatted, I smiled. I entertained. When a couple of girls complained about being harassed and asked me what to do when they got called *tortilleras* in the street, I suggested they handle it the New York way, and say, "¿Y qué? So what if I am? You got a problem with that?" We all knew they wouldn't do it, but it seemed to make them happy knowing somebody somewhere could talk back.

29.

I came back with different eyes, went into the Key Foods and had to walk right out, overwhelmed and a little disgusted by the gigantic slabs of pink salmon. Mounds of dimpled oranges. Entire shelves of plastic sacks of perfectly polished unbroken Uncle Ben's rice. The sidewalks were dangerously smooth. And compared to Cubans, the people were incredibly fat. And loud. Like a bunch of fat parrots chattering away. Despite the threat of TIPS, they still finished one sentence, went on to the next, then started another, spilling their absolute guts in the middle of the streets where anybody at all could hear them.

All we brought back was a bottle of rum and a handful of cigars. I found Al in front of the laundromat and gave him a big fat one, along with a pinch of Cuban dirt that he wanted for his secret mojo bag. We had a couple of friends over and lit a few. The smoke smelled good at first, all earthy, reminding me of that time my grandmother took me to the Kentucky State Fair and drug me around to see the biggest zucchinis and fanciest quilts, which were right next to these poles hanging with glistening brown tobacco. But when I woke up the next morning, the whole house still reeked, and my mouth tasted worse than vomit.

We all knew there was going to be another war. In Iraq, this time. Homeland Security kept issuing alerts, and Bush & Co. would follow them up with an exhortation to unite against that tyrant Saddam Hussein, who was responsible for everything bad in the world. He had secret weapons of mass destruction, secret bunkers, secret agents all writing in invisible ink, and training invisible missiles at us, subverting citizens. Like José Padilla. The guy was paraded around as if he were the biggest threat to Western civilization since Osama rode into the sunset, not just a small-time Chicago gangbanger who converted to Islam and got caught up in events way bigger than him. He actually hadn't lifted a finger when the government designated him an enemy combatant and dumped him into a military brig. We found out years later he got held in solitary with plenty of "enhanced" techniques that turned the guy into one big twitch. Yeah, Saddam and his minions were responsible for everything, just like Uncle Sam was the villain in Cuba. Only there, people had begun to roll their eyes at the propaganda. They knew who to blame.

I could feel it all accumulating, attaching to me like flies attach themselves to those gluey ribbons and die there. I tried to understand: "This is what America is, now," I told myself. "This is what I am. An American." I didn't know what that meant. It was more mysterious to me by far than what it meant to be a lesbian. I quit watching TV, again. I didn't read the newspapers that made your fingers all inky anyway. Just peeked at headlines online. Walked around with my guts as knotty as my brain. Got these incredible pains that had me bent over in the street looking worse than any drunk.

On February 15, 2003, we put on our warmest clothes and took the subway uptown towards the UN. There was supposed to be a big antiwar rally. No march, because the city had refused a permit, even if Bloomberg was mayor by then. We tried one street, then another. All were clogged with crowds. Cops had put up blockades, trying to prevent the demo from turning into a march. Later we heard they brought in the horses and trampled a few people, pepper-sprayed others, arrested a couple hundred who were mostly trying to get the hell out of there.

If you looked, you could still see the smoke rising downtown in two faint wisps.

Trapped, people started holding their rallies on whatever street corner they found themselves. I saw student groups and unions, people with enormous puppets. A lot of signs about Big Oil. Most people figured we were going into Iraq to get control of the oil fields for Cheney's old company Halliburton. Others thought Bush Jr. was trying to handle his father's unfinished business from the first Gulf War. I warmed my video camera inside my coat, shot a few minutes, then gave it up. We milled around, circling and freezing and stomping our feet and thwacking our hands together, before crawling back into the subway.

The organizers numbered us at three or four hundred thousand, which seemed a lot until we read that three million came out in Rome. A million and a half in Madrid. A million in London. All those people who had been horrified when they saw the planes hit the Towers were taking to the streets to beg us to stay home. Spain's Prime Minister Aznar and Britain's Tony Blair would be casualties later, kicked out of office at the first chance people got for being Bush's little warmongering lapdogs.

Maybe it would have been different if we'd come back the next day and the next day and the next, paralyzing our cities, like they'd do years later in Egypt, in Tunisia. And a couple times a year in France. But maybe not. When it came to Bush, news analysts had been using the word *unilateral* since he'd withdrawn from the ABM Treaty and the Kyoto Protocol. After the UN wouldn't approve his dirty little war, and he tried to blame the French, Bush offered an address stating we'd go it alone to protect ourselves. The new buzzword was *preventive*. As in "preventive war." It had ripples around the world. But instead of deposing tyrants, it unleashed them. While the global media had its eyes on Iraq, Cuba took its own preventive action, tossing seventy-five people in jail, including twenty-nine independent journalists, a bunch of human rights activists, and a couple of people who had set up libraries in their houses with banned books like *Animal Farm*. They'd rot in jail for a decade. In Russia, Putin went after his own enemies.

There were a few more days of international protests against the war, but they were bigger in Europe than in the United States, especially once bombs started falling on March 19. In New York, two hundred thousand took to the streets, half the number of the month before. The war didn't go well. American troops had been promised it would go quickly, and they would be greeted by Iraqi kids handing them bouquets of flowers, but they just weren't. Some even fired back. And pretty quickly soldiers were changing their view of Iraqis from poor oppressed victims to enemy combatants. You could tell Iraq was going to be another Palestine or Belfast, only bigger.

I had cousins in the military and they were sent over. My sister Kim had a troubled kid who didn't want to finish school or find a job, and she made him join the army, too, even though it meant hiding his history of mental illness. I could imagine all too well what the country was doing in my name.

In New York, my friend Al was dying. He'd been in the navy during Nam and gone to the VA, I think, with an infected toe-nail. He warned them to be careful. He had diabetes. But they screwed around, and a week later he had an infection and they had to chop half his foot off. There was the cancer, too. Lumps growing everywhere. I followed him from hospital to hospital, visiting when I could force myself, which was only every two or three weeks, though his other friends were even worse. There was this really good hospital in the Bronx where they'd give you wine with dinner if you wanted, but it was more of a hospice, and he wasn't terminating fast enough for them, so he got the boot and ended up at a nursing home on the Lower East Side. It stank of urine and shit and disinfectant, and the nurses were these evil West Indian women who would sit around blabbing about what they would do with machetes and gasoline and lighters if they caught themselves some faggots, some batty-boys. Like the songs said, "Boom Boom Bye" and "Bad Man Chi Chi Man." It was the first time in his life Al stayed in the closet. And I couldn't save him.

After that, it was back to the VA, where he swapped smokes with the other vets and tried to take a taxi to his apartment, just one last glimpse before he died, of the place stacked with photos, the darkroom. His home. He crawled up the stairs but only made it to the fourth or fifth floor before he was crying so hard with pain that his neighbors called an ambulance, and it hauled him back. I'd bring him stuff to eat, but he couldn't keep it down. It was the gesture he wanted. Like he'd grab my hand and hang on to it, desperate to be touched with anything resembling kindness. I agreed to put lotion on his back. When I smeared it around, chunks of scaly, gray skin came off on my hand. Al. Al. I met his sister or cousin or somebody when he was hooked up to the respirator. Told her how great he was. Used the word *gay* a few thousand times.

They had a memorial service at St. Mark's. Afterwards, his relatives and friends absconded with his rings. Other vultures had already gotten ahold of his estate, which was supposed to benefit queer children. They've shown his photos of the piers in a lot of exhibits since then, but I don't think gay kids ever saw a dime. His skin is under my fingernails still. That ashy-gray wizened back. Vulnerable to the hands of enemies. It was a few months after that, in the spring of 2004, that the photos started circulating of all those naked prisoners at Guantánamo and Abu Ghraib—filthy, piled up on each other in obscene pyramids, collared like dogs, with U.S. soldiers standing over them, giving a big thumbs up, proud as fishermen with a ten-foot marlin. Lots of Americans seemed to think it was okay. If we're good people, anything we do is good, too.

I reread James Baldwin, who declared it made sense to become "tough and philosophical concerning destruction and death, for this is what most of mankind has been best at since we have heard of man.... But it is not permissible that the authors of devastation should also be innocent. It is the innocence which constitutes the crime."

I remember fumbling around in my closet for a cigar box that had tarot cards and dusty fossils, a tiny gold cross this girl Lisa gave me at Myers Middle when I was still a twelve-year-old girl talking quietly about salvation and joy. I loved those fossils. Serrated teeth of ancient sharks. Remnants of plants that I'd gotten from a construction site in Florida once when they had the bulldozers in. I rolled them around in my hands like bones and tried to imagine time. Tried to put things in perspective. This America we live in is just a blip, I told myself. Full of tiny, transitory creatures.

But even a fly with its life cycle of thirty days or so from larva to adult resents the smashing fist. And I was neither the fly nor the fist with my own independent fate. I was powerless to stop anything, but still a part of the destruction like the tail on a rampaging bull. Faustina called in tears. America was getting too much like Cuba. Ana couldn't stop talking. About Bush. What we were doing to the Constitution, which had its flaws but was better than anything else going. I'd look at her tortured face while her mouth moved and big heart broke. She read all the papers of the world, wrote little, watched the news full of the battered bodies of all those men while we stood and watched. What did that silence make us? What were we doing to Iraq? What were we making of the kids we sent over there?

The bulletin boards were full of Bush bashers. But this wasn't entirely on him. The problem was all of us, offering our submission and consent by our silence. Which was like Cuba, too. Nobody called for a demo. Nobody took to the streets like they had trying to prevent the Iraq War, or even for Diallo, for Matthew Shepard. I was as bad as anybody. I wrote a couple of articles, but what I really wanted was for Ana to shut up already. But she never did. It was unbearable. I'd've chewed off a paw, left it in the trap to get out of there. I stood it for another year, rooting for the underdog Red Sox in the playoffs with the Yankees, hoping their victory was a sign, but Bush was reelected. Pro-torture Alberto Gonzales was confirmed as Attorney General of the United States. "Let's go to Paris for a year," I said finally.

A couple of days later, we started looking for a swap. It didn't take long, though Véronique tried to talk us out of it once she saw our place. "You understand my apartment is very small."

"We get it."

"Really small compared to this."

"It's not a problem."

"The whole thing could fit in your living room. Twice."

I applied for a Schengen visa and shut myself in the car with Berlitz tapes, snickering at the sounds my voice made in French. I loaded up an iPod with Cuban music and bluegrass. From Kathryn I borrowed Johnny Cash and that Icelandic art rocker Björk. Tried to find shoes that weren't sneakers so at least we wouldn't stick out as tourists. Bought tapes for the video camera. Speakers for the iPod. Backed up the computers. We gave a neighbor our car, shoved everything of value into one closet between us, and went.

.

IV. VIVAS TO THOSE WHO HAVE FAILED

It is unpractical, and it goes against human nature.
This is why it is worth carrying out, and that is why
one proposes it. For what is a practical scheme? A
practical scheme is either a scheme that is already
in existence, or a scheme that could be carried out
under existing conditions. But it is exactly the existing
conditions that one objects to; and any scheme that
could accept these conditions is wrong and foolish.

—OScar Wilde,
The Soul of Man under Socialism

30.

Véronique was right. The apartment was tiny. The kitchen no bigger than a bathroom stall, the toilet instructive, teaching me my first new word, *fuite*. Leak. Also, escape. We walked from dawn until dusk as if we were still in flight, returning only for Ana's quick translations and to sleep. The city smelled of sun and ripe fruit. It didn't rain for weeks. When we got hungry, we'd pop into a bakery and grab a croissant or baguette stuffed with *saucisson* or cheese. When we were tired, we'd sit in some crumbling church and listen to organists practicing on ancient tubes. Or slump in cold green metal chairs at the Luxembourg Gardens. The manicured trees didn't bother me anymore. I liked their knobby fists, the children pushing boats across a tiny lake with poles. I'd stop in front of *Le Triomphe de Silène,* watch Dionysus's drunken tutor try to get on the mule. We'd visit the bee-hives, greet the creatures aimed toward light, then walk to the little orchard of apples and pears. Even persimmons unfurled their bright green leaves.

In the afternoon, we'd stop for a beer or glass of wine and sit at a café watching the French go by. They seemed so serene, done with their guillotines and massacres and prayer break-fasts. All they had left were a few client states and the dirty linen of old men. We saw women riding bikes in high heels, pedestrians with their closed, impassive, but interested faces. Up at the bar, where it was cheapest, men with red noses stood arguing mildly over soccer or politics, or reading the paper, and sending up putrid smoke. We took refuge outside, even in win-ter, so we could breathe.

Sometimes in the subway we'd see a black kid, like the ones in Havana, uncomfortable in his new baggy jeans and bling. The white people on the platform would move away, not understanding he was just trying it on, like a young poet from Kentucky might sometimes sound like John Donne, sometimes Allen Ginsberg. Véronique's mom got this girl Babette to take us around at night in her enormous British checkered cab. Drunk from a picnic basket with wine and snacks, I stared at all the blazing palaces and cathedrals and hotels of the City of Light that were too beautiful to bear, and I started to bellow the one phrase I'd learned in case I was attacked as a Yank, "Je suis la bête américaine" (I'm the American beast), which Babette thought was hilarious and got me to say over and over.

Despite myself, little thready roots probed the soil. There was this skyscraper everybody hated for its ugly box-like shape rising out of nowhere, the Tower of Montparnasse. I imprinted on it like a baby bird. If I looked through our bedroom window at night, I could catch a glimpse of its lights. I imagined its twins.

Sundays were slow and empty when almost everything shut down. We'd get croissants. Maybe in the afternoon we'd turn on some music, some Al Green, and slow-dance together. Like we were nearly human. Like we loved each other and had permission for just a minute to let the world go to hell while we kissed.

We got library cards, and I took out mysteries and books on cheese and wine, learning a vocabulary of bullets, casings, autopsies, fog, vintages, varietals, mold, and molds. I listened to the radio half-heartedly picking out words. I didn't really want to understand French and mess up the pure, pure music of the human voice. Still, it happened. The people at the *épicerie* recognized me. Then the woman at the vegetable stand. And a neighbor who knew who I was but ignored me. Eventually, I registered with the prefecture, got X-rays made of my lungs, was duly interviewed (hoarse from screaming at a soccer game), produced proof of (borrowed) financial resources, swore up and down that I wouldn't look for a job, and was awarded a visa.

Ana called her friend Harriet Hirshorn, who had hooked up with a French girl, Marie de Cenival, and moved there before us. They were living near the Gare de l'Est along with Marie's teenage kid, Léa. I'd met Harriet once or twice at the Avengers and Dyke TV. She was this short, thin video maker with long blonde curly hair. We celebrated the Fourth of July together at the Luxembourg, where they gave a free showing of *Broken Blossoms,* the silent film with Lillian Gish and Richard Barthelmess as Cheng Huan, who saves her from her abusive alcoholic father and redeems the Asian race. I offered a profession of my fading American faith in the form of potato salad and hotdogs, which we gobbled as we waited. Surely, the truth would become self-evident again.

On the Fourteenth of July, we celebrated France's national day with liberty, equality, and fraternity, and bloody rage. "To arms, citizens! Let's march." We went to see the fireworks that night. Waiting, I had the impulse to reach out, participate. "The mosquitoes are awful," I said to an older lady near us in my halting French. "That's true," she agreed.

A week or two later, we all ate dinner at Chris and Giang's. I'd forgotten they had lent us their old apartment ten, twelve years before on our first trip to Paris. Since then they'd moved to a place near the Bastille with the Scientology headquarters across the street. We stared at it for a while but didn't see anything secret. Their hall was full of golf clubs and tennis racquets. We mostly spoke English, but they encouraged me to try my French. I'd blurt something out, then feel like an asshole making those strange sounds. Giang, a Vietnamese American brainiac, tortured me about my pronunciation of the vowels in *moules* (mussels). But I teased her back about her haircut, and just like that we became friends.

I started to work again, revising a book on Cuba, writing for *The Gully,* looking for grants. Words began to return to Ana, too, after we clocked enough miles circling the city. I pretended not to notice that she disappeared sometimes with a notebook. The days shortened. It started to rain. We had drafty windows.

One morning in late October the radio announced "disturbances" in a couple of *banlieues,* outlying neighborhoods where poor immigrants and their French descendants were shunted off. Two black teenagers running from ID-checking cops climbed a fence into an electrical substation and got electrocuted. Afterwards, there were a few large demos protesting racism and profiling and unemployment before the whole thing degenerated, and across the country young men of color started in on the French national sport of burning cars and breaking the shop windows of their own neighbors as a kind of autoimmune disease. It escalated for days until a group of youths in the Paris suburb of Sevran attacked a bus loaded with passengers. A disabled woman couldn't get out, and one kid doused her with gas and then threw in a Molotov cocktail. She survived, but with horrible burns. Nothing happened in our fancy corner of Paris. If we hadn't read the news online or listened to the radio, we wouldn't have noticed the difference. There was just a little shattered glass around one or two bus stops.

Ana wanted to go out to Clichy-sous-Bois and report on the riots for *The Gully,* but I threw a small fit remembering the dust-covered sight of her after she ran from a falling World Trade Center. Later on, though, we went to a community meeting out in one of the *banlieues* to hear a speaker who had something to do with Muslims and women. They had a dinner first, and we ate a whole Vietnamese meal with soup, then rice noodles, *bo bun.* And wine of course. They collected ten euros each. And we talked to a skinny imam who declared he was a feminist and lectured us at length. "A secular state is so important," he said, "especially for women. France already has a problem with misogyny. The last thing they need is conservative Muslims getting free reign. You heard about the woman in the suburb? Splashing acid on her for uncovering her face? Just terrible. Did you go to the march put on by *Ni putes, ni soumises*?" Neither whores nor doormats.

He was almost the only man there among the women of North African and East Asian descent. They were barely considered citizens by white French people but seemed unmistakably Gaulish to me. The way they organized things and argued and instructed. French people (like Cubans) are always explaining. That I even noticed was a sign I was becoming something more than a tourist, no matter how much I wanted to stay superfluous, let others agitate.

I liked being foreign. An undifferentiated American. Like James Baldwin and Gertrude Stein, I needed distance. I should have been warned when I began *The Gully* how painful it was to write as an American, an embattled queer. Every word you write about hate and violence will trace its own wound. I'd still double over with cramps in the street, practically crawl into a seat on the metro. Ana would haul me back home and up the narrow stairs past the glaring concierge and a puzzled, mossy statue of Neptune, god of the sea. Once, I woke up and couldn't open my eyes. There was this incredible gunk shooting out my pink eyes. A doctor made a house call, diagnosed conjunctivitis, and gave me a prescription for a bunch of orange drops. He only charged about sixty bucks. I staggered around with my hands out like you do in the dark.

I should have gone back to grad school, I thought. Gotten a job like Amy, who'd made a tidy sum with her stock options before the tech bubble burst. Sometimes I blamed Ana. I'd never have started *The Gully* if not for her continual rants about Elián. It was futile, anyway. We published the same stories over and over. Black men dead at the hands of cops. Dead queers. Dead civilians in Iraq and Afghanistan with their arms and legs blown off. Should I name the dead? Daniel Pearl, Pim Fortuyn, Sakia Gunn, all killed because of who they were. Then there was

Al, gone, too. In New York queers mobilized crowds against a white comedian doing blackface while ignoring a visit from Robert Mugabe, who incited violence against us, actually killed real black queers, slaughtered his opponents of all orientations. No gully in the rock. And for that I was broke in a world where, as Virgina Woolf wrote, only money dignifies work.

All I wanted to do was to walk, and sit, and swallow the beautiful sky. Even when Ana started spending her days at the library, we'd still stroll after dinner in the growing dark. Every shop window was as carefully composed as the Luxembourg Gardens. At the Seine, lights flickered across the black water. And the clouds were monstrously gray and white in the purple sky. You could imagine gods up there. They were doing Wagner that year at the Paris Opera, the whole Ring cycle with Robert Wilson directing. Ana splurged on tickets. And we saw every act of every opera from the forging of the ring to the Twilight of the Gods. Which seemed apropos of everything.

Then in February (now 2006), Ilan Halimi died. He was a young Jewish man who worked in a cell phone store. His kidnappers, the Gang of Barbarians, were mostly young African immigrants or their descendants who figured one of *them* can come up with some dough. For twenty-four days, they hurt him every way they could think of. Then they set him on fire and dumped his ravaged body by some railroad tracks. He wasn't quite dead yet. But almost. The cops tried to cover things up. And it took a while for journalists to break the story of the anti-Jewish rants the Barbarians made during ransom calls, the Muslim prayers they recited, and videos they made showing Ilan blindfolded with a gun to his head like the ones Iraqi kidnappers put out. The neighbors knew the whole time and did nothing. Some got in on the act.

We went to an SOS Racisme march on February 26. There were a lot of people. As many as fifty thousand. Most of the marchers seemed to be Jews, as if the rest of the city didn't care, despite all the plaques in front of elementary schools about deported children. On the rue du Temple I used to pass a panel to Raoul Naudet, resistance member, next to a window full of handbags. He lived in the building before he got arrested and exterminated in Mauthausen in 1942. It was a peculiar experience, being in a march like that in Paris. Probably some of the other people on our right and left had parents, or aunts and uncles or grandparents, who had been rounded up by the Vichy government or ratted out by their French Christian neighbors and sent to the camps. Ana wore a tag with a big pink triangle that said in French "Enough hate."

I had a sudden sense of the joint frailty of our human bodies, how easy it would be with a few guns to herd us all into cattle cars and kill us—that is, if you first reimagined us as animals. And if we continued to behave as humans, constrained by politeness, and respect, and our own optimism. We know we are humans like you, after all. Not beasts. You couldn't possibly...

Some teenage boys started running through the crowd, shouting and shoving and waving Israeli flags and Jewish Defense League banners. They had handkerchiefs drawn up over their faces like guerillas. At first, they just seemed high-spirited, asserting some power after years of being harassed. Then we heard the sound of breaking store windows. Some of the older protesters were shaken. Later, a Muslim shopkeeper was roughed up and a couple of passersby. It's so easy to become the thing you hate. Choose the opposite role for the moment that history repeats.

When spring rolled around, I decided to retire *The Gully*. Clear my head. Try to make some money for a change. I broke the news to Ana, then Amy, who was attending a music college in Sweden. We redesigned the thing and put it to bed on April 3, 2006, after more than six years. I shredded the book I'd been trying to write on Cuba, and the ridiculous mystery.

I turned forty. For my birthday, Véronique's mom arranged a boat trip around Paris at dusk. Lights shimmered on the water. The gold of my favorite, fantastical bridge glowed. We shivered and admired. Then drank hot chocolate. A couple of weeks later we headed back to New York, at least for a while.

31.

When I returned to Paris almost a year later, it was more home-coming than flight. A relief to be foreign in a place I actually was. In the East Village, the scraggly, weedy lots down the block had been pimped up to look like suburban office buildings but were actually luxury apartments for the horribly rich. Access to the river was blocked. Pissed-off people didn't take to the streets: they went online and shrieked at anti-Bush sites, which had no discernible impact on his illegal wars, the torture, the domestic spying, the disastrous handling of Katrina.

In the fall, Democrats had finally taken a stand with the midterm message "Vote for us. We're not Republicans." They would have lost again except the GOP's Mark Foley got caught drooling over boy pages. He and his Republican homoscan-dal turned the tide. Not the economy or Iraq or Halliburton or the Constitution lying at the bottom of the American bird-cage. I didn't know why queers were thrilled. Antigay marriage amendments passed in seven out of the eight states at issue, making it twenty-seven states where same-sex marriage was expressly banned.

I belonged back in France. Yearned for it when they threw another riot in the *banlieues,* smashing everything in their paths. So much blab from the elite, and the rest left with either silence or paving stones. Why not try to bash your way into their monologue, change an abstract discourse about jobs and racism and immigration into something a little more real? Maybe with your face on it. Read my lips. Except, except, except...the guys setting stuff on fire were almost always thugs, jumping onto busses with weapons, scaring the crap out of innocent people, their neighbors mostly, just so they could drive the thing a few yards away and set it on fire. It reeked of macho satisfaction. Look what I did. My fire's bigger than yours. Which I guess is why Bush showed around that picture of Saddam, his face all bloated and dead after the execution.

I got a gig to cover a huge agricultural fair in Paris and went back alone in the spring. The paper was the *Louisville Courier-Journal*. I thought it was hilarious my byline would read "columnist for *Gay City News* in New York." Yes, Missus Cogswell's daughter is a big fucking dyke. Ana was supposed to follow almost immediately. When she got delayed, our swap fell through, and I spent the next couple of months in déjà vu mode, changing neighborhoods as often as I did fresh off the bus in New York. First, Harriet and Marie put me up in their new place in back of Père Lachaise Cemetery. We visited Oscar Wilde's kiss-covered monument, and the bullet holes in the wall where the last rebels of the Paris Commune were lined up and shot. Then I watered plants for three or four weeks at Mathilde's while she went off in a ship to dig up oceanic rocks. She was Marie's cousin, and a dyke, too.

She lived in a high-rise in Belleville with these big drafty windows showing enormous apartment buildings stuffed with immigrants, remnants of the old city, and some pointy church. Clouds would get stuck in the spires and break free in a rage of double and triple rainbows. A block away was an enormous market filled with women from Morocco and Algeria and Senegal. The nearby rue de Belleville changed from West African to Chinese and South Asian, with pockets of white working-class French in between.

To get anywhere, I had to run the gauntlet of old Arab men. They stared at me. Sometimes with indifference. Sometimes hate. Maybe they hated everybody. They wanted to go home but were stuck in Paris. Maybe they just hated me. I wasn't crazy about them either. Some of their sons were brutal assholes, knocking blonde Harriet off her rollerblades. "N'importe quoi!" She was an affront, a high-flying woman. I went to this one Moroccan bakery where the men were unusually nice to me. But then I figured out that they figured I was a guy. They seemed pissed off when they realized the mistake. I went back anyway when I had the nerve because they had these great cheap fried buns full of tuna and olives and boiled eggs. Also, I thought it did them good to see me, with my polite-dyke "Bonjour" and parting "Bon journée" on the way to the Salon de l'Agriculture.

God, I like my fairs, especially ones with wine. Not long after my grandmother died, I dragged Ana and her brother Pablo to a fair in upstate New York and made them look at chickens and eat corndogs and go to a demolition derby. The crowd rose to their feet and covered their hearts as a canned soprano wailed "The Star Spangled Banner," and the waiting cars below shot flames from things that looked like organ pipes. Then Pablo and I rode something that bucked and curved and screwed so thoroughly with my equilibrium I was still nauseated the next day. That's Amurrica.

Chirac opened the fair as current president, nostalgic that this was his last time to kiss old Bessy between her well-groomed bovine ears before somebody else took over. I pressed through the scrum of journalists and bodyguards who all pretended that it was perfectly normal to see this power-suited politico surrounded by hay and manure, and the ruddy white faces of farmers who spent all their days outdoors. This was the message: that at heart, France was still some rural idyll where even the most sophisticated Parisian is only one step from a farm where milkmaids frolic and grandpa distills his own fruit spirits. No matter that ninety percent of the French shop in supermarkets and kids in the *banlieues* speak only the language of burning cars.

All the presidential candidates came afterwards. Nicolas Sarkozy was a law-and-order guy, like Giuliani, and about as bad tempered. When he got heckled from the crowd about his handling of the 2005 riots, he shot back, "Shut up, you stupid asshole." It made headlines for days. Ségolène Royale was there, too, after squeaking through the primaries to be the Socialist candidate. And I stood in line with the other journalists for a chance to video her chewing steak with the beef lobby.

I got pulled into her campaign when Mathilde came back and I stayed with Harriet and Marie again. It had taken them a while to get onboard, even if Ségo was gay friendly. Maybe because the whole stiletto heel thing doesn't go over well with dykes. Or because she spoke out against crime, which always horrifies the bourgie Left, and got painted as a provincial mother of four sure to drag the Party to the Right. Ségo did grow up in a right-wing Catholic family with a father who kept his sons in military buzz cuts, but I grew up Southern Baptist in Kentucky, so what does that prove? I liked her message that France was for everybody.

The misogynist hacks in her own Socialist Party were even more skeptical than the dykes. Former PM Lionel Jospin was such a dick that when he withdrew from the primaries, he declared he'd support anybody but "la candidate," the female candidate. Ségo's only chance was to reach out to ordinary people, taking a page from Hillary Clinton's senatorial campaign with "listening tours" and town hall–style meetings. "I've become convinced that citizens . . . are the only real legitimate 'experts' on any of the questions facing us."

That's when I fell in love—with that word *citizen*. In the United States, we don't use it much unless we're talking about immigration. National politicians usually stick to "My fellow Americans," implying a kind of geographical craps game you just happened to be a part of. In France, politicians all said, "My fellow citizens," draping us with obligations, and making me feel like a part of this enormous human project whose goal still is to construct a state aiming toward Liberty, Equality, Fraternity.

It worked for Ségo, anyway. She packed whole stadiums. People from the *banlieues* cheered next to formerly cynical French dykes. Even the jocks got involved, like Chris and Giang, their daughters behind them, already in scarves, looked warily at brothers half their age but already with sharp little fists. These were the girls glad to go to French public schools where they could skip the head schmatta only because it was banned, be like everybody else. It's never them you see in riots. Though maybe you should.

I tried not to see them. Had my own problems. I'd get harassed by the guards at the Monoprix up at Place des Fêtes. They'd take one look at my German army fatigues and spiky dyke hair and stop me at the door. "You have to check your backpack." And my French was good enough to scream at them, "Why pick on me when you just let that other woman go by? She had a backpack, too, only hers was leather, and she was dressed nicer. Is that it? And what about that handbag there that just slipped by as you hassle me? Hers is three times bigger than my tiny sac. Why didn't you stop her?"

Sometimes people would pause in my defense, though that had its own pitfalls because sometimes they'd start to imply the guards were wrong because they were black. Not because they were assholes. I got tired of the show and walked an extra couple of blocks to the grubby little Monoprix in the other direction where nobody cared if I had one backpack or ten.

Often the nineteenth seemed like Cuba, a neighborhood f men, and I had no business there. There were a lot of West frican guys who lived in single rooms. I'd see them in the laun- omat doing their own wash for the first time ever, struggling h the machines. There were transgendered women, too, aking Latin American Spanish. North African guys, both slims and Jews, would walk back and forth on the sidewalk, ig to get glimpses of them. Sometimes we'd hear about dy fights between rival gangs. All that testosterone put to ise under that ascending star Sarkozy, who got his own off setting quotas for deporting undocumented immi- , twenty-five thousand by the end of the year, and they ehind schedule.

and their friend Valérie, a book restorer that I'd started to hang out with sometimes. I'd meet her at her workshop full of old paper and glue pots and weights, then we'd pick up sandwiches and play boules at the Roman Arena nearby.

I joined them when they went flyering at the Gare de Lyon. I felt like a citizen myself, at least of Paris. I'd earned my papers walking the streets, arguing in cafés, marching for Ilan Halimi. Hell, I patted cows at the fair. Knew where dozens of public libraries were and all the Monoprix supermarkets. I even asked Véronique's mom to ask St. Geneviève—who watches over the city—to bring Ana back safe and sound. This was my fight, too. Even if I hoped nobody would hear my accent and accuse me of interfering where I didn't belong.

Luckily, people just took the damn pamphlets and didn't bother me, though Chris got harangued a couple times by a certain kind of white man who would get all red-faced when he saw Ségo's face on the brochure. Or maybe it was Marie who got called "Dirty cunt," "filthy whore." It was around then that I woke up one night to howling from the other room. Harriet was out of town, and Marie had been out with a fag friend. They went to a gay bar where they just had time to order a drink before this big brutal bouncer said Marie had to go, and when she asked why, just grabbed her and tossed her out. They didn't want any females in there. His fat fingers left incredible bruises. Distracted, she had an accident on her rollerblades and broke her wrist—hence the howling. She had to have surgery and a couple of pins. I harassed the nurses in my bad French, "Be careful. She has trouble with anesthesia. Almost died once. Understand?" After that, Marie worked harder than ever for Ségolène.

On election night, we all went to a party at Chris and Giang's. We were hopeful at first, drinking wine, making jokes, then the depressing results poured in. Tears rolled down Giang's face as Ségo gave her concession speech on a balcony outside her headquarters, promising she wouldn't disappear. Was in it for the long haul. And she did hold more public meetings trying to find a new direction, but she was trapped by the Socialist ball and chain. All that misogyny.

Heading to the train to go home after the party, I got caught in a demo at the Bastille, yanked my camera out of its case, and started to film. The cops were heaving tear gas at protesters, lanky white boys mostly, a few girls. The thin column with the gold figure on top disappeared in smoke, along with the cops moving around behind it. The gas wasn't so close at first, just a faint burning of lungs and eyes. I pulled my shirt up over my mouth. Then one canister hit almost at my feet and I was blinded, stumbling around like I had conjunctivitis again and could only open my eyes for a fraction of a second at a time. I'd get a glimpse of things, then dash away with my eyes shut tight. Life is like that, I thought.

32.

My eyes were still tearing when I got back to our two-room duplex on rue Cadet. "What happened to you?" Ana had just arrived a day or two before, underwhelmed at our new dump that had wires dangling in the hallways. I'd only grabbed it because th decent, cheap places had lines around the block of clean-c white kids with dossiers proving they had good job contract that their parents were stinking rich. Landlords didn't want eigners, even white ones, without fat assets in France.

A couple of days later, when an enormous storm bunch of puddles all over our stuff upstairs, our friend lent us a temporary place in the fifth arrondissemen kids shrieked in the schoolyard behind and kicked ball against our wall. We'd sit drinking at the chear borhood place, L'Inévitable. The Institut du Monde nearby, and we'd see young Muslim women in and expensive shoes sailing down the street wi clenched. I figured some were true believers; ot' their headscarves to flip the bird at French soc voted for Ségo, dragging their mothers and g rallies, willing to be citizens of a France that in just demanding obligations but sharing righ†

Those young Muslim women were a worl ures covered head to toe in black who woul when we finally found a place in the nir fat and ravaged and mute. Teeth were r million years old but were probably my a like mules, used as breeders. They hadr

By then I wasn't a visitor anymore, no matter what my visa said. I got interested in immigrant issues, like the danger of open windows. There was that Russian kid who cracked his head open falling from one while trying to elude police. The North African man slipping from a window ledge and fracturing his leg. A Chinese woman ended up in a coma after plunging from a window. She got spooked, thinking they were coming for her when the cops started knocking on the door of a neighboring apartment. At least Parisians were a little like us East Village types who used to scream at cops and take badge numbers when they were rousting young men in the neighborhood. And in Paris, passersby would gather spontaneously to stop cops as they moved in for raids. Passengers on planes would throw fits when deportees were on them and sometimes ground flights for hours.

Ana and I went to a couple of marches. I'd take my video camera, and once a woman gave me a teary, "Thanks for coming. No one is paying attention." Looking around, I thought about a doctor who told me his usual gig was working with poor immigrants. "You never know what you're going to see when they undress. Old bullet wounds. Scars from machetes. Others scars you can't see. You should write about that." Harriet and Marie went, too. Marie was an AIDS activist with Sidaction and did a lot of work in Africa. She saw the effect of Sarko's policies. But she and Harriet were just as angry at the Socialists. All the misogyny the election had uncovered—it poisoned everything.

Marie finally circulated an e-mail asking if any other women out there were just as pissed off and got enough responses to form La Barbe, which means the Beard, but also Enough. Marie had been in ACT UP Paris. Harriet in the Avengers and Dyke TV, and a million feminist groups. They were also fans of Billionaires for Bush, who had punked the Republicans. La Barbe was based on an equally simple idea: invading men's spaces like board meetings, slapping on beards, then "congratulating" the assholes for keeping out girls.

Before the first action, Harriet and Marie came over and squeezed themselves around our tiny table to eat. "You guys should participate." I felt guilty but declined. I had all the confrontation I could handle every time I left the house, and my papers weren't quite in order. I was suddenly the cautious immigrant. I also wanted to think about other means of resistance that cost me less. Writing, thinking, art maybe. My brain as a laboratory. Ana might have been interested in the group if it were for dykes, but it wasn't. She also didn't want to be the one immigrant. The one person of color. Besides, she'd already done her bit for France the first time she'd lived there, working in women's and gay groups, Les Gouines Rouges, the Red Dykes. She also didn't want to lose focus on her book. She'd finally let me take a look, six or seven drafts on. It was as strange and angry as *The Invisible Man*. And hilarious in a bitter Rabelaisian sort of way.

It seemed timely. Still does. How it grapples with identity. The '08 presidential election was under way in the United States. And Hillary Clinton, the first serious female candidate for the Democratic spot, got treated about as well as Ségolène in France. *South Park* writers hid nuclear weapons in Clinton's cartoon vagina, and men howled their disgust at Clinton's shrieking harpy, schoolmarmy voice, those fat, childbearing, repulsive hips. But then I noticed plenty of dykes in the chorus even if they had hips, too. And were furious and shrill and aging fast.

Not that she was perfectly clean. Every now and then, one of Clinton's people would float a trial balloon mentioning offensively how well-spoken Obama was or something. But then even Obama's guys indulged in a little immigrant bashing, briefly trying to demonize Clinton's South Asian contributors as economic bogeymen, dumping American workers for Indian techies.

And when Sarah Palin got picked as John McCain's VP, NOW actually issued a press release to say they didn't support women candidates just because they were women. Because and their friend Valérie, a book restorer that I'd started to hang out with sometimes. I'd meet her at her workshop full of old paper and glue pots and weights, then we'd pick up sandwiches and play boules at the Roman Arena nearby.

I joined them when they went flyering at the Gare de Lyon. I felt like a citizen myself, at least of Paris. I'd earned my papers walking the streets, arguing in cafés, marching for Ilan Halimi. Hell, I patted cows at the fair. Knew where dozens of public libraries were and all the Monoprix supermarkets. I even asked Véronique's mom to ask St. Geneviève—who watches over the city—to bring Ana back safe and sound. This was my fight, too. Even if I hoped nobody would hear my accent and accuse me of interfering where I didn't belong.

Luckily, people just took the damn pamphlets and didn't bother me, though Chris got harangued a couple times by a certain kind of white man who would get all red-faced when he saw Ségo's face on the brochure. Or maybe it was Marie who got called "Dirty cunt," "filthy whore." It was around then that I woke up one night to howling from the other room. Harriet was out of town, and Marie had been out with a fag friend. They went to a gay bar where they just had time to order a drink before this big brutal bouncer said Marie had to go, and when she asked why, just grabbed her and tossed her out. They didn't want any females in there. His fat fingers left incredible bruises. Distracted, she had an accident on her rollerblades and broke her wrist—hence the howling. She had to have surgery and a couple of pins. I harassed the nurses in my bad French, "Be careful. She has trouble with anesthesia. Almost died once. Understand?" After that, Marie worked harder than ever for Ségolène.

On election night, we all went to a party at Chris and Giang's. We were hopeful at first, drinking wine, making jokes, then the depressing results poured in. Tears rolled down Giang's face as Ségo gave her concession speech on a balcony outside her headquarters, promising she wouldn't disappear. Was in it for the long haul. And she did hold more public meetings trying to find a new direction, but she was trapped by the Socialist ball and chain. All that misogyny.

Heading to the train to go home after the party, I got caught in a demo at the Bastille, yanked my camera out of its case, and started to film. The cops were heaving tear gas at protesters, lanky white boys mostly, a few girls. The thin column with the gold figure on top disappeared in smoke, along with the cops moving around behind it. The gas wasn't so close at first, just a faint burning of lungs and eyes. I pulled my shirt up over my mouth. Then one canister hit almost at my feet and I was blinded, stumbling around like I had conjunctivitis again and could only open my eyes for a fraction of a second at a time. I'd get a glimpse of things, then dash away with my eyes shut tight. Life is like that, I thought.

32.

My eyes were still tearing when I got back to our two-room duplex on rue Cadet. "What happened to you?" Ana had just arrived a day or two before, underwhelmed at our new dump that had wires dangling in the hallways. I'd only grabbed it because the decent, cheap places had lines around the block of clean-cut white kids with dossiers proving they had good job contracts or that their parents were stinking rich. Landlords didn't want foreigners, even white ones, without fat assets in France.

A couple of days later, when an enormous storm left a bunch of puddles all over our stuff upstairs, our friend Valérie lent us a temporary place in the fifth arrondissement. School kids shrieked in the schoolyard behind and kicked a soccer ball against our wall. We'd sit drinking at the cheapest neighborhood place, L'Inévitable. The Institut du Monde Arabe was nearby, and we'd see young Muslim women in headscarves and expensive shoes sailing down the street with their fists clenched. I figured some were true believers; others just used their headscarves to flip the bird at French society. Many had voted for Ségo, dragging their mothers and grandmothers to rallies, willing to be citizens of a France that included them, not just demanding obligations but sharing rights.

Those young Muslim women were a world away from the figures covered head to toe in black who would pass by sometimes when we finally found a place in the nineteenth. These were fat and ravaged and mute. Teeth were missing. They looked a million years old but were probably my age. They'd been worked like mules, used as breeders. They hadn't chosen anything. And their daughters behind them, already in scarves, looked warily at brothers half their age but already with sharp little fists. These were the girls glad to go to French public schools where they could skip the head schmatta only because it was banned, be like everybody else. It's never them you see in riots. Though maybe you should.

I tried not to see them. Had my own problems. I'd get harassed by the guards at the Monoprix up at Place des Fêtes. They'd take one look at my German army fatigues and spiky dyke hair and stop me at the door. "You have to check your backpack." And my French was good enough to scream at them, "Why pick on me when you just let that other woman go by? She had a backpack, too, only hers was leather, and she was dressed nicer. Is that it? And what about that handbag there that just slipped by as you hassle me? Hers is three times bigger than my tiny sac. Why didn't you stop her?"

Sometimes people would pause in my defense, though that had its own pitfalls because sometimes they'd start to imply the guards were wrong because they were black. Not because they were assholes. I got tired of the show and walked an extra couple of blocks to the grubby little Monoprix in the other direction where nobody cared if I had one backpack or ten.

Often the nineteenth seemed like Cuba, a neighborhood of men, and I had no business there. There were a lot of West African guys who lived in single rooms. I'd see them in the laundromat doing their own wash for the first time ever, struggling with the machines. There were transgendered women, too, speaking Latin American Spanish. North African guys, both Muslims and Jews, would walk back and forth on the sidewalk, trying to get glimpses of them. Sometimes we'd hear about bloody fights between rival gangs. All that testosterone put to bad use under that ascending star Sarkozy, who got his own rocks off setting quotas for deporting undocumented immigrants, twenty-five thousand by the end of the year, and they were behind schedule.

By then I wasn't a visitor anymore, no matter what my visa said. I got interested in immigrant issues, like the danger of open windows. There was that Russian kid who cracked his head open falling from one while trying to elude police. The North African man slipping from a window ledge and fracturing his leg. A Chinese woman ended up in a coma after plunging from a window. She got spooked, thinking they were coming for her when the cops started knocking on the door of a neighboring apartment. At least Parisians were a little like us East Village types who used to scream at cops and take badge numbers when they were rousting young men in the neighborhood. And in Paris, passersby would gather spontaneously to stop cops as they moved in for raids. Passengers on planes would throw fits when deportees were on them and sometimes ground flights for hours.

Ana and I went to a couple of marches. I'd take my video camera, and once a woman gave me a teary, "Thanks for coming. No one is paying attention." Looking around, I thought about a doctor who told me his usual gig was working with poor immigrants. "You never know what you're going to see when they undress. Old bullet wounds. Scars from machetes. Others scars you can't see. You should write about that." Harriet and Marie went, too. Marie was an AIDS activist with Sidaction and did a lot of work in Africa. She saw the effect of Sarko's policies. But she and Harriet were just as angry at the Socialists. All the misogyny the election had uncovered—it poisoned everything.

Marie finally circulated an e-mail asking if any other women out there were just as pissed off and got enough responses to form La Barbe, which means the Beard, but also Enough. Marie had been in ACT UP Paris. Harriet in the Avengers and Dyke TV, and a million feminist groups. They were also fans of Billionaires for Bush, who had punked the Republicans. La Barbe was based on an equally simple idea: invading men's spaces like board meetings, slapping on beards, then "congratulating" the assholes for keeping out girls.

Before the first action, Harriet and Marie came over and squeezed themselves around our tiny table to eat. "You guys should participate." I felt guilty but declined. I had all the confrontation I could handle every time I left the house, and my papers weren't quite in order. I was suddenly the cautious immigrant. I also wanted to think about other means of resistance that cost me less. Writing, thinking, art maybe. My brain as a laboratory. Ana might have been interested in the group if it were for dykes, but it wasn't. She also didn't want to be the one immigrant. The one person of color. Besides, she'd already done her bit for France the first time she'd lived there, working in women's and gay groups, Les Gouines Rouges, the Red Dykes. She also didn't want to lose focus on her book. She'd finally let me take a look, six or seven drafts on. It was as strange and angry as *The Invisible Man*. And hilarious in a bitter Rabelaisian sort of way.

It seemed timely. Still does. How it grapples with identity. The '08 presidential election was under way in the United States. And Hillary Clinton, the first serious female candidate for the Democratic spot, got treated about as well as Ségolène in France. *South Park* writers hid nuclear weapons in Clinton's cartoon vagina, and men howled their disgust at Clinton's shrieking harpy, schoolmarmy voice, those fat, childbearing, repulsive hips. But then I noticed plenty of dykes in the chorus even if they had hips, too. And were furious and shrill and aging fast.

Not that she was perfectly clean. Every now and then, one of Clinton's people would float a trial balloon mentioning offensively how well-spoken Obama was or something. But then even Obama's guys indulged in a little immigrant bashing, briefly trying to demonize Clinton's South Asian contributors as economic bogeymen, dumping American workers for Indian techies.

And when Sarah Palin got picked as John McCain's VP, NOW actually issued a press release to say they didn't support women candidates just because they were women. Because they're apparently the National Organization for Only Those Women Who Agree with All Our Policies. And queers went after queers. Democratic activists yanking Republican fags out of the closet, inciting homophobia that they hoped would blow back against the antigay McCain. At the same time, their candidate in chief, Barack Obama, was campaigning with some of the same gay-hating preachers who supported Bush and promised to dump way more money than the Texan oilman into faith-based programs. Obama would also flip-flop on primary promises and voted for bills broadening the powers of Homeland Security. Which I still hated, even if no one else did.

I got pissed, then even more depressed. Went through a bad patch. My last ties to the United States were frayed and fragile as my new roots in France. My whole way of life was a waste. Should be ended somehow. Killed. Reborn, maybe. Rewritten at least. It's not enough to resist what is.

I thought about Rimbaud who wrote all that luminous poetry and got shot and drank and fucked and made scandals, then fell ostentatiously silent. Camus also went mum on the issue when he got tired of arguing that the French shouldn't shoot all the Arab Algerians or keep them in thrall, and that the Arabs shouldn't force all the French Algerians to flee to a country they'd probably never seen. He advocated for a third way, but nobody listened. Finally, he put down his pen. And that was a message, too. I wanted to do the same, fall silent, women attacking women, queers attacking queers, people of color attacking immigrants. But to do that, and have it mean anything, you have to already have a booming voice. People have to know you exist. And what was I? The girl getting thrown out of the Monoprix. Who never made a dent in anything.

I didn't really belong anywhere, but in the street, deserted football fields, creeks. I wondered if it were a mistake to kill *The Gully,* that whole world I'd made where identity was complex, interwoven with everything, and resistance could mean just opening your mouth. It was the only place my life made sense, though we got it wrong sometimes. Like when we sneered at Bush's "cabinet of color." Even if Powell or Rice were window dressing, what windows they looked out of, preparing the way for Obama. Sarko had done the same thing. Packing his administration with brainy, beautiful, big-mouthed women of color like Rachida Dati, Rama Yade. He even dipped into the Left, recruiting Fadela Amara, a feminist activist from the projects.

But it was too late. I'd put *The Gully* to bed, shredded my books. Allied myself with Gerardo in Cuba with his ellipses and shrugs. I walked obsessively. At night I'd crawl into bed beside Ana and feel the curve of her back under my hand and the heat coming off it, but the sensation would stop at about my wrist. Before, it would have gone all the way past my elbow, and shoulder, clear to the pumping muscle of my heart.

In January, we'd taken the train to the empty forest of Fontainebleau and hiked around the trails using a map we printed out from the Internet. When we were good and lost, we caught a glimpse of a wild boar running through the trees. But all that beauty had nothing to do with me.

In the spring of '08, I was sitting on the couch and saw a bug jump up on my ankle. Then found one in the bed. We'd gotten fleas, *les puces*. We fumigated the whole place, washed every scrap of cloth but were so disgusted we gave notice. And after a couple more weeks, we fled.

33.

By June, after a stint in New York, we'd installed ourselves in two unfurnished rooms in a seventeenth-century building on rue Visconti, a long gray street in Saint-Germain des Près. At the rue de Seine end, there were a couple of cheesy galleries with sculptures that were supposed to be from Benin but arrived one by one in shopping bags carried by shady skinny men. At the other end was a convent. And across from it, Balzac's failed printing concern that cheered me up a little. I wasn't the only writer that sucked at making money.

Tourists clogged most of the cafés nearby, taking discreet pictures of Karl Lagerfeld at the Café de Flore, or posing like Sartre and de Beauvoir in Les Deux Magots, though without the cigarettes, because the smoking ban had just gone into effect. Which meant when Ana and I discovered a cheap café, we could finally sit inside. In the laundromat up rue de Seine, the Spanish and Americans and provincial French would mistake me for an employee and try to give me orders. I'd be nice to them anyway and use every language I knew to explain how the machines worked. "No, that's a washer." And I'd warn them not to leave clothes alone in the dryer because they'd magically disappear.

We'd take refuge in the movie houses and bookstores. They stayed open later than some of the cafés in case you had a sudden urge for the latest Fred Vargas mystery or a reprint of Marx's essay on the French Civil War. Or a translation of Willa Cather. Or a novel by Marie NDiaye. They were all so carefully designed. I'd pick them up just to admire how they fit in my hand. Ready to open my heart to some writer's world. I felt like we belonged, Ana and I. Or should have in a neighborhood that once welcomed Janet Flanner, Colette, and Sylvia Beach. Gertrude Stein had lived not too far away, and she actually got a plaque on her house, though it didn't mention Alice.

And in our own apartment, we had this airshaft-patio sort of thing that had an open brick wall in back. Just behind that was a private park where *über*Sapphist Natalie Clifford Barney had her Temple of Friendship, throwing literary soirées and outrageous parties. A couple of trees were visible over the top of the wall. I remember a peeling sycamore with fat gray leaves and once or twice considered borrowing a ladder from somebody and peeking over. Instead, I'd stare at the bricks and imagine what it was like. Colette running around the neighborhood half-naked with bliss. What would it feel like to be so utterly unself-conscious? I wanted to snog Ana on a street corner. Throw wild parties that scandalized the bourgeoisie that hadn't improved any.

There was that guy on a fancy motorcycle barreling down the sidewalk. When he almost ran over Ana, and we chased him down, he insulted us first as women, then dykes, then foreigners. And the crowd snickered when we called him a misogynist, turned away when we called him a homophobe, and ran back into the cafés to get their smelling salts when we called him a racist xenophobic dickhead who was the shame of France. I missed lesbians. We had our friends, of course, but hardly ever saw dykes on the metro or in the street. At the time, the only two with a national profile were an anonymous couple suing the state for the right to adopt or inseminate. I got teary the night we saw the dyke rocker Beth Ditto do a cheesy music program on TV. She'd gotten chic all of a sudden, and her curvy naked body was on the cover of a fashion magazine.

We created a group, Goudou Explosive (Explosive Dykes), just to march in Pride. I spent two days sewing and painting a red and gold banner fit for a king, bought a bunch of toy trumpets at a novelty shop, and the whole dirty dozen of us from five different countries made a hell of a lot of honking, squealing noise, and every girl in the crowd cheered, demanding our Goudou Explosive stickers and pamphlets, and joining in for several blocks. Marching, the goudou were reminded why they were explosive. One homo on the sideline made snide comments about how well we blew our trumpets and what we could do with them later on. Young straight boys kept dodging in between us as we marched, making equally clichéd suggestions. A fag marshal lectured us about preparing for the moment of silence as if we were infants, while ignoring the big loud float full of men ahead of us. Meanwhile, the two white guys announcing the participants refused to acknowledge we existed until we took a couple of menacing steps toward them, blowing our horns.

Ana and I capped off Pride weekend by attending a neighborhood talk about Barney's Temple of Friendship. But instead of juicy details about crazy liaisons and wild dyke parties, the guy giving the lecture focused on the original, boring owner and dismissed Barney as some rich American dame who gave literary soirées for important straight men. He only hinted at her being a dyke with the coy, "Remy de Gourmont called her the Amazon. I'll leave it to your imagination as to why." So at the end, when he was taking questions, the explosive Ana Simo stood up and asked why he was so reluctant to pronounce the word *lesbian,* and why he ignored Barney's importance in her own right as a literary pioneer and dyke icon. Then the crowd started murmuring, some in favor, some outraged that she'd brought up those dirty lezzies. "What does that have to do with anything?" Though if Barney had been a guy, you can bet the speaker would have mentioned he'd conquered Colette, not to mention Liane de Pougy, the famous courtesan.

Our Internet wasn't working yet, so I went to one of the municipal offices to use their free WiFi and file a story about all this. That's when I discovered that the city of Paris with its gay mayor was blocking every Web page with the words *lesbian, gay,* or *goudou.* You'd get this message declaring it pornographic. All my own articles were censored, my blog apparently obscene. Even the *New York Times'* coverage of the Paris Pride march was ostensibly a threat to public morals and the delicate sensibilities of children. Where were the outraged queers? I wondered. I called up the mayor's office, but they didn't call me back until I'd already written a furious article. Their main point was that Mayor Bertrand Delanoë couldn't be homophobic. "He's gay, you know." "So what?" I said. They unblocked my site, but that was it. The antigay filter stayed.

The fall was cold and gray. We put plastic on the windows, wore the sweaters I knitted obsessively after 9/11. Ana was plotting a new book. I was trying to rediscover my essence, writing for myself, shooting video, changing the equation of the fight. I left messages in the street on little stickers that remained for weeks. *Quand la Beauté défait son corsage, ce n'est pas pour nous. When Beauty unbuttons her shirt, it is not for us.* I was planting my own flag in the city. I exist, I said. Or will.

In the spring we went south to Toulouse. La Barbe had been invited to a lesbian conference, and Harriet and Marie suggested they ask me and Ana to do something on the Lesbian Avengers. The theme was Lesbians and the Weapon of Laughter, and I suspect the organizers in Toulouse expected us to be light and funny, the superheroish dykes from New York. We agreed to do it, but neither of us felt like dykes in France had anything to laugh about. U.S. queers surely didn't. The same day Obama got elected, same-sex marriage got banned in California with the passage of Prop 8. A black man could finally be president, but queers couldn't even file joint taxes. Obama hadn't evolved very far yet on LGBT rights. In fact, he rubbed salt in the wound by inviting Rick Warren to bless his inauguration, even if the reverend had helped roll back AIDS programs in Africa, fueled antigay campaigns in Nigeria and Uganda, unleashed mobs with machetes.

Still, crowds of queers demonstrated after the Prop 8 fiasco. And the press as usual started heralding a new movement, Stonewall 2.0, which would be mobilized by e-mails and tweets, not phone trees. But it fizzled pretty quickly because it wasn't rooted in anything. Our national organizations had stuck to their de-gayed approach: putting nice hets front and center, talking about generic rights, reinforcing the idea we were a bunch of pervs too disgusting to show ourselves. We forgot that we didn't need their permission to knock on doors, stand on street corners. That it paid off to court the poor, and people of color.

It was a case for the Avengers. But the Avengers were dead. Not just dead, but obliterated. After the election, I Googled them, and there almost nothing online except an article of Sara Pursley's in *The Nation* about organizing in Idaho. It should be required reading for every queer activist. The Wikipedia entry was worse than none. There was nothing anywhere about the dozens of chapters worldwide. All those actions. The tens of thousands of dykes who marched behind Lesbian Avenger banners in D.C., New York, and San Francisco. A few cities had Dyke March Web sites, but they rarely mentioned their origins, as if they were ashamed of them. Sometimes I was. All that ugliness at the end. In the beginning, so much hope, and for what?

Getting ready for the conference, I e-mailed Su Friedrich, and she sent me a DVD of *Lesbian Avengers Eat Fire Too.* It was only the second time I'd seen it. I felt a little nervous just slipping it into my laptop. My god, what a Pandora's box. What a relic. We'd gone from the War on Culture to the War on Terror. From my work at *The Gully,* I knew dykes were still in the street, but in Guatemala City or South African townships, not New York. It was ancient history. Almost indecent to watch. But then I started seeing these familiar faces. The Irish dyke Sheila Quinn and cabbie Phyllis Lutsky. The filmmaker Su Friedrich. Ana was there in the Plaza Hotel talking to the camera about the Colorado boycott as a security guard tried to haul her away.

My young, bald self ate fire. I'd forgotten how much fun it was, how brave we were. How much we accomplished going on the offensive, reimagining dykes. "Look at them," I said, when Ana came home from the library. "Just look." We reunited the statue of Alice with Gertrude. We danced in the snow. Twenty thousand dykes marched in D.C. There was such joy on their faces.

But that led almost to a new kind of grief. And a kind of fury. Our history had disappeared. First, Natalie Barney. Then the Avengers. Now, we were even filtered out of the Web, and nobody seemed to notice or care.

The train to Toulouse was late, and the weather was awful. More or less reflecting our mood. Imagine it: trying to work up a smile after all that and find some way to celebrate dykes in a world blessed by Rick Warren. Where the Avengers fighting so long for lesbian visibility had been made invisible themselves. Lesbians were back where they were twenty years before. More like amphibians than citizens. Sitting like frogs in a vast vat of water as the temp slid up to boiling. Sedated with their potlucks and sports associations and conferences and Web sites. Tech advances that shared information at the speed of light but didn't always have ripples in the real world.

We couldn't do it. Laugh.

In fact, we sucked all the air out of the room when we took our place on the panel of activists, which included Madrid's Toxic Lesbians, and Harriet and Marie representing La Barbe, even if it wasn't a dyke thing. With our dueling accents in French, Ana and I went at the audience with sharp sticks. Tried to wake them up. We incited desire, showing video snippets of Avengers taking over Fifth Avenue to protest the murders of Hattie Mae Cohens and Brian Mock, the vast Dyke March in D.C. in '93, and fire-eaters in front of the White House. We even showed Avengers giving schoolchildren balloons that said, "Ask about lesbian lives."

But we also pissed them off, declaring how insignificant we were. How hated, actually, when push came to shove. Let's admit it: if *lesbian* was a dirty word, what were lesbians in the flesh? We announced the dirty secret that it wasn't just bigots to blame. It was dykes hiding in corners. And taking it. Refusing to claim a place in society.

I suppose we could have put a different spin on it. Made a joyful call to action. The conference was kind of cool. The organizers were committed to lesbians. But celebrating the power of laughter seemed almost obscene when anger was as taboo as pedophilia. When we'd abdicated the street. Neither seen nor heard. Not demonstrating. Not running around half-naked with bliss. No public platform even for satire. Not like Rabelais poking fun at clerics, or Mel Brooks forcing Torquemada and Hitler to sing and dance.

The response was mixed. Love for the images of activist dykes. Anger at our declaration that lesbians could disappear and nobody would notice we'd gone. One woman said lesbians weren't that invisible in her city; they'd actually held one whole demo not long ago. Another woman seemed to come out against activism altogether: "Shouldn't we stop and think about our goals first?"

I was accused of being evangelical about street activism. "It's not the only way," she said. I didn't disagree, but my point was that direct action was a tool. Everybody should know how to use it. Especially dykes who rarely have lobbyists or representatives or cultural power. Like the poor of the world, all we have are our loud, annoying voices. Our bodies that take up room in the street. Every time the Avengers pulled off an action, we weren't just making lesbians visible or trying to change society. We were changing lesbians. Creating a new kind of dyke who saw public space as hers, who could step out into the street and make noise, be herself, feel at home in the world. In some ways, we were the last utopian group of the millennium, aiming not only for justice, but pure freedom.

It was the whole point of the first Avenger manifesto. We could be as camp as we wanted, as ridiculous, as angry, as serene. You could get from the lesbian feminists of the seventies to all the equality-focused projects without groups like the Avengers, but probably not to a dancing dyke like Ellen. Or a wise-cracking Wanda Sykes. Forget *The L Word.*

By chance, the director Rose Troche was at the conference, too, and we went to see her presentation the next morning. I had flashbacks to the East Village circa 1994. She'd been a friend of Anne d'Adesky and had been to a couple of parties in the loft at Avenue B that were full of fashionable queers drinking jewel-colored martinis. She talked about her recently defunct TV show *The L Word* featuring Pam Grier, whom Carrie Moyer had made an Avenger icon, and her film *Go Fish.* Before she was done, Rose managed to inspire finger-pointing, threats, and a near fistfight, at least in the back of the room where we were. The women were arguing about whether *The L Word* was a sell-out or not. Is something better than nothing? Would you really sleep with Shane? Was *Go Fish* truly an embarrassment with its scruffy butch dykes? Don't those *L Word* bitches ever work?

It was my birthday, again. After watching Rose, Ana and I played hooky and went to a restaurant in the market in Place Victor Hugo, eating the best cassoulet in France, and gulping the local wine like we'd been parched for a month. We'd been there our first year in France on a trip to the southwest that included Carcassonne where the heretical Cathars had a stronghold before they were targeted by the Inquisition. I got obsessed with them, that whole wide-eyed desert-dwelling puritanical strain. Thousands were burned at the stake by the equally fanatical Church that liked nothing better than freeing people of their disgusting flesh.

Maybe the attraction was that I could have been either. The heretic or the inquisitor, inflamed by rage, by hate, by a vast consuming love.

34.

It was still under my skin when we got back home to Paris—how we could just disappear and nobody would notice we'd gone. One year for Christmas, I gave Ana a book called *The Commissar Vanishes,* about doctored photos in the USSR. One sequence showed a photograph of Stalin with three other leaders of the Russian Revolution. One by one, they were airbrushed, cropped, and clipped out of the picture until only Stalin remained, so it seemed like he alone was responsible for the revolution. That was us, on the cutting room floor. The Lesbian Avengers. What an embarrassment we were to everybody. So brash. So lesbian. So un-American, rooted in the East Village art scene where people got up to all sorts of embarrassing things with chocolate, and dyke artists weren't ashamed to portray raunchy sex, or even two girls duking it out in a bad relationship. I couldn't believe we were ever featured in *Newsweek.* Yeah, the Avengers were gone, and who cared? Our goal now—a mature equality, cultivating our grandmothers' gardens.

Even if it had its practical side, I wasn't content, wanted room for somebody to cry out in the queer wilderness, "LESBIANS! DYKES! GAY WOMEN!...We're wasting our lives being careful. Imagine what your life could be. Aren't you ready to make it happen?" Why had we dumped that utopian road? That powerful call to reimagine our lives?

I was too tired to start over, but I couldn't stand how small they'd made us. I hate constraint. Always had, scratchy little tights. Social boxes that appear as soon as the world takes note of you. I wanted to take up space. On my next trip back to New

York, I scanned a bunch of stuff and added it to the tiny Avengers site I'd posted for the conference. I wrote a little article. Then two. Then I enlisted Carolina Kroon for some of her photos. Look. There's proof. We existed. It's my world, too. My own goal: to be a splinter under society's fingernail, create an annoyance for the forces of invisibility. While I was still in New York, Amy Parker invited me to give a talk on activism up at Harvard, where she'd become an administrator for the women, gender, and sexuality department. The stock market had crashed by then, and some of the students were organizing demos around the mass firings at Harvard but couldn't come up with much except walking around in circles with signs. Even though some of them had studied queer activism. In actual classrooms.

I thought about activism in the United States, and how it hadn't begun or ended with MLK. There were abolitionists, and union organizers, and the Boston Tea Partiers who would soon be hijacked, and the group from my own neighborhood, Up Against the Wall Motherfuckers, and went up there and showed the documentary and fielded questions. And generally felt like I should be in the Natural History Museum. Afterwards, an archivist up there asked me for my papers, and it was like proof I really was a fossil, a street activist in the age of the Internet. With a gap growing between my generation and theirs, so vast that a couple of Avengers I talked to actually sounded a little embarrassed at having shouted in the street. Though they were glad I had started documenting the Avengers. Of course, that was important. For the sake of lesbian history.

No one else, though, seemed to feel it was as urgent as I did. Maybe because their voices weren't as faint as mine, they didn't feel as invisible. Or maybe they remembered how it ended and were afraid somebody would find out that lesbian activists weren't always pretty. As if we were supposed to be immune to the usual activist infighting, the American curse of race. Not part of that enormous evolving story. My friend Martha Burgess reminded me that the Avengers fought about a lot more than that. Like when those girls came and tried to get us to take on the case of Aileen Wuornos, the death-row dyke who killed all those men in Florida. The problem was the girls weren't steady Avengers and seemed to pack the room with their friends. Martha turned up for the first time during this mess, and after opening her mouth to speak in favor of doing something for Wuornos was accused of being one of the people there just to swing the vote. She almost didn't come back. She was still pissed, telling me about it, though at least nobody did a Stalin and put an icepick in their rival's head. We just wanted to.

For a while now, people have also been rolling their eyes a little at the goal of visibility. Like the idea is passé. They'd expected it to do tricks. Roll over and beg. Save avalanche victims with a tub of rum. And all it did was lie there. I always thought about visibility as a jumping-off place, a precondition for having a voice. Because if you aren't visible in the culture, or in politics, or even on the streets, how can you demand anything or participate like a grown-up in the ongoing narrative of your country? We could disappear, and who'd know we'd gone?

In Paris, I remembered visibility could be even more basic: the simple desire to see a face like yours, hear your name pronounced. I really was thrilled to see the American dyke rocker Beth Ditto on TV, her body on the cover of that fashion magazine. After Obama got elected in the fall of '08, it seemed like every person of African descent in Paris walked just a little straighter. Some actually grinned from ear to ear, carrying newspapers with his face on it. Whatever I thought of him as a politician, he gave people hope, stiffened their spines. Visibility isn't change itself, but a kind of wedge others can follow. Though we don't know toward what. "The door itself / makes no promises. / It is only a door," says Adrienne Rich.

We went back to New York in the spring of 2010. Six months later, I made a trip to Louisville. My mother still lived there, as well as my father, his second wife, and my sister Kim's family. Vikki came in from Colorado with her husband and kid. It was the first time in thirteen years. On the plane I noticed all these guys with racing forms. The "reunion" coincided with the Breeders' Cup at Churchill Downs, and I spent the next few days imagining a baby-popping competition.

Things had changed, kind of. An out gay guy, Jim Gray, had just been elected mayor of Lexington, Kentucky. One teenager I met, lured into the ROTC by promises of rock-climbing trips, passed a semester or two driving her colonel crazy, defending gays in the military and women's rights. Though across town, another young girl spent several weeks circulating a petition to preserve the ill-fated Don't Ask, Don't Tell policy of the military, and she wasn't even in the ROTC yet. She wore bits and pieces of her brother's uniform, and the two did drills when they were bored. That was my niece, and everybody said she's exactly like me.

Then there was my mother. When my cousin Donna picked me up at the airport, she told me she'd been lecturing my mother to be more accepting, or failing that, to bite her tongue. "I don't know how I'd feel if one of my kids had made that choice, but you still have to love them and welcome them into your house. And their companions, too. Even if you don't agree with their lifestyles." Donna meant it kindly, but all I wanted to do was turn around and head back to my home planet, which dared rotate around the sun, like Galileo's Earth, without anybody's approval.

Still, whatever she said to my mother worked. Mom didn't exactly ask after Ana, even if we'd been connected at the hip for eighteen—eighteen!—years, but she did button her lip, and because I did, too, we passed our visit together in a relative truce. It was what I was there for, to visit parents who were aging at an accelerated rate. To show my face. Which was the literal truth, especially for my mother, who can't stand the rest of me, particularly the rebellious brain packed with a lesbian *life*. Very little *style* involved. We looked at photos. She showed me her art. She'd taken classes at U of L and begun painting again years before. She'd drawn and done watercolors as a young woman, stopped when her new husband made fun of her. I tried to encourage her. We should have had this in common. But I heard after I left that she had resumed her diatribes against her no-good, sinful daughter.

The visit with my father was equally calm. I'd decided to let go of the grotesqueries of the past and was rewarded with a martini. Three, actually.

After a couple of nights in a hotel, and all I could gorge at the Dairy Queen, I went to stay with Adrienne. She was a girl from grade school who tracked me down at *The Gully* and wasn't at all put off by reconnecting with a big dyke. She had one for a sister-in-law, in fact. And she and her husband had actually gotten together when they both agreed some gay-baiting guy at their church was an idiot. Her husband, who teaches social studies at a high school for at-risk kids, told me the girls there were incredibly open, going around arm in arm, declaring they were lesbians, partly to provoke, partly to experiment, without knowing entirely what it meant. Queerish boys, though, were more reticent. When one kid from a troubled family came out as bi, his family was awful. A couple days later he disappeared from school and hadn't been heard from since. Maybe they sent him somewhere else. Maybe he got the crap beat out of him and was in the hospital. Or was dead.

I was back in Louisville just a couple of months later, not as a daughter but to talk about the Lesbian Avengers. Another classmate, Leigh, had invited me to do something for Women's History Month at the university where she taught philosophy. So much had happened in the world, it seemed more like a decade had passed since I'd been there. Though I wasn't sure they'd noticed. Did students at an out-of-the-way college know the Arab world had busted out in what was getting called a glorious spring? That the triumph of nonviolent organizing was getting called a "revolution by Internet" (despite the crowds in the street day after day, despite the years of activism)? Kids had occupied Wall Street. Or tried to. Direct action was relevant after all. Like the traditional media that amplified all the action on Facebook and YouTube and Twitter. Like making yourself visible to get support from the whole fucking world. It was already clear they'd need it. Trying to remake entire nations. Egypt and Tunisia stood a better chance, anyway, than Iraq, where change had been artificially imposed.

I chatted with the burly, bearded tech guy and discovered that he used to hang out in my neighborhood because his dad was a musician at the Toy Tiger Lounge, which I'd been told was a den of iniquity. And after we laughed about that, he said, "You're awright. I didn't know what to expect, but you're awright." Which is high praise in that part of the world, where they're freaked out as much by New York as the lesbian thing.

When it was finally time, I gave my spiel and showed the movie. Afterwards, a couple of young lesbians in the audience talked about how a gay student was beaten up in a school bathroom recently while a whole gang of kids looked on. Cops refused to classify it as a hate crime. Then a dyke activist from Louisville gave me a CD of Yer Girlfriend, a lesbian band she'd played in during the early nineties, about the time I went to New York. Somebody else asked about the lesbian lifestyle, and I gave a lecture on the lesbian oatmeal I ate and lesbian jeans I put on, because I hadn't barbequed any infants in decades.

The next day, the aging, twanging mother of a lesbian shop owner actually recommended a gay-friendly church. And at a party, a young black lesbian said she'd finally worked up the nerve to come out but was totally deflated when her father said it was no big deal. Ditto for when she announced she wanted to be a drag king. "Well, we better go buy you some clothes," was the response. At a dyke bar, she didn't know anybody, but her dad spotted a friend and her partner: "Look, there's so-and-so." She said the worst of it in Louisville was the racial segregation among queers. Her closest friend was a young white fag, and they got hassled a little whenever they went together to bars and clubs. "What are you hanging with him for?" "Why are you with her?" The two shared a house with his white boyfriend, who was from rural Kentucky. He told me he came out with no problem, though his father was still struggling with it. Online, he'd found other young queers from the same region, and they had a little network. Some of them had even begun moving back home. He was considering it himself and planned to enlist the help of progressive nuns to get something going in the area if he did return.

We stared at each other in mutual awe. They thought it was cool I was living in New York and had been a Lesbian Avenger and had made it as far as Paris. I was impressed that they were still at home. In Kentucky. Smack-dab in the middle of the Bible Belt. I could never have imagined their lives. I could never have imagined my own. After all, I was going to be a medical missionary. A doctor, pouring out the balm of Gilead. Instead, there I was outside the city. Blowing a toy trumpet, staring at crumbling walls.

NOTES AND ACKNOWLEDGMENTS

Readers should be aware that this is not an exhaustive history, especially of the New York Lesbian Avengers. Far more people contributed than are mentioned here. For the sake of the book, I had to make cuts, not additions. On the other hand, what I did include is as accurate as possible, though in a few instances (for example, when I was informed that I once had three roommates instead of two) I decided to let the original description stand. Our lives are shaped as much by the stories we cobble together with our memories as they are by the actual details.

Partly for this reason, I made a conscious decision to use full names only for people who are public figures, at least in a limited sense. It can be unsettling to see your name pop up on Google or in a book, especially if you don't remember things quite the same way. The only two pseudonyms in *Eating Fire* are Faustina and Kathryn.

In general, this book owes a great deal to ideas explored in *The Gully* online magazine and New York's *Gay City News,* but my biggest thanks go to those joyful troublemakers and unapologetically big-mouthed dykes the Lesbian Avengers. This book is for you.

Born in Louisville, Kentucky, **Kelly Cogswell** is a journalist, blogger, and prize-winning columnist at *Gay City News* in New York. A longtime lesbian activist, she worked briefly with the Irish Lesbian and Gay Organization in New York before becoming a founding member of the Lesbian Avengers in 1992. She cofounded and edited *The Gully* online magazine, offering "queer views on everything."

Born in Louisville, Kentucky, **Kelly Cogswell** is a journalist, blogger, and prize-winning columnist at *Gay City News* in New York. A longtime lesbian activist, she worked briefly with the Irish Lesbian and Gay Organization in New York before becoming a founding member of the Lesbian Avengers in 1992. She cofounded and edited *The Gully* online magazine, offering "queer views on everything."